Praise for *Live at the Cellar*

"In *Live at the Cellar*, Marian Jago deftly explores the phenomenon of co-operative jazz clubs, a neglected area in the study of jazz. While her book focuses on the fertile scene surrounding Vancouver's Cellar Club and, to a lesser degree, parallel clubs in Edmonton, Calgary and Halifax, her methodology, insights, and conclusions provide an excellent basis for comparative work on co-operatives in the United States and Europe. A pioneering work, this book makes a substantial contribution to jazz scholarship."

– ROB BOWMAN, Grammy Award–winning musicologist and professor of ethnomusicology, York University

"I grew up in Vancouver during the formative years of 'the new jazz,' and I was fortunate enough to be at the 'right place and time' to watch jazz history being made. These clubs were our jazz 'school,' where we learned all about this North American art form. Our music was formed in a 'crucible' of jazz, where all of the elements fused together to form something new. In *Live at the Cellar*, Marian Jago perfectly chronicles this chapter in Canadian jazz, something that few have revealed in such detail. Her amazing book captures the spirit and essence of that time and that experience."

– TERRY CLARKE, C.M., drummer and Canadian jazz icon

"The Cellar on Watson Street was a huge part Vancouver's jazz history and had an obvious influence on my own club, The Cellar on Broadway. I would've given anything to be around during the heyday of Vancouver's jazz co-ops – this book helps me close my eyes and imagine what it was like to be there!"

– CORY WEEDS, jazz musician and owner of The Cellar on Broadway

MARIAN JAGO

live at the CELLAR

vancouver's iconic jazz club
and the canadian co-operative
jazz scene in the 1950s and '60s

UBC Press • Vancouver • Toronto

27 26 25 24 23 22 21 20 19 18   5 4 3 2 1

Printed in Canada on FSC-certified ancient-forest-free paper (100% post-consumer recycled) that is processed chlorine- and acid-free.

Library and Archives Canada Cataloguing in Publication

Jago, Marian, author

Live at the Cellar: Vancouver's iconic jazz club and the Canadian co-operative jazz scene in the 1950s and '60s / Marian Jago.

Includes bibliographical references and index.
Issued in print and electronic formats.
ISBN 978-0-7748-3768-2 (hardcover). – ISBN 978-0-7748-3769-9 (softcover).
ISBN 978-0-7748-3770-5 (PDF). – ISBN 978-0-7748-3771-2 (EPUB).
ISBN 978-0-7748-3772-9 (Kindle)

1. Cellar (Jazz club: Vancouver, B.C.: 1956-1964). 2. Jazz – British Columbia – Vancouver – 1951-1960 – History and criticism. 3. Jazz – British Columbia – Vancouver – 1961-1970 – History and criticism. 4. Jazz – Canada – History and criticism. I. Title.

ML3509.C28V22 2018   781.6509711'3309045   C2018-904482-9
C2018-904483-7

Canadä

UBC Press gratefully acknowledges the financial support for our publishing program of the Government of Canada (through the Canada Book Fund), the Canada Council for the Arts, and the British Columbia Arts Council.

This book has been published with the help of a grant from the Canadian Federation for the Humanities and Social Sciences, through the Awards to Scholarly Publications Program, using funds provided by the Social Sciences and Humanities Research Council of Canada.

UBC Press
The University of British Columbia
2029 West Mall
Vancouver, BC V6T 1Z2
www.ubcpress.ca

For all the players.

And particularly for Lance,
who got this all rolling so many years ago.

And also for Mark Miller,
whose work on Canadian jazz lit the way.

It's been an honour.

Contents

Illustrations

Foreword

I've long had this theory that people do a lot of the things they do simply because they are bored. After dinner and a long day at work, they just want to go out and do something. "Let's go to a movie," "let's go out for a drink," or maybe "let's get together with some friends and listen to jazz." This is what I did when I was about seventeen years old. Two or three friends and I would get together a couple of nights a week and play jazz records till about one in the morning. We would listen to every track, read the liner notes, and look at the pictures. There was something mysteriously exciting about it. Musicians like Dizzy Gillespie, Thelonious Monk, and Charles Mingus almost seemed to be from another planet where people were smarter and hipper. I had this feeling that they knew a lot of stuff that ordinary people like me just didn't know and I really wanted to be one of them. My friends all had an interest in the music and we really enjoyed our evenings together, but for me jazz and the whole jazz world became an obsession. I always wanted to find a way to get to know the guys on the records so I could really understand them and their music. While we were listening to our jazz records, my work-mates would often drift off to the local pub and drink beer for a few hours. But I was content to stay and listen to the music.

I'd heard so many stories from some of the older guys I've known about how, in the 1940s, every bar in town had a jazz group playing, and they would be packed till the wee hours of the morning. It sounded great but keep in mind that these places were not really "jazz clubs" – they were simply bars that had a jazz band playing. And a lot of the musicians were probably fooled into thinking that the people listening to their music were real jazz fans who had come to hear them play – when, for the most part, they were there for a drink and a good time. I suspect that this was the case in all the bigger cities in Canada and the United States.

When I moved to Vancouver in 1960, there were quite a few bars where jazz groups played. Then there was the Cellar. The Cellar wasn't just a bar or a restaurant like the others. It was a place that featured real jazz and where people came to *listen* to the music. I never played the Black Spot, but I played many times at the Flat Five, which later became the Blue Horn. Both the Black Spot and Flat Five were like the Cellar inasmuch as they were run by musicians and featured real jazz. But the Cellar was still "the place" to go for jazz in Vancouver. There was something strangely exciting about going down those stairs, paying the admission, and waiting for the door to open so you could enter. I remember standing outside listening to the band playing and feeling a thrill go through me because I knew that I was about to hear some fantastic music.

In reading Marian Jago's book, I was a bit surprised to find out that the Cellar had only been open for ten years. For me now, ten years goes by in the blink of an eye. But when I was twenty years old, ten years was half of my life time, and I just figured that the Cellar had been there forever. Anyhow, when I left Vancouver in 1965 and moved to San Francisco to play with John Handy the Cellar was still going, and I wasn't around when it closed. But in reading the accounts by John Dawe and the others in this book, I can see how, after ten years, it wasn't much fun anymore. I just used to show up and play and have a great time. It never occurred to me just how much work it was to keep the place going and how John Dawe, Dave Quarin, and the rest of them were doing all that stuff to make it such an enjoyable experience.

Back then, the jazz scene was still going strong for a while in other places. San Francisco, in 1965, was sort of like jazz heaven. There were clubs everywhere and everyone was playing all the time. Up on North Beach there was Basin Street West, the Jazz Workshop, El Matador, and a couple of other places all on Broadway. We were playing over in the Fillmore at the Both/And on Divisidero, and just a block away George Duke had a great trio at the Blue Note. Over the bridge in Sausalito, there was the Trident where Denny Zeitlin played every Monday night, and there was one club in town that had a twenty-four-hour jazz policy. Six bands played four hours each and apparently there were people there all the time!

Basin Street West was a big sort of supper club with a stage at one end. They always had great music and featured people like Count Basie, Woody Herman, Jimmy Smith, Ahmad Jamal, George Shearing, and all the rest of the big names. I went to hear Ahmad Jamal one night but the audience was so noisy he refused to play. George Shearing was faced with the same situation when I went to hear him and he just sat on stage at the piano for a long time until the people in the audience noticed him. I only played El Matador once (actually we closed the place) and I don't remember much about it, but the Jazz Workshop was everything I'd hoped for in a jazz club. It was a listening room and people came in there for the music. They would line up around the block every night for two weeks to hear John Coltrane or Miles Davis. The Both/And was a real listening room too but most of the other places were just really nice bars or restaurants.

I returned to Canada in the spring of 1967 and by then the Cellar I knew was closed. By all accounts, most of the clubs in San Francisco were gone buy the mid-70s too. These closings were not just a San Francisco phenomenon though. Shelly's Manne-Hole closed in Hollywood in 1972, as did the Penthouse in Seattle in 1968 and the old Half Note in New York in 1974. Toronto's Town Tavern closed in 1971 and the Colonial Tavern in the late 1970s.

So what happened? In my opinion television happened. TV had been around for a while. When I was a kid we got our first set in about 1954 and I remember sitting there night after night watching *Father Knows Best, Leave It to Beaver, Zorro*, and wrestling. Back then, we only were able to get black-and-white TV with three channels, and there was one channel that had a movie on at 11:30 every night after the news. In other words, TV was pretty boring and it didn't take long before we just stopped watching it and went back to our jazz LPs. So, with TV being what it was, people were still showing up at the clubs and everything seemed to be okay with the jazz scene. But then came colour TV. With the change to colour everything looked better and people started watching again. There were more channels and some pretty good shows, so a lot of people just stopped going out at night. But I think what really finished it off was cable and satellite TV, which became popular starting in the 1970s. All of a sudden there were many channels to choose from and people were happy to stay home. And now with YouTube and all the digital music services available, you can watch or listen to any artist in any kind of music genre whenever you like. Everyone has their iPhones and they can watch movies, listen to music, play games, text one another, and sometimes even make a phone call. They don't get as bored now and no longer have to go out. These days there are only a few jazz clubs left and the audience is getting old. The last gig I played was a solo piano set for an hour and there were only two people in the place younger than me (one was a former student and the other was his girlfriend) and I'm seventy-eight!

The Cellar was a club started up by a few young jazz musicians who just wanted a place to play. It was open for ten years and for the first eight or nine years was host to some of the greatest jazz musicians in the world – Charles Mingus, Ornette Coleman, Art Pepper, Lee Konitz, and Harold Land, just to name a few. It was an amazing accomplishment when you think about it. My first gig there was with Conte Candoli. Then I played with Barney Kessel and Jimmy Lovelace. I remember two gigs there with Ernestine Anderson and quite a few with my own band. But the gig that sticks in my mind the most was the two-week one I played with an alto player from California by the name of Monty Waters and with Jimmy Lovelace again on drums. Our gig was from 9:00 pm to 1:00 am and then around 1:30 there would be a session that would go on until about 4:00 am. Every musician in town would be there and we would play all night. This was what the Cellar was all about for me. As a young musician it was a chance to meet and play every night with some of the greatest players in the world. It was like the music would never end.

I think it's amazing that Marian has basically preserved an important bit of the history of jazz in Canada. We owe her and Mark Miller a huge thank you for what they've done. As time goes by, things are often forgotten but thanks to them our jazz history and the musicians that created the music will live on.

Don Thompson, O.C.
Award winning multi-instrumentalist and Canadian jazz icon

Preface

This book is the first to detail the remarkable decade of activity (roughly between 1955 and 1965) that saw the emergence of several important co-operative jazz clubs across Canada. It also represents the first inclusion into the historical record, in many cases, of Canadian jazz players who, because of their relative regional isolation, have had a limited profile and impact in Toronto and Montreal, where so many Canadian jazz stories are situated. This book illustrates in part how the privileging of recorded output so common to the construction of jazz hierarchies can diminish the importance of localized musical practice, involvement, and discourse. Being an important musician does not always mean being a well-recorded one, particularly in Canada. In focusing so frequently on those who have the most significant discographies, existing accounts have largely overlooked those musicians who may have profoundly influenced local, regional, and even national forms of jazz expression, despite receiving little or no recognition outside their home communities, particularly in popular terms. My work then is the result of many years of thinking about and talking to Canadian jazz musicians – of fitting their stories into the wider narrative of jazz to discover not only what this musical genre has meant to Canada, but also how the formation of vibrant local jazz scenes has served to give it voice.

Though now much more an academic and scholar of jazz, I also consider myself a jazz musician, and, as a Canadian player, in this exploration of co-operative spaces and the communities they engendered, I was engaged in the unearthing of my own origin story. The clubs detailed here gave early starts to many of the players I have spent hours listening and talking to and learning from; gave rise to many of the local myths and "were-you-there-when-stories" that have animated local and national musicians' "hangs"; and supported the development of the jazz societies, festivals, and university-level programs that helped me get where I am today. However, unlike the authors of other recent works on the concept of "scene" in popular music – including Sara Cohen, author of *Rock Culture in Liverpool: Popular Music in the Making,* Barry Shank, *Dissonant Identities: The Rock'n'Roll Scene in Austin, Texas,* Aaron Fox, *Real Country: Music and Language in Working-Class Culture,* Alex Stewart, *Making the Scene: Contemporary New York City Big Band Jazz,* and Travis A. Jackson, *Blowin' the Blues Away: Performance and Meaning on the New York Jazz Scene* – I was not a direct participant in any of the scenes examined in this book and have no direct experience of the culture of the 1950s and 1960s that shaped them. I could not look around to soak up the scene, so to speak, but only backwards, relying on such historical documentation as exists and upon the recollections and experiences of my interview subjects, themselves also looking backward.

The research for this book combines historical and ethnographic approaches, and relies in large part upon interviews with dozens of musicians conducted over a period of several years. What little had been written on the musicians involved in these clubs has come via the pioneering efforts of Mark Miller, in particular his *Jazz in Canada: Fourteen Lives* (1982), *Boogie, Pete, and the Senator: Canadian Musicians in Jazz: The Eighties* (1987), and *The Miller Companion to Jazz in Canada and Canadians in Jazz* (2001). Following from Miller's work, I conducted numerous interviews in person as well as over the phone, via Skype, and in email and letters. Wherever possible I spoke with surviving members of the clubs in question, with family members of the musicians, with jazz fans who attended these clubs, and with non-musical artists featured at these clubs.

I was based in Toronto when most of these interviews took place, and they were often conducted in a peripatetic style that involved my sleeping on the couches of friends and family, crisscrossing the lower mainland of British Columbia by car, bus, and, for a memorable few days, travelling Vancouver Island via bicycle. Interviews were conducted in a casual, ad hoc manner in locations ranging from coffee shops and restaurants to performance venues, and very often in the homes of unfailingly generous musicians. I chose to forgo a formal list of questions for these encounters, preferring a more open conversational approach, which permitted free-flowing, wide-ranging discussions, and which often brought to light things I would never have thought to ask. That said, despite this somewhat improvisational approach, all interview subjects were asked similar questions having to do with racial and gender issues, their thoughts on influential or formative musical experiences, and their knowledge of the Canadian jazz scene beyond their home communities.

To help corroborate the recollections of my interview subjects and to piece together a chronology on which to base my questions, I searched back issues of the Canadian jazz magazine *Coda,* the *Vancouver Sun,* the *Ubyssey* (University of British Columbia student newspaper), the *Edmonton Journal,* American jazz magazine *Downbeat,* and the *Halifax Chronicle-Herald.* I also conducted research at the CBC Archives and the City of Vancouver Archives, both of which helped to fill in the gaps regarding the musical and cultural life of the city.

Memory can be as much an act of construction as it is faithful recollection, and so I made sure to double-check information from interviews against as many other sources as possible. Dates and other factual data could usually be verified in local newspapers and magazines, or other written sources. Often, however, the only way to cross-check information was to ask the same or similar questions to a number of people and to eliminate or highlight, as the case may be, anything that seemed outside the common consensus. When recollections of events were similar, I chose to quote from the most colourful or most contextually appropriate sources. Whenever doubt persisted regarding factual information, such as exact performance dates, I simply narrowed it down as much as possible.

This ethnographic cross-checking is best seen in the discussion surrounding Charles Mingus's 1961 appearance at the Cellar, where there were varying interpretations of the high-profile conflict between Mingus and some BC Lions football players (see Chapter 5). None were necessarily contradictory, but recollections of the Mingus episode illustrate the complicated nature of memory, nostalgia, and context as details were emphasized or omitted based on where people had been sitting in the room, how closely connected to the on-stage activities they were, how old they were, and whether they'd witnessed the incident firsthand or knew it only as a piece of Cellar lore. So interesting was the picture this painted that I have chosen to include several versions of the story here. Cross-checking was also important for the discussion surrounding the playing style of drummer Bill Boyle, one of the few Vancouver-based players to be reviewed with any detail in *Coda* magazine (see Chapter 5). In this case, I identified a possible stylistic disconnect between the correspondent from *Coda* (which was primarily devoted to traditional or Dixieland jazz at the time) and the modern jazz style featured at the Cellar. Without recourse to recordings, I sought a variety of opinions on the matter.

I spoke to numerous people involved with the Vancouver scene, including Chris (Hole) Birdseye, whose marriage to entrepreneur and musician Ken Hole provided insights into the origins of the Cellar, Victoria's Scene Club, and later Vancouver venues such as the Inquisition and Espresso coffee houses; celebrated poets bill bissett and Jamie Reid; area resident Lyvia Brooks; author Adrienne Brown, whose father Harry Webb played an important role in designing the Cellar's advertising; stalwarts of the Vancouver scene Lance Harrison, Dal Richards, and Bob Hales; clarinettist Phil Nimmons, who got his start out west; CBC producers Jack Reynolds, George Robertson, and Neil Ritchie; anthropologist Adrian Tanner; visual artist and musician Gregg Simpson; and founding co-op members, musicians, and scene participants John Capon, James Carney, Jim Chivers, Terry Clarke, Tony Clitheroe, Don Cumming, John Dawe, Bill Fawcett, Don Francks, Joe Geszler, Ricci (Quarin) Gotsch, Ken Hole, Jim Johnson, Cliff Jones, Jim Kilburn, Claire Lawrence, John LeMarquand, Frank Lewis, Walley Lightbody, Chuck Logan, Lynne McNeil, Al Neil, Ed Roop, Paul Ruhland, Mike Taylor, Don Thompson, Gavin Walker, Blaine Wikjord, and Doreen (Williams) Young. Vancouver broadcaster and musician Al Reusch was interviewed by Mike Beddoes in 1999 (and excerpts are used here with permission).

In Edmonton, I spoke with pianist and co-founding member of the Yardbird Suite Tommy Banks, as well as with Tom Doran, and documentary filmmaker Collette Slevinsky. I also spoke to Dennis Slater and Sheila Thislewaite from Calgary, and Charles "Buddy" Burke, David Caldwell, Warren Chiasson, Terry Hill, Pat LaCroix, Bob Mercer, Don Palmer, Don Vickery, and Stan Perry from Halifax. In a welcome stroke of luck, many of those involved with Halifax's 777 Barrington Street, such as Don Palmer, Stan Perry (who was also active at the Cellar), and Don Vickery, had moved to Toronto, and I caught up with Warren Chiasson in New York. In Toronto, I spoke in person to leading Canadian jazz writer Mark Miller, and saxophonist and educator Mike Murley.

The well-documented activities at the Cellar, combined with the active participation in this study by so many members of both the Cellar and Vancouver's other major jazz co-operative, the Black Spot/Flat Five, provide rich perspectives on the history of the co-operative jazz scene in Vancouver while also shedding light on the activities of co-operative jazz clubs elsewhere in Canada.

Acknowledgments

This book is the work of many years and wouldn't have been possible without the assistance of countless musicians, librarians, archivists, jazz enthusiasts, academics, writers, painters, friends, and family members.

Though I made initial contact in 2001 with the musicians who are integral to this book, the bulk of the work was completed between 2010 and 2014 at York University, where I worked with professor of ethnomusicology and Grammy-Award-winning music writer Rob Bowman, musicologist Rob van der Bliek (editor of *The Thelonius Monk Reader*), and ethnomusicologist Robert Witmer, whose name also graces these pages as a bassist on the Vancouver jazz scene in the 1960s. Their support and good-natured reality checks helped immensely in the shaping of this book.

I would also like to thank Mark Miller for responding to my repeated calls for help with good humour and a wealth of knowledge; Colin Preston at the CBC Archives in Vancouver for making a great many photos and films available to me; and Gavin Walker for repeatedly lending his astonishing memory for the sounds and sights of Vancouver.

Most importantly, I would like to thank each and every person who took the time to speak with me for this project. Without exception, they proved overwhelmingly generous with their time, their memories, and their keepsakes. All of them are listed at the end of the book, but I would like to single out Lance Harrison for getting this all started in 2001, John Dawe for responding to my constant questions so quickly, Jim Kilburn for access to recordings (and for putting me up after a long bike ride up the coast of Vancouver Island), Tony Clitheroe and Paul Ruhland for their good company, James Carney and Walley Lightbody for providing many of the photographs found here, and Al Neil for his support and encouragement.

I have not even attempted to compile a list of all the musicians involved with the co-operative clubs I researched – far too many people would be omitted through ignorance, and this is as much their story as those whose names are in these pages. Anyone interested in contributing to what I hope will be further work in this area can reach me at liveatthecellarbook@gmail.com.

live at the CELLAR

Introduction

We started from nothing. We just had this record store. We met there. It didn't have that many customers, either, come to think of it.

– Al Neil

In the mid-1950s, something new was happening on the Canadian musical landscape. In smaller urban centres far from the hub-bub of Toronto and Montreal, musicians interested in "modern jazz" – the sort of jazz that had developed in the wake of bebop and the Second World War – were coming together to create places in which the music could be celebrated, practised, listened to, and performed. "Do-it-yourself" affairs of the highest order, the clubs these musicians formed were borne of shared interest, and mutual support. Against a social backdrop that offered few other options, these players and enthusiasts rented rooms, built stages and tables, formed alliances, leveraged connections, practised hard, and brought forth an exceptional burst of musical activity that still reverberates today.

This book looks at a unique ten-year period (roughly 1955–65) that saw the inception of artist-run, co-operative jazz clubs in four Canadian cities: Vancouver, Edmonton, Calgary, and Halifax. Though these clubs developed in regions of Canada marginal to the jazz activity of Montreal and Toronto, they had a profound influence on the development of jazz in Canada. By providing performance spaces for jazz where none existed previously, these clubs made it possible for Canadian musicians to stay home, at least regionally speaking, while actively pursuing an interest in jazz and developing themselves as performers. The creation of these strong regional nodes for jazz performance in many ways laid the groundwork for the pan-Canadian jazz scene we now take for granted, with its attendant festivals, societies, and various college and university jazz programs.

In these clubs, young musicians worked on their music free from the commercial constraints of the hotel dance band, free from the generic restrictions of traditional (Dixieland) and big (dance) band jazz, and, for the most part, free from the professional pressures and obligations of the studio orchestra musician. At the same time, these co-operative spaces provided a nexus for the development of postwar countercultural expression in other arts such as poetry, literature, theatre, and film, all of which were similarly marginalized outside Canada's major urban centres. Nowhere was the importance and cultural influence of these spaces more evident than in Vancouver, where the Cellar provided a welcoming and collaborative home for experimental arts practice during the late 1950s and early 1960s.

This book was initially conceived as an examination of five jazz cooperatives across four Canadian cities from the mid-1950s through the mid-1960s. They were the Cellar and Black Spot/Flat Five in Vancouver,[1] the Yardbird Suite in Edmonton, Foggy Manor in Calgary, and 777 Barrington Street in Halifax – all important regional hubs for jazz development during the period and home to important jazz festivals, societies, and educational programs since the 1980s. This goal quickly proved unfeasible due to the dearth of scholarship and scanty surviving evidence about the majority of these clubs. Regrettably, therefore, while the Foggy Manor, Yardbird Suite, and 777 Barrington Street were doubtlessly significant spaces for their local jazz communities, they play a less prominent role in this book, and much about their structure and operation must be inferred from what we know about the better-documented clubs in Vancouver: the Cellar and the Black Spot/Flat Five.

Of all the co-operative clubs discussed in this book, Vancouver's Cellar has simply left behind the most evidence. A majority of the founding members of the Cellar were still alive and were willing to be interviewed;[2] the club advertised regularly in local newspapers; several club members were enthusiastic photographers; and promotional material for the club, including concert posters, has survived. As a result, a considerable amount of archival material is available, including several photographs of the club's interior taken by CBC photographer Franz Linder in 1961. In addition, a 1964 National Film Board documentary on Vancouver's arts scene titled *In Search of Innocence* contains film footage of the Cellar, which includes a short performance by the Al Neil Trio with Don Thompson (bass) and Glenn McDonald (saxophone).[3] This short sequence offers a valuable glimpse into the atmosphere of the Cellar, its audience, and contemporary attempts to merge jazz and poetry (see Chapter 4).

Significantly, the Cellar also provided me with the only opportunity to *hear* contemporary performances by the musicians involved in one of these co-operative ventures. The surviving recordings were not made at the Cellar itself, nor are they contemporary commercial releases, but privately held copies of three live CBC radio broadcasts from 1956 and 1957 did offer a rare opportunity to hear key members of the Vancouver co-operative playing jazz (standards and original compositions) at the same time they were active at the Cellar. Additionally, three recordings featuring American guest artists at the Cellar exist. The first one is a rare bootleg recording of saxophonist Harold Land's otherwise unrecorded quartet featuring Elmo Hope (piano), a young Scott LaFaro (bass), and Lennie McBrowne (drums), released by Spanish label Fresh Sound in 2007 as *Harold Land: Jazz at the Cellar 1958*. The second, *Kenneth Patchen Reads with Jazz in Canada* (Folkways, 1959), features pianist Al Neil with a group of Cellar-based musicians backing American poet Kenneth Patchen (see Chapter 4). And the third is *The Montgomery Brothers in Canada* (Fantasy 3323, 1961), which was recorded after hours at the Cellar specifically for commercial release.

As a result of a conscious attempt by the Cellar's membership to connect to the jazz scene beyond the confines of Vancouver, the club hosted touring American artists with remarkable frequency. Many, like Harold Land and Art Pepper, were notable stars of the day, and others, such as Scott LaFaro, Don Cherry, and Ornette Coleman, were significant emerging artists. More than simply stopping by for a jam session or a single evening's performance, these visitors were often booked for lengthy engagements at the Cellar. Their extended stays in Vancouver led to the formation of personal relationships with local musicians, and to an organic interaction with the Cellar membership, which would often include rehearsals, jam sessions, formal performances, pedagogy, and informal discussions or "hangs."

Before proceeding further, it would be best to consider exactly what a "jazz co-operative" is and how it differs from commercial jazz clubs and other venues, such as cafés and restaurants, that also provide a welcoming space for jazz performance but operate as for-profit businesses. For the purposes of this book, a jazz co-operative is defined as a club that is conceived, operated, and managed by the musicians themselves with only nominal outside help. The rent and other operating expenses are borne as a shared risk by members of the co-operative without significant outside help, government funding, or private or commercial sponsorship. In addition, major decisions pertaining to booking, advertising, and the like are reached via consensus through an official board of directors, designated club manager, or some less formal means of group decision making. The clubs function as not-for-profit organizations, whether or not formally incorporated as such (several were formally registered). Though some key individuals may receive compensation for taking on particularly time-consuming roles in the operation of the club (manager, cleaner, etc.), the emphasis is on a volunteer-based, shared distribution of the workload.

Because the central role of the musicians themselves in the venue's establishment and operation is the main feature of jazz co-operatives, some important early Canadian jazz venues that were operated primarily by jazz enthusiasts rather than jazz musicians are excluded here. These include venues such as Victoria's Scene Club, Vancouver's Espresso Coffee House and Inquisition Coffee House, Winnipeg's Rando Manor and Stage Door, and most of Toronto's well-known jazz clubs.

This book is also largely unconcerned with club activities in such major urban areas as Toronto and Montreal, in part because jazz in these cities has been fairly well documented,[4] but mainly because these cities provided enough commercial opportunities for jazz and jazz-related music that self-organizing, co-operative performance spaces were unnecessary. In other words, both cities enjoyed populations and urban density sufficient to support nightclubs, coffee houses, and other performance venues, and jazz, to a large extent, was an economically viable pursuit. This is not to suggest that jazz performance in Montreal and Toronto was necessarily a lucrative venture, or even that numerous dedicated jazz venues existed at all times in these cities, but simply that there were enough performance spaces available to forestall the need for the establishment of artist-run co-operative jazz spaces.

One notable exception may be Toronto's MINC (Musicians Incorporated Club), which opened in 1959. This club existed largely to provide a performance venue for those musicians excluded from the local Toronto branch of the American Federation of Musicians Union, and thus from much paid work in the city. The majority of these musicians were American, others were newly arrived from other Canadian cities, and almost all were waiting to clear the union's six-month waiting period before they could join the Toronto local.[5] For many of Toronto's black musicians, the MINC also served as a venue in which they could practise and perform jazz, rather than the R&B, blues, and dance band music that formed much of their staple employment. Some, such as guitarist Sonny Greenwich, used the creative freedom offered by the MINC to evolve an interest in more avant-garde forms of jazz, the sounds of which were often absent from Toronto's major jazz venues.[6] The MINC therefore served a decidedly different purpose from the co-operative clubs, such as the Cellar, that are the focus of this book and which often represented the only performance opportunities for jazz in the cities where they operated.[7] As something of a unique case, Toronto's MINC is discussed in some detail in Chapter 7.

Unlike many music scenes that have recently been the focus of musicological enquiry,[8] the jazz scenes described in this book existed outside the concerns of the contemporary commercial recording industry, and were largely unaffected by the desires and ambitions of musicians trying to establish "professional" recording careers. Musicians interested in jazz understood that this genre of music occupied a decidedly marginal place within Canadian popular culture, and the Canadian recording industry. Local record stores did not generally stock jazz recordings, and albums of even the "big" American jazz artists often had to be specially ordered. And while American recordings may have had limited availability in Canada, domestically produced Canadian jazz recordings essentially did not exist.[9] Oscar Peterson was recording commercially as of 1945 (largely in the United States), but few domestically based Canadian jazz artists were commercially recorded before the mid-1960s. Significant exceptions were clarinettist Phil Nimmons who recorded out of Toronto for Verve and RCA in the late 1950s and 1960s, multi-instrumentalist Lance Harrison who recorded for RCA in 1965, and, later, saxophonist Fraser MacPherson in 1973 and again in 1976 when he released *Live at the Planetarium,* notable for its release three years later on American jazz label Concord Records.[10] Despite their popularity, CBC Vancouver stalwarts such as Chris Gage, Ray Norris, and Eleanor Collins did not record commercially at all.

While the domestic recording industry in Canada as a whole was admittedly rather limited during this period, it had flourished during the 1920s, particularly in Montreal. Several companies were active in the classical, folk and popular music fields, their catalogues including the novelty rags of pianists Willie Eckstein, Vera Guilaroff, and Harry Thomas, and the efforts of such jazz (or, more accurately, "hot dance") bands as the local Melody Kings and the Toronto band of pianist Gilbert Watson. The Apex subsidiary of Toronto's Compo records, for example, was recording Canadian artists as early as 1920, and released some three hundred Canadian recordings between 1921 and 1925. The extent to which these recordings were distributed outside Toronto and Montreal, however, remains unclear, and none of my interview subjects recalled any Canadian recordings as having been significant to their early musical exposure and development. It is worth pointing out that while Jack Litchfield's excellent *Canadian Jazz Discography, 1916–1980* lists numerous recordings made by Canadian jazz groups and orchestras,[11] the vast majority of these were commissioned for broadcast use only, and were never commercially available. Similarly, many jazz musicians (based primarily in Montreal and

Toronto) recorded from 1962 to 1966 for the not-for-profit Canadian Talent Library, but once again these were intended only for radio broadcast and were not distributed commercially.[12]

As a result, any professional ambitions that were harboured by the young jazz musicians involved with these co-operative clubs were focused more on securing musical jobs within the lucrative studio scene centred at or around the CBC (television and radio), or with the remaining dance bands that worked the hotels, ballrooms, and supper clubs in most Canadian cities.[13] In Vancouver, a well-recognized split developed between those musicians who inhabited the world of studio employment offered by the CBC and those who focused their musical energies around the jazz scene based out of the Cellar (initially) and the Black Spot and Flat Five clubs (later on).

The music presented on CBC television also rarely ventured into the realm of postwar small group jazz (bebop) as performed by the members of the Cellar and other co-ops. When the CBC did air such programming, it was generally with a well-known American star headlining. The local CBC radio station in Vancouver was a slightly different story, due in large part to the sheer amount of content required to fill the airwaves, and several of the Cellar-based groups did receive airplay as early as the late 1950s on programs such as *Jazz Workshop,*[14] or on other programs as guests performing opposite American artists booked to play the Cellar.

As a result, performance practice at the Cellar (and at other Canadian jazz co-ops) was for the most part free from pressure to conform to a particular definition of jazz, or to seek a middle ground between jazz and more popular programming in the hopes of finding wider popular and commercial success. Rather, the construction and performance of musical identity at these co-ops was self-regulating; it depended upon the internal consensus of the scene itself rather than on external, economically driven pressures. Indeed, the one major organizational breakdown at the Cellar occurred over one faction's desire to broaden the appeal of the club and "go commercial" against the wishes of the majority of the membership. This is not to say that the Cellar or the other jazz co-ops operated completely free of the jazz marketplace, but only that market pressures were largely secondary concerns connected to the American recording industry and its influence on the shaping and making of taste and performance repertoire.

Before considering the activities of the Cellar and the other co-operative jazz scenes specifically, Chapter 1 of this book explores the concept of "scene" in general, along with its relationship to a methodological tool known as the "scenes perspective." We all understand the use of the word "scene" in everyday language, but when considered more critically, examinations of "scene" and the community-based (and community-building) activity it engenders can be a powerful tool for understanding the emergence of varied, localized musical practices against notions of musical homogeneity. This introductory consideration of the scenes perspective is followed in Chapter 2 by a brief look at the socio-cultural climate in postwar Canada that contributed to the development of co-operative jazz clubs, including improvements in regional and national transportation systems and radio broadcasting, as well as an examination of the state of the Canadian jazz scene more generally. Given the book's focus on the Cellar, particular attention is paid to the early history of jazz in Vancouver and to the convoluted history of liquor regulation in British Columbia, which had a significant impact on live music venues in the city.

The bulk of the book is concerned with Vancouver's Cellar club (Chapters 3–6), and its evolution from the day it opened its doors in 1956 to its eventual closure in the mid-1960s. In charting the Cellar's roughly ten-year lifespan, this book considers the various ways in which the Cellar and the actions of its members created and enacted a jazz scene; its expansion of activities to include regular appearances by well-known American jazz artists; its role as a multi-disciplinary arts space that combined jazz with poetry, visual art, and theatre; and the ways in which this egalitarian co-operative venture remained very much a largely white, largely male-dominated space.

The success of the Cellar had a profound impact on the musical landscape of Vancouver, which by the early 1960s had expanded to include such clubs as the Inquisition Coffee House and the Espresso Coffee House, as well as the Black Spot/Flat Five, a co-operative jazz venture modelled expressly upon the Cellar. The rise of these new venues, along with the Cellar's slow decline as the key jazz space in Vancouver, are explored at length in Chapter 6. Chapter

7 then looks at the parallel establishment in the late 1950s of Edmonton's Yardbird Suite, Calgary's Foggy Manor, and Halifax's 777 Barrington Street, as well as briefly considering the contemporary jazz landscapes of Toronto and Montreal.

In detailing the ways in which musicians came to create performative communities, this book offers evidence of musical lifeways that have become increasingly rare. It also provides a counter-narrative to the dominant discourse of jazz centred in America, and on American jazz practices. Taken together, the actions and activities of these early jazz co-operatives created a new and infectious energy for jazz in Canada, one which I argue had a lasting impact through the 1990s and early 2000s, a period that Mark Miller has called a "golden era" for jazz in Canada. These unique co-operative ventures and the grassroots processes at the heart of regional jazz practices in Canada are a vital and previously unexamined part of the history of jazz in this country.

part one

Setting the Scene

1

Are You In or Out?

The Nature of the "Scene"

> *They just wanted to go out and play, and so we [made] these places so that we could go out and play. We could play whatever we damn well pleased, you know. And we didn't have to be beholden to anyone else.*
>
> – *Stan Perry*

The term "scene" has long enjoyed widespread use in everyday speech. We can easily refer to music scenes, art scenes, or the scenes associated with myriad other interests, which we then immediately understand to be both part of wider society and simultaneously marked, through dress, social behaviour, artistic output, or any combination of these factors, as representative of a smaller subset within society. However, though we are easily understood when we refer to the punk scene, the country scene, or the poetry scene, we are using the term only in a loose, superficial sense. By taking firmer hold of the word "scene" and considering just what, *exactly,* the term describes, it becomes a powerful tool for examining the ways in which people construct and enact meaning: in the case of this book, the ways in which groups of people construct and enact meaning through jazz music.

Briefly, the scenes perspective can be seen as a way of locating and describing the essential human relationships and social structures that enable particular localized forms of socio-cultural activity – here particular sorts of musical activity – to occur. At the same time, it allows for exceptional broadness of scope in considering the ways in which local scenes interact with and are part of wider musical communities with shared values (such as individual jazz scenes in other cities and, more generally, as represented by the jazz industry – records, magazines, etc.). From a research perspective, the word "scene" is particularly effective because it has a rich history of colloquial use and was immediately accepted and understood by everyone I spoke to. While some of the deeper theoretical nuances explored by scene theory might not have been conveyed in these exchanges, everyone was immediately able to understand more or less what I was interested in, and therefore what sort of information might be pertinent.

The term "scene" is also useful in that, much like Christopher Small's neologism "musicking,"[1] it includes those who participated in the activities of co-operative jazz clubs through vital, though non-musical, means. These non-musical participants in the scene form the complex milieux of the audience, fulfill necessary support roles, and produce complementary, yet non-musical, art. They are as vital to the scene as those who perform the music, and indeed, the constant and complex dynamic of these overlapping roles and responsibilities allow the scene to emerge and sustain itself. As we shall see, when the urgency of maintaining these relationships declines – when the need to be "on the scene" wanes – the scene itself starts to dissolve.

What Is a Scene?

Scenes are complex and fluid constructions that express themselves in myriad forms as they overlap, compete, and co-operate with one another for the use of shared resources (such as venues, media sources, musicians, and audience members). Members of one scene may also participate in other scenes (e.g., jazz players who also work in the studio world, audiences with varied interests), and multiple expressions of a single scene may exist within one local area (e.g., multiple jazz clubs in one city). To help navigate these modes of scenic expression, musicologist Andy Bennett suggests a division into three major types: the local, the translocal, and the virtual.[2]

Local scenes have a specific geographic focus and involve the relationship between music making and the lifeways of specific communities. Works such as Sara Cohen's study on rock music in working-class Liverpool and Barry Shank's exploration of music scenes in Austin, Texas,[3] are prime examples of local, geographically specific scene studies, as is my focus on the co-operative jazz scenes in certain Canadian cities, particularly the scene centred on the Cellar in Vancouver.

Bennett's second category, the translocal, concerns scenes that are widely dispersed geographically but drawn together around a particular music and/or corresponding lifestyle. These translocal scenes then make contact with one another through such resources as magazines, fan clubs, recordings, films, the passage of bands and fans through local scenes, and, more recently, via the Internet. Through these contacts, a sense of membership and identity may transcend local borders, enabling scene members to feel "at home" in diverse geographical settings. The jazz scene, for example, is not necessarily bounded for its participants by one particular venue, city, or country, but by certain codes of social and musical behaviour that are generally consistent from scene to scene and place to place. Audience members and performers can attend and engage with jazz at venues around the world with a sense of general continuity and belonging. Though active participation in the individual local scenes that make up the translocal jazz network would require local knowledge (the long process of "paying one's dues" and integrating into the community), more casual interaction as a fan or a peripatetic musician playing a short engagement is largely effortless, based on a shared understanding of the scene.[4]

One example of a translocal scene in operation is the touring pattern of jazz musicians from cities in California up the coast to the Cellar in Vancouver during the 1950s and 1960s. Through this movement of music and musicians, repertoire was spread, news shared, employment acquired, instruments bought and sold, and a sense of a musically bounded community fostered – all despite distance and regional difference. In a larger context, the spread of news and critical assessment through magazines such as *Downbeat, Metronome,* and *Coda* represents another way in which scenic jazz activity transcended local boundaries and participated in a network of complementary scenes, which were then informed and reaffirmed by news of one another.

Participants in Bennett's last main category, the virtual scene, are likewise often separated from one another by vast geographical distance. However, unlike translocal scenes, participation in virtual scenes may involve little, if any, in-person contact.[5] Rather, conversations are held and information is traded on the Internet through chat rooms, forums, blogs, and the exchange of media. Often these Internet meeting spaces are established and run by members of the scene themselves, and as such are generally less mediated by market and industry concerns than venues tied to commercial live performance (the club, the concert, the festival, the convention) or fan sites facilitated by record labels and management companies. A virtual scene is therefore a unique reflection of the desires and interests of its members, desires that may fluctuate organically over time as the scene evolves.

Virtual scenes are of course less pertinent to my historical discussion of co-operative jazz clubs in Canada, yet the relationship between the translocal and the virtual is relevant. In *Coda* magazine during the 1950s, for example, readers regularly received news and announcements from jazz scenes in the UK, Argentina, and Australia, as well as from the United States and other parts of Canada.[6] Information from these international scenes, many of which offered little or no possibility of direct interaction to the bulk of *Coda*'s readership, can perhaps be seen as a precursor to digitally virtual scenes. Certainly such news would have stood in contrast to regional and national news that offered readers the prospect of in-person interaction via touring and tourism.

Making the Scene

In many ways it is perhaps better to ask "Who is a scene?" rather than "What is a scene?" In order to function, any scene relies upon a confluence of musicians, fans, family, friends, recordists, journalists, producers, managers, agents, graphic designers, music store employees, back-line providers, and venue owners.[7] The activity of the scene's members serves both to create place (a venue or venues for the scene's activity) as well as space (the time and will to regularly enact it). Subsequently, scenic resources – be they people, venues, or goods – are frequently shared across art worlds (to use Howard Becker's term), a situation that permits scenes to exist *within* other scenes. For example, the Cellar in Vancouver functioned as a nexus for the burgeoning postwar counterculture and became a space where emerging musicians, poets, painters, architects, activists, actors, and filmmakers communed.

Through repeated acts of co-operation and mutual support, scenes create complex networks, which include both the interpersonal and the institutional, and which over time develop common conventions. These conventions provide the scene with boundaries and expectations to which members conform, and also with a sense of stability: the roles and co-operative acts necessary to the activities of the scene are able to continue despite turnover in the specific makeup of the scene's membership. Although scenes are formed through shared conflict with convention, paradoxically, it is when the shared conventions of the scene begin to fade that scenes themselves begin to lose their relevance.[8] In the case of jazz, such conventions can relate to repertoire (the Cellar was very much a bebop-oriented space), level of professionalism (jam sessions versus formal performances), and expectations for audience behaviour (some venues are "listening" rooms, while others reduce performances to background music). Local cultures of regular participants create and maintain a shared understanding of how music *means* within the context of the scene and what constitutes "good" within the parameters of scenic expression.

Multiple scenes accommodate multiple interpretations of authenticity, and the scenes perspective enables minority forms of musical expression to be granted validity even in the face of an overarching or dominant set of performance expectations.[9] At a time when the commercial jazz industry centred in the United States presented the dominant or most widely recognized set of jazz practices, Vancouver housed a modern jazz scene centred at the Cellar, as well as a traditional jazz scene, a dance band scene, and the scenes centred on nightclub work and commercial studio work, respectively. Each of these scenes in turn had sub-scenes based around specific venues and areas of the city. The Cellar and the Black Spot, for instance, catered to similar tastes in bebop-oriented jazz though to different age demographics, while the Espresso Coffee House was the after-hours spot for Vancouver's studio musicians.

What one does while not on the scene – when not physically present in the scenic space – is still informed by the scene and by one's level of identification with it. There was a marked difference, for example, between those who attended Vancouver's Cellar once or twice for an evening out and those whose lifestyle choices as artists and musicians co-operated with and were commensurate with the scene. Deep associations with a scene are often extended and expressed through the actions of daily life and the accoutrements – the records, books, clothes, friends, and jobs – that act in some measure to enact and signal one's sense of self (e.g., jazz fan, jazz musician). This sort of identification with the scene – with jazz as a lifeway – was remarked upon repeatedly in the interviews I conducted. Musicians, artists, and co-operative members recalled a self-conscious understanding that the scene wasn't just a matter of what they did, but a fundamental and foundational element of who they were. Scenes thereby function as an intersection between the realities of public life and the imagined interiors of constructed identity. Even when temporarily divorced from scenic activity (the periods between gigs or other scenic events, the "regular" life of jobs and school, etc.), an individual maintains a sense of identity that is in large part predicated upon involvement with the scene. Over time, these forms of expression and behaviour may take on ideological and political overtones that, in some cases, are transmitted beyond the confines of the scene and are "read" by larger society.[10]

While these social readings may be more obvious in relation to such visibly expressive scenes as punk, metal, goth, or hip hop, in the postwar period bebop was subject to similarly politicized associations with regard to morality, racial politics, countercultural attitudes, the beat aesthetic, and the changing socio-political landscape in the United States. Vancouver's Black Spot club, for example, catered to a slightly younger demographic than the Cellar. Poet Jamie Reid saw it as "a beatnik club ... Everybody in black turtleneck sweaters and pretending to write poetry and getting up and reading poetry and drinking awful coffee and so on."[11] However, at the Cellar, "a thing that was interesting costume-wise," commented poet bill bissett,

> was that a lot of the guys wore grey flannel suits. And it was considered extremely hip, and I think it was somehow modelled after ... the guy that jumped from his hotel in Amsterdam – Chet Baker. I think it had something to do with Chet Baker, I think. So I got myself a grey flannel suit. I think I didn't wear a shirt and tie under it, I wore, like, a T-shirt under it. Majorly cool.[12]

For many of its participants, a scene functions as a lifestyle rather than a pastime – music making is then a socio-cultural experience predicated upon the entwined practices of listening and performing, of seeing and being seen, and of a sociability imposed by the constraints of space and place. Scenes, however, are not necessarily places of universal positivity or inclusion, and the politics of economic class and gender expectations may affect the musical activities of the scene and the behavioural codes that govern it.

While multiple factors conspired to bring about the eventual closure of Vancouver's Cellar club in 1964, a sense of decline in shared conventions was commonly remarked upon by those I interviewed. The scene began to hold less relevance for those who had had founded and participated in it, and this gradual decrease in scenic energy, coupled with continually evolving cultural tastes in wider society, meant that the scene also began to hold less allure for those on the outside – the more casual audience previously drawn by the scene's sense of cool and cultural relevance as much as by the music. What resulted was a sort of scenic entropy: the eventual dissolution of the scene as newer forms of musical expression and their attendant scenes began to take on the role previously performed by clubs such as the Cellar and the Black Spot. One participant of the scene pointed a finger at "Rock and roll. What's his name ... Elvis. The Beatles. There was no money and there was no up-and-coming jazz musicians, really. They were all going with the crowd."[13] As musician John Dawe told me, "It was all over. The fun was over," adding later, "We'd all grown up a bit, in some ways.

Everybody was starting to mature a bit and get other ideas."[14] Scenes, then, are pushed and pulled by a kind of social gravity; they rise, fall, and overlap until their eventual entropic decline.

The Scenes Perspective at Work

The scenes perspective has been prevalent in musicology since the early 1990s, with Will Straw's 1991 work "Systems of Articulation, Logics of Change: Communities and Scenes in Popular Music" generally cited as the first article to use the word "scene" in this more specific sense. Straw posited that scene study offered a means to undermine "assumptions of uniformity within local music cultures," a tendency that he felt had been encroaching into popular music studies.[15] Rather than one homogenous musical expression that arose from and was marked by space or place, multiple local musical tendencies were visible even in those areas dominated by an overarching, often historically linked musical culture. Furthermore, these local tendencies overlapped and interlocked, a process through which the local became global (or translocal) with astonishing speed. Indeed, within a year of the Cellar's opening in Vancouver, the Yardbird Suite was established in Edmonton, followed shortly by the Foggy Manor in Calgary, a direct result of the translocal – of scenes interacting with and influencing other scenes. Further, the contemporaneous existence of 777 Barrington Street in Halifax suggests that socio-cultural conditions common to a region or nation may lead to the emergence of similar scenes even though they are not in direct contact.

Through their *construction* of identity rather than the *inheritance* of identity, scenes are self-conscious attempts by their members to create a space for the performance of cultural activity that lacks an outlet elsewhere (the Cellar, the Yardbird Suite, 777 Barrington Street) or where the outlets are inadequate to accommodate all those interested in the activities of the scene (Black Spot/Flat Five). Scenes are initially volatile spaces seeking to establish and perpetuate boundaries of affect and influence, yet they are guided by an internal logic that amounts to a microsociology of advance and retreat, resulting in a somewhat predictable life cycle of birth, expansion, and contraction. As a scene stabilizes, it develops an infrastructure of venues, publications, and media that integrate it into the wider marketplace. Through such infrastructure, scenes enable local practices to be reproduced on national and international scales, often with the result that multiple musical vernaculars are enacted in multiple locales.[16]

The jazz scenes in this book, for example, relied upon local media, such as student and city newspapers, local radio, and local record stores, to promote their activities. Eventually, some of these activities were reported through nationally available sources such as *Coda* and *Downbeat* magazines, and infrequent CBC national broadcasts that sometimes included some of the musicians involved in these co-operative clubs (though usually not in the same musical context). At the same time, the widespread reach of the dominant American jazz culture ensured that a knowledge of emerging musical practices and the existence of major American clubs were shared themes for desire and emulation. The nature of identity formation, group dynamics, the role of insiders versus outsiders, the importance of place, and the tension between art and the commercial marketplace are explored with varying degrees of focus in work by musicologists Sara Cohen, Barry Shank, Andy Bennett, Aaron Fox, and Ruth Finnegan, as well as sociologist Alan Blum, who offers insight into the symbiotic relationship that exists between scenes and the modern city.[17]

Whereas several scene studies have examined not only the inner workings of scene formation but also the ways in which scenes interact with the demands of the commercial marketplace,[18] Aaron Fox's *Real Country: Music and Language in Working Class Culture* focuses on musical practice as a form of social interaction. Fox concentrates on the country music scene he finds located or situated in the honky-tonks and bars of rural Texas, the last vestiges of a commercially marginal scene forced out of Austin, the nearest large city. In examining musical practices that are self-conscious in their lack of commercial viability, he concentrates upon how musical practices come to *mean,* and the ways in which they may come to occupy the central place in the culture of a particular group.[19] Additionally, because country music is simultaneously the basis of a highly lucrative commercial enterprise with marketable stars (in Nashville) as well as the means of expression for a non-commercial yet vital local scene (the honky-tonk), Fox examines the distinction "between genres of popular music as fields of production and consumption, mediated principally by the relationships of economic exchange they structure, and genres of popular music as fields of popular practice, mediated primarily by ritualized forms of intimate social interaction."[20]

Jazz is, similarly, a genre in which local or marginal forms of jazz expression compete with the dominant (American) jazz culture, a process that is perhaps more urgent when one considers that localized expression in Canada must compete with American jazz influence *within* the scene as well as without. In the case of the scenes that sprang up around Canada's jazz co-operatives, the adoption of an autonomous, anti-commercial artistic aesthetic was conscious, and repeatedly remarked upon by my interview subjects. As drummer Stan Perry told me,

> The average Joe – Mr. and Mrs. Smith, they don't have a clue about jazz, and they can't get up and dance to it, and us guys, at least when I was young, and the other people like me, when they were young, they didn't give a sweet pippy about the general public, they just wanted to go out and play, and so we [made] these places so that we could go out and play. We could play whatever we damn well pleased, you know. And we didn't have to be beholden to anyone else.[21]

The oppositional quality of scenic activity is a powerful force in shaping community and in forging identity – the scene is as much defined by what it isn't as by what it is. Jazz has perhaps never had the same broad popular profile as the music examined by Cohen, Shank, and Fox. Nonetheless, marginal sub-genres and sub-scenes within the larger jazz world have long had to fight for traction against both the popular perception of jazz (as exemplified by, say, Miles Davis or Dave Brubeck) and dominant performative norms within the scene (the contentious reception of Ornette Coleman in 1959 is perhaps the most famous example).

In examining the songs and artists considered part of the local canon, the socio-cultural codes of behaviour that surround the musical space, and how scene participants come to express themselves, Fox's study of country music also describes how lines of affiliation may be drawn and defended *within* musical genres with as much vehemence as between them. The "hipness" or "squareness" demarcating those within the jazz world from those without may also exist *within* a jazz world itself, divided into internal microgenres or styles, yet largely seen as homogeneous by those outside the scene.

The nature of the urban environment is such that multiple scenes exist simultaneously in any one city, and at times overlap in terms of their venues, resources, and active participants. Much of the musical activity produced by these scenes is what musicologist Ruth Finnegan has termed "hidden,"[22] musical practices by largely amateur or semi-professional players and by those who must balance their participation in the scene with work, family, and other social obligations that at times take precedence. Such situations are normal for many participants of commercially marginalized music scenes, even at the highest levels. Many scene members must take work unrelated to their musical interests. For instance, Ornette Coleman was an elevator operator in Los Angeles during the 1950s; many of the Cellar members had day jobs. Many other participants may work within the music industry, though perhaps outside their preferred mode of artistic expression, in order to make a living.

Musical activities are not spontaneous occurrences, but are "made to happen" through the efforts of their respective scenic communities,[23] and must be located in time, space, and place with enough regularity to develop their own mythology, local history, and sense of stable social structure or community. The maintenance of scenes is only possible through the presence of an audience and the actions of support personnel who continue to secure a space/place within which the musical practices may occur (these roles are, of course, not mutually exclusive). Through these acts of collective "musicking," the scene brings itself into being, and its members are connected not "just by shared views or emotions but by social *practices*" that occur along "socially recognized pathways which systematically [link] into a wide variety of settings and institutions within the city."[24]

The Jazz Scene

The term "scene" has long appeared in jazz literature, and while one advantage of this longstanding association is the extent to which the term is accepted within the jazz community, its methodological efficacy is at times muddied by its frequent colloquial use. Indeed, the term "jazz scene" is commonly used somewhat interchangeably to refer to all jazz practices in a global sense, differentiating jazz from other forms of musical expression; to refer to the jazz community in a certain country (the American scene versus the Japanese scene) or region (the west coast scene or the east coast scene); or to refer to jazz practices within whichever city is being discussed (the New York scene). Very rarely is the term used in a hyper-specific sense to refer to the various overlapping scenes that may coexist in a city or region at the same time, and which simultaneously co-operate and compete with one another.

Eric Hobsbawm's 1960 landmark work *The Jazz Scene*, for example, is rightly interested in the widespread intersection of jazz practice with other elements of popular culture and modern life. It was one of the first works to turn the lens of scholarship from the stage toward the audience, and from the named stars of jazz to those toiling in relative obscurity for little obvious gain.[25] The work is rarely specific as to how the sites of jazz practice are organized, relate to each other, and gain meaning for their participants; however, its sections on "Popular Music" and "The Jazz Business" are nuanced,[26] and those on the "Jazz Public" and "Jazz as Protest" were remarkable for their time. Though Hobsbawm used the word "scene" colloquially, without the specificity or rigor with which it is currently employed, his title does suggest how easily, and for how long, the term "jazz scene" has had traction within both the academic community and the jazz world.

Indeed, the majority of works that invoke the term "jazz scene" are wide-ranging studies of jazz practices in individual cities or regions. Often the only works of their kind, these studies are invaluable repositories of jazz history, but often do little to increase our understanding of the self-organizing principles at work within specific sites of engagement for jazz.[27] A notable exception is Clora Bryant's *Central Avenue Sounds: Jazz in Los Angeles,* which addresses the concept of "scene" more narrowly, examining the spaces, musicians, and other resources particular to the city of Los Angeles.[28] She highlights "The Watts Scene," providing an in-depth discussion of an area (not officially part of Los Angeles in the 1920s) that was becoming a major site of settlement for the black community. Free from many of Los Angeles's restrictions on alcohol and nightclub activities and home to many black performers, Watts became an area of significant jazz activity that operated under unique, scene-specific conditions. Recent scholarship has refined the use of scenes in jazz even further, intersecting with the sociological roots of scene theory as well as its application in other areas of musicology to produce such significant works as Alex Stewart's *Making the Scene: Contemporary New York City Big Band Jazz* and Travis Jackson's *Blowin' the Blues Away: Performance and Meaning on the New York Jazz Scene*.[29]

Stewart's work, which combines oral history, ethnography, and self-ethnography, examines the ways in which big bands in New York City during the 1990s were meaningful to the musicians who played in them and to the audiences who came to hear them. He looks at the different scenes centred on rehearsal bands, mainstream jazz orchestras (such as the Vanguard Jazz Orchestra), Latin bands, repertory bands (those playing the works of Duke Ellington and Charles Mingus, for example), experimental ensembles (such as William Parker's), and orchestras that perform contemporary compositions (such as Maria Schneider's). In so doing, Stewart addresses the complex and intersecting nature of scenes, and how multiple scenes can coexist, overlap one another, and share members. In describing the complex world of big band musicians in New York, Stewart brings in notions of authenticity and legitimacy, the seemingly irreconcilable notions of individuality (a jazz hallmark) and the blend required to play in a section, as well as issues of race and gender particular to the big band scene. Nonetheless, while Stewart admirably describes and explores the scenes he encounters, he uses the term without addressing what it might mean beyond its colloquial applications.

However, Travis Jackson's careful consideration of performance and meaning on the New York scene of the 1990s locates the concept of "scene" within the pre-existing sociological and musicological literature, refining his own use of the term while describing its wider application and roots as a methodological tool. Jackson highlights the multiplicity of scenes available in the same urban location at the same time, and considers how the energy and importance of scenes alters over time. A scene may pass out of a position of ascendancy without passing out of being, and may continue to have local relevance and influence long after it has ceased to be a site of wider aspiration or imitation. Significantly, Jackson also looks at the ways in which jazz journalists provide perhaps the best and most insightful work on individual jazz scenes, concerned as they are with the day-to-day and month-to-month activities of their local areas. Finally, Jackson reminds us, scenes are not simply spatial phenomena but historical ones. The human interactions at the heart of scenic activity resonate beyond the specific spatial limitations of the scene (the venue), extending across history both through the evolving structures and activities of the scene, and the shared mythologization of prior scenic activity.

A City of Scenes

Scenes, sociologist Alan Blum tells us, are essential to how the city itself becomes a humanized space or a place,[30] and the language of scenes is irrevocably tied to the language of urban geography. One cannot consider the question of cities without running across settings identified, with varying levels of specificity, as "scenes." Repeated and often generic references to such socio-cultural groupings as the theatre scene, the literary scene, or the music scene in descriptions of urban life suggest that scenes, in the life cycles of cities, function as cultural commodities and "circulate in ways that might bring them to some cities rather than others or to all cities in varying degrees."[31] Indeed, the extent to which a city possesses such scenic elements helps position it in relation to other cities for attracting residents, tourists, and certain forms of urban investment and development.

If "space" is an often generic physical or geographical location, "place," for the purposes of this discussion, is "humanized space," somewhere that is emotionally significant or resonant for an individual or group.[32] Whereas *spaces* provide a structure through which processes and events flow, *places* are "particular moments in ... intersecting social relations ... which have over time been constructed, laid down, interacted with one another, decayed and renewed."[33] Where musicians perform affects what they perform and how, because the intersection of space and place is defined socially, as well as physically. While scenes are dependent upon economic viability as they pass through urban space in search of resources, the innovation and particular character of scenes follows from the *places* they inhabit, from the construction of a community in which the constraints of economic viability are lifted, even if only temporarily.[34]

Scenes, then, are heavily, even intimately weighted with the idea of the local, with not simply the concept of space, but of socioculturally specific place.[35] The places that scenes inhabit then become repositories for localized histories, for the relevant "socio-musical codes," which are lived as much as learned. Past performances of scene and some shared understanding of that history or mythology enables the current practices of, and within, the scene to be locally situated – to be meaningful – as they engage with other sociohistorically located practices.[36] In the case of local jazz scenes, this often takes the form of frequently shared stories about who played where and when; this storytelling allows for the construction of myth and identity. Key events in the history of the scene (such as a particular Mingus engagement at the Cellar discussed in Chapter 5) are shared and retold by those who witnessed them, and over time pass into the wider lore of the scene, possessed by all scene members and not just those who witnessed the event. Possession of the story then equates, to some degree, with possession of place – with membership in the scene, and a connection to the scene's history.

Scenes often become associated with certain performance venues, but also with particular record shops, book shops, and music stores. Participation in the scene is thus staged across these various spaces. Scenic coherence and the ability of a scene to provide a place of stability and resonance for its members becomes harder to achieve the more fragmented these associated spaces become across the urban environment. While Blum suggests that such movement encourages the exploration of boundaries,[37] Straw makes a convincing counterargument that fragmentation occurs when greater time and effort must be expended to participate in a scene. Without the frequent experience of seeing and being seen, individuals cease to be recognized within the scene, and their sense of attachment and identification with the scene weakens. The scene loses its "visibility, dispersed within multiple sites of encounter and consumption."[38] As we shall see, this describes how the scene centred on the Cellar club waned in the face of increased opportunities for jazz expression in Vancouver, even though those opportunities had been prompted by the Cellar's initial success.

Scenes exist, then, as brief, ephemeral occurrences. Even though the sense of identity and community may linger between scenic events, the scene itself comes together in mutual semiotic expression only at brief, though perhaps regular, intervals: the scene itself is only fully realized at the gig, the concert, or the festival. As such, scenes are a product not just of space and place, but of temporality. Even once a scene has lost its power, having become less significant or dissolved entirely, the social connections formed through participation in scenes do much to enable the social interactions upon which urban living depends.

> Scenes are, much of the time, lived as effervescence, but they also create the grooves to which practices and affinities become fixed. Chance encounters on a street or in bars often require, to be smooth and successful, the resuscitation of connections or mutual interests now marginal to the rest of our lives. In such encounters, and in their repetition, knowledges are reinvigorated and the peripheries of our social networks renewed. Such occasions are like the sedimentation of artifacts or architectural forms within cities: through them the city becomes a repository of memory.[39]

At their heart, scenes may best be considered a form of musical phenomenology; performance that does not merely give voice to memory, but that simultaneously creates and embodies it. Scenes exist at the intersection between global flows of media and local cultural expression, where they wrestle with notions of authenticity, mythology, identity, place, and belonging. In some cases, the qualities of a scene are compelling enough that it spills out of its local setting to inform connected scenes elsewhere, simultaneously transcending the need for face-to-face interaction while multiplying the opportunities for it to occur. The activities of a scene provide avenues for discourse through which scene members engage in a process of identity formation upon which a sense of collective belonging or community is built. Nonetheless, the term "scene" remains vague, still as likely to be used to describe the local coffee shop as the ways in which musical practices and socio-cultural behaviours come to have meaning for those who share them.

Some fifty years after the closure of these Canadian co-operative jazz clubs, I found no shortage of participants able and willing to recall their experiences, and my research was greatly aided by the fact that many members of these scenes had remained in some sort of contact over the intervening decades.

2

Laying the Groundwork

The Early History of Jazz in Canada

> *I remember working up in a survey crew in the middle of the province in Tweedsmuir Park with my radio, and I could set up an aerial, and ... strangely enough [deep in the woods] I could pick up that signal and listen to Bob Smith on CBC.*
>
> – *Walley Lightbody*

In the early decades of the twentieth century, jazz scenes in Canadian cities (and regions) tended to be insular.[1] This was due in large part to the vast distances between major Canadian cities and relative dearth of quick, reliable transportation across the country via automobile or rail. In addition, domestic recording opportunities for jazz artists were limited, and there was no nationally broadcast jazz programming. Most Canadian regions in the 1950s boasted only one major urban centre, particularly in the East, where Halifax's 1951 population was only 86,000, and the West, where, in 1955, Edmonton's population stood at 210,000 and Vancouver's at 588,000. In contrast, New York City was home to some 7 million residents during the 1950s, Boston some 800,000, Chicago 3.6 million, and Los Angeles 1.9 million. Outside more densely populated central Canada (Toronto and Montreal), the music scenes of Canadian cities were often far more attuned to musical activity in the nearby United States. American music exerted a huge influence through radio stations broadcasting over the border, the dominant American recording industry, publications such as *Downbeat* and *Metronome,* and the large percentage of American artists who were featured on Canadian radio broadcasts. Canadian jazz culture in the postwar period, therefore, faced huge logistical barriers to the dissemination of Canadian content.

Canada has had a long relationship with radio, receiving the first transatlantic wireless signal in 1901 at Signal Hill in Newfoundland and launching one of the world's first radio stations – XWA in Montreal – in 1919.[2] National broadcasting was first attempted by the Canadian National Railway in 1923, a move that also marked the unofficial beginning of public radio broadcasting in Canada. Available on the main CNR trains and at CNR hotels in its major destination cities, the CNR's broadcasting efforts sought to provide regular, consistent, and engaging programming to its customers from coast to coast. Programming was originally provided by harnessing and rebroadcasting high-output Canadian and American stations. Ultimately, the CNR set up a national network of stations and began to supply these stations with programming it deemed to be of suitable quality. On December 27, 1928, the CNR network broadcast the first coast-to-coast Canadian national network radio program.[3] Generally speaking, however, CNR broadcasts were national only in that they were available to patrons throughout the national railway network. They were not broadcast simultaneously across the country.[4]

During the 1920s, Canada could boast only a few dozen radio stations, the most powerful of which were operated by the CNR and the rest by a mix of newspapers, universities, and private companies. Broadcast hours were limited, though Canadians living close to the border were often able to tune in to more regular US-based programming. Following the recommendation of a royal commission, the Canadian Radio Broadcasting Commission was established in 1932, and was replaced in 1936 by the Canadian Broadcasting Corporation. Though today the CBC is popularly perceived as promoting nationalism in its representation of Canadian interests, it has, historically, just as often served to promote an insular regionalism in the performing arts. Certainly this was true for jazz in the decades before such popular national jazz programs as *Jazz Beat* (1983–2007) and *After Hours* (1993–2007), both of which tried to strike a regional balance in the presentation of Canadian recordings and live broadcasts.[5] In the early decades of Canadian radio the focus was local; by 1936, Manitoba, Saskatchewan, Alberta, and British Columbia were receiving their own programming produced in the West, rather than the same programming as the rest of the nation. This situation was formalized in 1939 with the establishment of regional networks within each of the country's five time zones that sought to cater to regional interests.[6] There was of course national programming, but the programming of popular music was generally left to local taste, and musicians on one side of the country rarely heard those from the other. Compounding the issue was the prevalence on Canadian airwaves of US broadcasts that featured American bands. In 1939, columnist Don McKim proclaimed in *Downbeat* that "Canadian bands are still in diapers," due in part to the CBC's policy of broadcasting American bands some five times as often as Canadian ones.[7]

Even orchestras at larger hotels with radio broadcast capabilities received limited national airplay,[8] and as a result, while certain groups and bandleaders enjoyed regional success due to live performances, no Canadian orchestra emerged with the national popularity of, say, Benny Goodman or Glenn Miller in the United States. This characteristic regionalism did, however, enable artists to acquire a local popularity and profile they may not have had otherwise, and left room for the emergence of local and regional media personalities, some of whom had a lasting impact on the development of jazz in their communities.

British Columbia radio broadcaster and columnist Bob Smith began his career while still in high school during the mid-1930s, hosting a program on local station CJOR that focused on the popular American big bands of the era. During the Second World War, Smith joined the Royal Canadian Air Force, and was eventually posted to the South Pacific where he served with US forces, returning to Canada in unique possession of a large collection of contemporary American jazz recordings. In February 1947 he broadcast the first instalment of *Hot Air* on CBC Vancouver, a program that became perhaps the longest-running jazz radio show in the world. Initially a half-hour broadcast, in May 1948 *Hot Air* was extended to a full hour, and quickly became an important part of the jazz scene in Vancouver.[9]

As CBC producer Neil Ritchie recalled, Bob Smith was

> just one of these delightful individuals who was very personable. He had an incredible memory. I guess originally the show was done live on Saturday nights from the Hotel Vancouver. I think it was at eleven or twelve on Saturday night. And the thing about the location was that a lot of the visiting musicians that were playing the Cave or Isy's would walk up to the studio. Bob would always have a bottle stashed somewhere, and they'd have a drink and chat a little bit and then go back to the gig. So it was very much a live show, and over the years the musicians ... it became part of their itinerary. When they were in Vancouver, they would see Bob. And of course Bob could remember every detail of every record they'd made and every city they'd visited since he'd last seen them. So the musicians really responded to him, and would go out of their way to come in for a chat.[10]

Broadcast over Vancouver's powerful CBC station and passed through repeater stations in smaller communities, *Hot Air* was heard throughout British Columbia's rural interior and enabled young musicians outside the metro Vancouver area to develop an interest in modern jazz.[11] Jim Carney, trumpet player and eventual charter member of the Cellar, recalled that *Hot Air* enabled him to keep up with developments in jazz even from a distance.

> [Nelson, BC] is where we first heard Bob Smith's show *Hot Air.* At that time in our school we – those of us who were interested in music – we would listen to Benny Goodman and Tommy Dorsey and Harry James and all the big band guys, and then one night I was listening in my bedroom to this wonderful new kind of music, and it was actually Warne Marsh, and maybe Lee Konitz, I don't know, but it was then the theme for *Hot Air,* called "Wow." That was my introduction to [modern jazz]. It was an epiphany. It was not an acquired taste, it was something that just hit me between the eyes.[12]

Likewise saxophonist (and later Queen's Counsel) Walley Lightbody, who would help to co-found both the Cellar in Vancouver and the Scene in Victoria, recalled that

> Bob Smith was the big guy when he started his *Hot Air* [program], and he became a close friend. I remember working up in a survey crew in the middle of the province in Tweedsmuir Park with my radio, and I could set up an aerial, and I would listen to Bob Smith's *Hot Air* which I think came on a Friday night at that time, though I could be wrong about that, and so strangely enough [deep in the woods] I could pick up that signal and listen to Bob Smith on CBC.[13]

However, despite the important role that *Hot Air* played in exposing young BC musicians to more modern forms of jazz, the programming was overwhelmingly American in content.

> In those days our local musicians didn't have records, so the show changed and it became more about BC artists [later on], but of course in those days jazz was American. And there were lots of BC musicians, but they didn't get very many jazz gigs. It was mostly television gigs and dance gigs, and lots of club gigs and things, but really the jazz gigs were rarer ... None of the local musicians, really, had recorded as jazz artists.[14]

The general lack of Canadian jazz on radio and the highly regionalized nature of the Canadian content that did exist was compounded by the difficulty of regional and national transportation imposed by Canada's sheer size and relative underpopulation. Until at least the time of the Second World War, travel from Toronto, Montreal, or Halifax to such American cities as Chicago, New York, and Boston was much easier than travel to western Canadian destinations. A daily rail service was available from Montreal to Chicago on the International Limited as early as 1900, and while service from Toronto and Montreal to Vancouver began in 1916, the proliferation of short, regular train service south to such US destinations as Washington, DC, Boston, New York, and Chicago in the East and Seattle, Portland, San Francisco, and Los Angeles in the West meant that it remained much easier for music and musicians to traverse the American landscape than the Canadian.

Though the last spike on the Canadian Pacific railway (the first trans-Canadian rail line) was not driven until 1885, travel across the northern United States had been possible since 1883 via service on the Northern Coast Limited, which connected Chicago with Seattle and included branch line service into Winnipeg, Manitoba, and Sumas, British Columbia.[15] Additional national service did not operate in Canada until the 1916 completion of the Canadian Northern Railway, though regular service between Edmonton and Vancouver (three times a week) on portions of Canadian Northern track started in 1915.[16]

The state of the highways in western Canada was even worse, and contributed to the movement of music and musicians *around* Canada, rather than across it. In the early decades of the twentieth century, it was essentially impossible to cross the province of British Columbia east to west by road, and the only north-south motor route into the province's interior was by way of the Cariboo Road, a rough and unpaved route that was "very much in the same form in the 1920s as it had been in the 1800s."[17] Even as late as the 1950s, road travel across British Columbia was so treacherous that resident Leah Shaw recalled that a relative travelling to Vancouver from the prairies became so horrified by the road conditions that they attempted to hire a local driver and, when that proved impossible, preferred to ship their car ahead and take the train rather than drive the rest of the way to Vancouver.[18] By contrast, a patchwork system of highways led across the northern United States from Chicago to Seattle, and by 1926, US Highway 99 stretched from the Canadian border down the US west coast almost to Mexico. While the Trans-Canada Highway did not begin construction until 1950 and did not open until 1962, by at least 1940 the completion of the King George Highway in British Columbia's lower mainland provided an easy connection from Vancouver to the US border and the American highway and interstate system.

Even if eastward transport across and out of British Columbia had been easily accomplished, population density still complicated things for most touring musicians. The drive from Vancouver to either Edmonton or Calgary (some nine to twelve hours even today), offered few performance opportunities on route; the same was true of the journey further eastward to Regina or Saskatoon, and so forth. By contrast, the drive from Vancouver to Seattle is approximately three hours, followed by Portland, Oregon, in another three hours. While the drive further south to Los Angeles takes more than a day, the trip would have offered the possibility of performances in some of the larger cities along the way such as Sacramento, San Francisco, Oakland, San Jose, and Fresno.[19]

As Mark Miller details in *Such Melodious Racket: The Lost History of Jazz in Canada 1916–1949,* it was simply quicker and more cost-effective to cross from the Canadian East to the Canadian West via the United States than through Canada itself. This routing also afforded travelling musicians more cities and towns as possible venues while on tour. The net result was that stronger, more important musical ties were often formed along a North-South axis, rather than an East-West one. Indeed, Vancouver journalist Patrick Neagle recalled that in the years following World War Two, a veritable "show business railway" existed, moving American performers from Las Vegas, Los Angeles, San Francisco, and Seattle northwards up the Pacific coast to Vancouver.[20]

Early Jazz in Vancouver

Vancouver's relationship with American performers and with American jazz-oriented music began early in its civic history. In 1914, less than twenty years after the city's founding, the Original Creole Orchestra, featuring trumpet legend Freddie Keppard, appeared at the Pantages Theatre on Hastings Street in Vancouver's bustling East End.[21] In September 1916, the group returned, now billed as Johnson's Creole Band, and was described in the local press as

> a headline attraction ... [which is] where they belong, for a more novel and amusing turn has not been to the Pantages circuit for some time. [The band consisted of] six instrumentalists of ability and class ... [and] the selections were well rendered, even though a trifle weird at times, the various pieces in the band though [account] for this as there is a trombone, a cornet, a clarionet [sic], a violin, a bass fiddle,

> and a guitar. The musical numbers are all of the latest syncopated class and keep one's feet busy on the floor.[22]

These engagements took place at one of Vancouver's two outlets for the popular North American Pantages vaudeville circuit, which, under the direct management of George Pantages, nephew of chain founder Alexander, competed directly with the Imperial, Avenue, Crystal, Royal, and Orpheum Theatres, all of which occupied a narrow corridor along Hastings and Pender Streets in Vancouver's East End. Taking full advantage of its position at the heart of Vancouver's thriving commercial centre, the area also cultivated innumerable pool halls, beer parlours, hotels, and cafés. It was surely no coincidence that Vancouver's first automatic traffic lights were established at the intersection of Main Street and Hastings.[23]

In addition to the Original Creole Orchestra, these Vancouver theatres hosted many early jazz performers, including the "Largest Jazz Band in the World," a twenty-five piece orchestra of recently demobilized American servicemen,[24] and the Jazz Hounds, a duo comprising pianist Shelton Brooks and "clarionettist syncopationist [sic]" Horace George, who opened at Vancouver's Orpheum.[25] Brooks was a songwriter of considerable fame, having composed such popular tunes as "Darktown Strutters' Ball," "Walkin' the Dog," and "Some of These Days" – the last made famous by Sophie Tucker, who had visited Vancouver in 1914. Perhaps most famously, Vancouver's East End played host to pianist Ferdinand "Jelly Roll" Morton, one of the early giants of jazz. Speaking to Alan Lomax in 1938, Morton recalled that "on the streets of Seattle I ran into ... an old New Orleans sporting-life friend ... now a big time gambler ... [who] brought me into those circles and I started losing money. About the time [I] got down to my last dime Will Bowman asked me to bring a band into his cabaret in Vancouver, Canada."[26]

In operation since 1917 to service the booming commercial corridor along Hastings Street, the Patricia Hotel and Cabaret passed into the hands of William Bowman on August 12, 1919, and by September of the same year, had installed a group that included both Morton and pianist and clarinet player Oscar Holden.[27] According to Morton, although the band was capable, "somehow that cabaret didn't do so good"; he suggested that in Vancouver, "folks there didn't understand American-style cabarets." In any case, Morton took leave of Bowman and the Patricia by the summer of 1920.[28]

From 1920 through 1922, the Patricia Cabaret also presented other entertainers, among them vocalist Ada "Bricktop" Smith, whose biography offers some insight into the atmosphere of the Patricia. "Bowman's biggest customers, and I do mean big," relates Bricktop, "were Swedish lumberjacks who came into Vancouver on their time off ... [and] pretty soon they'd be drunk and ready to fight."[29] Such fights were apparently not restricted to the patrons, as Bricktop herself suffered a broken leg in one such melee on New Year's Eve of 1920. Rumours of this activity eventually found their way out of the clubs, which may explain how a music that had earlier been lauded in the press for its ability to "stir real enthusiasm in a world wearied by a long and ghastly war," was now considered a dynamic nuisance that ought, as in Portland to the south, to be banned. Jazz, along with its popular dance companion the shimmy, were seen by many as the "twin sisters of corruption."[30]

Hogan's Alley and the East End

The eastern portion of downtown Vancouver, which has been alternately known as the East End and as Strathcona (after 1950), stretched roughly from Main Street east to Campbell Avenue, and from Powell Street near the Ballantyne wharf in Coal Harbour south to Prior Street, ending near the rail yards and False Creek (see Figure 1).[31] This area, which encompassed Chinatown, the stretch of Cordova Street known as Japantown, and a largely black neighbourhood known as Hogan's Alley, was home to Vancouver's largest concentration of working-class residents. B.C. Electric had its headquarters on Hastings Street, and the bustling rail and dockyards lay only a few blocks away. Indeed, so great was the concentration of working-class citizens in the East End that in 1923, Louis D. Taylor, soon to become one of the city's most colourful and beloved mayors, lost an election because a power failure that immobilized the streetcar network prevented the bulk of his blue-collar electorate from reaching the polls.[32]

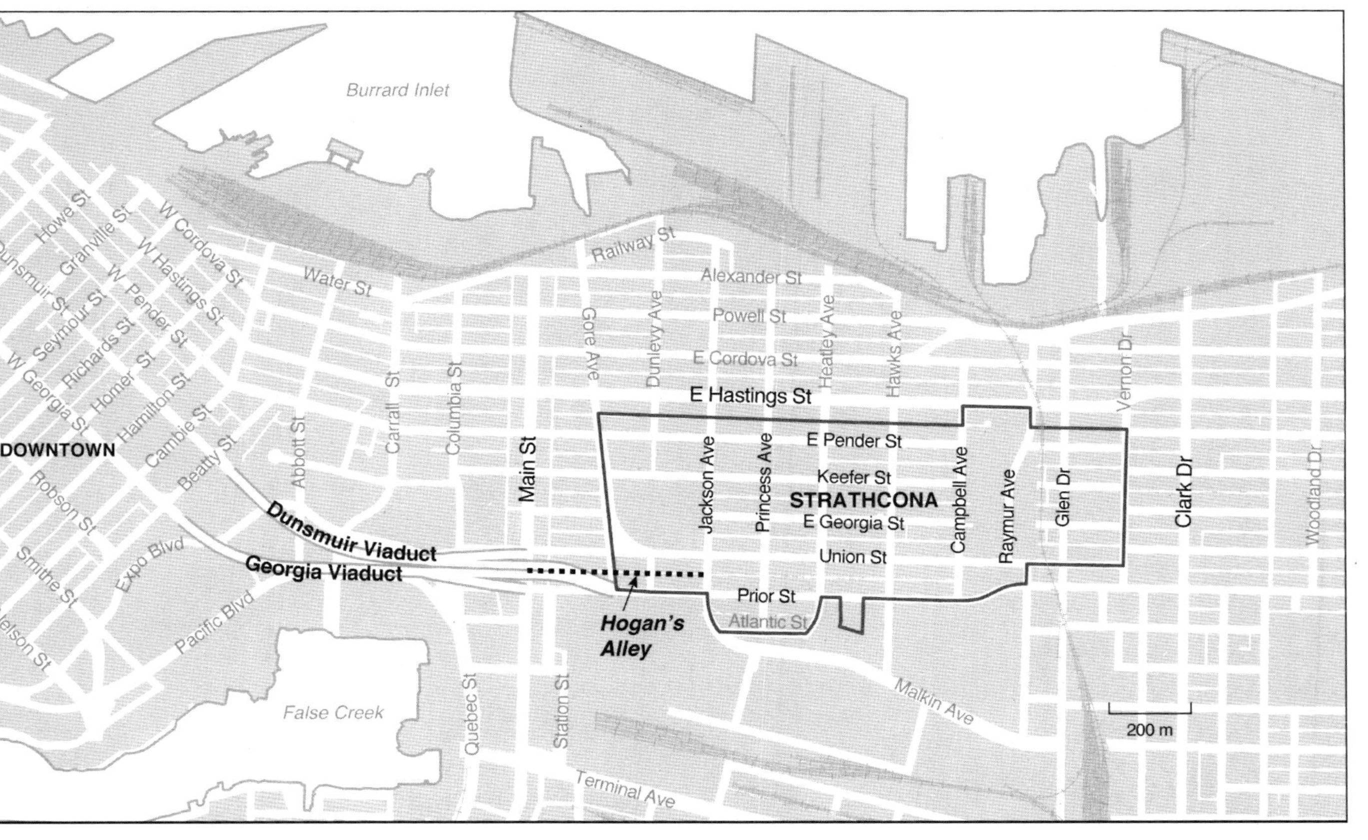

1 Vancouver's Strathcona neighbourhood and Hogan's Alley. Hogan's Alley was located where the Georgia Viaduct is now.

Something of a rough and tumble area, the East End had as many as ten thousand on the relief rolls in 1920, and crime was both casual and common. Gambling, prostitution, and bootlegging were rampant, and dead bodies in alleyways were not unknown.[33] In 1920, for example, an average of sixty to seventy auto thefts occurred each month, motorized hold-up gangs emerged, 108 bootleggers were raided, and $9,750 in liquor fines was collected. This level of crime prompted the implementation of armed street patrols in the winter of 1922 and, by 1925, a regular police prowl-car service.[34]

The cosmopolitan East End saw the bulk of Vancouver's working-class ethnic minorities living within blocks of one another, often in cultural ghettos such as Chinatown and Japantown. Though Vancouver's largest ethnic concentration was Asian, considerable numbers of ethnic Europeans and East Indians, and a reasonably large Jewish population, also resided in and around the bustling Hastings Street corridor. Though little historical evidence of early black history in Vancouver remains, a community of blacks was also centred in the East End by at least 1923, at which time a group purchased the Norwegian Lutheran Church at 823 Jackson Avenue and established the Fountain Chapel, an African Methodist Episcopal Church that flanked Hogan's Alley. While a strong black community existed, the congregation relied on pastors imported from south of the border.[35]

The black community in Vancouver remained a relatively small subset of the population. Due to the Second World War, no census numbers were recorded in the 1940s, but in 1951 the black population in all of British Columbia was listed at just 438, and in 1961, at just 572.[36] More than half of the province's black population resided in Vancouver, yet in 1951 it represented less than 2 percent of the city's total population, and in 1961 less than 3 percent.[37] Writer Wayde Compton concludes,

> Hogan's Alley was not at all an exclusively black neighbourhood: it was also home to Italians, Asians, First Nations people and others. It seems most correct to say that Hogan's Alley had a black community within it, and one that was conspicuous enough that some do refer to the neighbourhood itself as a racially black-identified space.[38]

While some *Chicago Defender* reports seem to suggest an atmosphere of relaxed acceptance toward blacks in Vancouver, others indicate that racial barriers, though less extreme than those in the United States, were nonetheless still evident north of the border. Some black American musicians referred glowingly to Canada as "like coming home to your mother's arms ... [because] [t]he white musicians wouldn't let anyone call us those names."[39] Others mentioned racism, specifically with regard to the actions of Canadian branches of the American Federation of Musicians, many of which, like Local 406 in Montreal, stopped accepting black members during the Depression.[40] Racism encountered by black musicians in Canada may have been mild in direct comparison to the intolerance of the Jim Crow South and the politically hostile environment of the northern industrial cities, which culminated in widespread race riots in the 1910s.[41] However, these positive statements concerning racial tolerance may be best viewed as experiences of *relative* toleration, rather than as evidence for an absence of prejudice. Though largely unofficial, racism toward blacks in Vancouver was prevalent, and in 1952, following the high-profile beating death of a black longshoreman at the hands of white police officers, the Negro Citizens League was formed in an attempt to combat anti-black racism in the city. This move was followed in 1958 by the formation of the British Columbia Association for the Advancement of Coloured People.[42]

Indeed, throughout the 1930s, 1940s, and 1950s, black patrons of the province's beer parlours were often denied service for no reason other than their race. One can easily surmise that for each case brought before the courts and therefore written into the record, many more went unreported. Unsurprisingly perhaps, the issue often had less to do with single men of colour than with social proscriptions against mixed-race couples. Though no law banned black patrons from beer parlours or outlawed mixed-race couples, beer parlour owners were free to deny service to whomever they chose. Mixed-race couples were as a result routinely barred from such establishments, many of which cited discomfort among their patrons as a rationale. The parlours tended to define a mixed-race couple as a white woman with a man of colour, while women of colour with white men and mixed-race couples that included no white parties were of little or no concern.[43] Such discrimination against people of colour under the guise of freedom of commerce was widespread. For decades black patrons had been routinely denied admittance by Vancouver area hotels, and black visitors needing overnight accommodation, particularly those who lacked the marquee recognition of a Duke Ellington or Louis Armstrong, were often forced to book at smaller hotels downtown or in the East End or go to motels along the Kingsway strip.[44] The issue of discrimination by Vancouver hotels is a complicated one, as there was no official policy of segregation in Vancouver and such decisions were often made on an ad hoc basis.[45]

The 1920s and 1930s saw the slow demise of vaudeville and a concurrent maturation of the entertainment industry through talking films, wider dissemination of phonograph records, the advent of stronger radio signals, and, in music, the evolution of jazz from ragtime to early swing. New venues sprang up in the city to take advantage of these developments, such as the Commodore Ballroom (1929–present), Alma Academy (ca. 1930s), and the Alexandra Ballroom (ca. 1930s–1940s); the Hotel Georgia (1937–present) and the Panorama Roof at the Hotel Vancouver (1939–present); and nightclubs including the Cave (1937–81), Palomar Supper Club (1937–1951), Penthouse Cabaret (1947–present), and Isy's Supper Club (1958–76). In the East End, smaller cabarets such as the Patricia Hotel (1917–present), the Smiling Buddha (1953–89), and Mandarin Gardens (ca. 1945) provided less formal opportunities for an evening's entertainment. Most of these venues had house orchestras of varying sizes that were tasked with providing music for dancing, accompanying the floor show, and backing up any travelling talent. It was, at least for a time, relatively easy for a capable musician to find work in Vancouver.[46]

By the late 1930s, the swing dance craze was so well entrenched in Vancouver that both the Palomar Supper Club and the Beacon Theatre hosted competitions with prizes as high as one hundred dollars, and images of tuxedoed and gowned youths stepping out in lindy-hop fashion featured prominently in the *Vancouver Daily Province*'s coverage of 1939's debutante balls.[47] Indeed, such was the popularity of swing music that the *Province* ran a front-page interview with Viennese conductor Walter Herbert that sought to assuage fears about the perceived impropriety of the new entertainment. "Swing music ... may now be taken up by the more conservative set," declared the article's opening line, continuing:

> Walter Herbert, world-famed as chief conductor of the Vienna Civic Opera gave [swing] his endorsement as he sat in the lobby of the Hotel Georgia today. "Swing – I like swing," he said. "It also has an influence on classical music. Its rhythms have a definite effect. Look at Stravinsky, he employs the tempo of modern jazz in some passages of his work."[48]

Bandleader, arranger, saxophonist, and recording studio operator Al Reusch recalled the hectic schedule that the popularity of swing and other dance music afforded working musicians throughout the 1930s:

> Wednesday, Friday, and Saturday nights, this was when we played the average ballroom. When I came out here in 1934, the Alexander was big, which was later known as Danceland, at the corner of Robson and Hornby, and a fellow named Len Chamberlin had the band there. Then there was the Alma Academy, which was out at Broadway and Alma, on the northeast side of Alma ... Stan Patton and his band played there. There was the Hollyburn Pavilion ... there was also the White Rose, and a little nightclub, the El Morocco above the Capitol Theatre. There was the Commodore ... a very popular place. The Cave of course, late 1930s. The Palomar ... for burlesque, there were theatres downtown. The Beacon Theatre had a sort of burlesque, and there were two other theatres on Hastings Street. They had strip shows, and old drunks were sitting in the front rows. The Beacon was a really good spot, a lot of the musicians used to go there because a lot of the big bands used to play there ... The Beacon was located at Carrall and Hastings, right near the old interurban station. Woodward's was on the corner, and it was across from the Army and Navy ... We got to meet a lot of the musicians that come [sic] from out of town ... but the

> burlesque places, they were actually in the sleazy part of town.[49]

As the entertainment industry heated up in Vancouver's downtown core, musical entertainment in the less affluent East End kept pace. Austin Phillips, a black guitarist who had moved west from Alberta's Athabasca Landing, arrived in Vancouver sometime in 1935 and recalled the vibrant and bawdy nature of the East End during the period.

> Oh the things that used to happen there! ... There was nothing but parties in Hogan's Alley night time, anytime, and Sundays all day. You could go by at 6 or 7 o'clock in the morning, and you could hear jukeboxes going, you [could] hear somebody hammering [on] the piano, [or] playing the guitar, or hear some fighting, or see some fighting, screams, everybody carrying on.[50]

Outside of the stable combos employed by the Scat Inn, Buddy's Beer Garden, and other hotels or cafés, musicians in the East End, like Phillips, often plied their trade without benefit of contract or guaranteed wage:

> I used to go from one place to another playing guitar. They never paid you a salary. They had what you call a kitty, a little tin box with a horn like a phonograph on it. People wanted to tip you ... a buck, 10 cents, whatever it was ... they'd throw it in the kitty. That was your money. That's what you made ... I was making money going from place to place ... There used to be a bunch of chop suey houses on Pender Street, always has been, and I would go from restaurant to restaurant and play from booth to booth. I've seen myself make as high as $25 a night in those days. And then go back down and go into the bootlegging places again.[51]

As he travelled from restaurant to restaurant and from bootlegging joint to beer parlour working for tips, Phillips would play the popular songs of the day. An evening's repertoire may have included such tunes as "East of the Sun," "Am I Blue?," and "It's Only a Paper Moon," in addition to jazz numbers such as "Don't Get Around Much Anymore," "Beale Street Blues," and "St. Louis Blues." Phillips recalled one Mrs. Pryor, a large black woman who would visit the alley every few months, bringing with her a leather sack full of fifty-cent pieces and silver dollars.[52]

> She used to weigh 350 pounds ... and she would set me on her knee, say "Play my song! You come on and you play 'Maggie.'" I didn't know 'Maggie,' I'd just sing what I knew of it, and every time I'd sing [it] for her, she'd give me a silver dollar. And curse me out, curse me out all the time! "Oh, play me that song 'Maggie' again!" Probably have to play it for her about fifteen times a night, but if you got through, you got a dollar for every time you'd sing it.[53]

In such a manner, Phillips and those like him were able to eke out a sufficient, if not significant, living during the depths of the Depression. The colourful Mrs. Pryor aside, the ability of musicians to make ends meet often depended upon the largesse of those members of Vancouver's more affluent circles who visited the East End to indulge in liquor, gambling, and music of a less polished variety than that offered uptown at the Commodore, the Cave, or the Palomar. In addition to providing a place for musicians to work, even those establishments that did not operate as gambling halls were more than willing to participate in the Alley's number-one industry, bootlegging. Phillips recalled, "Every place in Hogan's Alley bootlegged. If you could afford a high-class place, you went to the Scat Inn, [or] you went to Buddy's Beer Garden. He served beer and he'd serve hard stuff – rum, gin, whisky."[54]

Liquor and the Law

Vancouver and its regional districts have had a tumultuous relationship with the regulation of alcohol. Still very much a frontier town in the late 1800s, saloons in Vancouver dispensed all forms of alcohol and remained open twenty-four hours a day, seven days a week until as late as 1900. In an attempt to break from this rough and tumble situation, by 1911 the BC government had amended the legislation to require that saloons be housed in hotels, a move that curtailed the number of such establishments. In 1916, when the move toward temperance was successfully linked with propaganda in support of the war effort, the prohibition of alcohol was successfully enacted. Though the purchase and consumption of alcohol for recreational use was illegal, alcohol was permitted for medicinal purposes and could be obtained via medical prescription. This loophole was widely exploited, with one doctor known to have written some four thousand such prescriptions each month.[55] Saloons stayed open through the brewing of "near" or non-alcoholic beer and through the sale of whatever bootlegged product escaped the attention of the inspectors.

That alcohol was easily accessible in Vancouver despite legislation to the contrary was evidently common knowledge, as reflected in a 1920 letter to the *Chicago Defender* wherein the correspondent states that in Vancouver, one is able to "crook [one's] elbow and never be molested."[56] Ada "Bricktop" Smith recalled that

> it was the craziest law. You can't stop people from doing what they want to do. If you try, you just make them want to do it more ... Prohibition made a lot of people *start* drinking, and it didn't make anybody stop ... There was no Prohibition in British Columbia, but the liquor laws were so complicated that Vancouver was what we called a dry town. Outside of the private clubs and speakeasies, the only place you could buy a drink was at someone's house. It was like those after-hours places in Chicago, only in Vancouver you could buy a drink night or day at someone's house ... so [my roommate] and I started selling a shot of whiskey for fifteen cents, or two for a quarter.[57]

Indeed, the ever-widening gap between Vancouver's ostensible lack of alcohol at nightclubs and the less than sober reality prompted several police crackdowns, and all accounts seem to agree that prohibition in Vancouver was honoured more in the breach than in the observance.

The year 1920 saw the repeal of prohibition in favour of controlled alcohol sales through government outlets, though as the cost of a yearly permit to purchase alcohol was roughly equivalent to an average day's wages for a blue-collar worker, the new law did little to eliminate bootlegging and surreptitious drinking at ostensibly "dry" establishments.[58] Though drinking in public was still expressly illegal (including saloons, hotels, restaurants, and cafés), private clubs were able to skirt this rule and there was a sudden boom in such establishments, memberships of which were often freely and easily obtained. These private members' clubs were granted business licences by the city, which by 1923 had established a separate club licence, reflecting their popularity.[59] Because the clubs were considered private rather than public spaces, members were permitted to store and consume personal alcohol on the premises. The club itself could not sell alcohol, and all the booze was officially presumed to have been dutifully and legally purchased from government outlets.

The establishment of the "beer parlour" in 1925 enabled British Columbians to drink in public again, but the rules governing such consumption were austere. Beer parlours were forbidden from serving anything other than beer, including soft drinks. There could be no stand-up bar, and patrons had to be seated at tables, where they were limited to one drink at a time. No food was served, and no entertainment was allowed to be provided or encouraged. Though women were permitted to enter beer parlours, they had to use a separate entrance that gave single women and women with male escorts access to a separate area of the parlour.[60] Ladies had to keep to this partitioned space, and single men were strongly discouraged from crossing to the ladies' side, an issue that was raised with more urgency if race entered the equation.[61]

In 1947, the government amended the legislation to allow licensed private clubs to sell liquor to members, thereby providing a legal alternative to the beer parlour for the purposes of social drinking. This change prompted a mammoth upswing in membership at a wide variety of private members' establishments. The Pacific Athletic Club on Howe Street, for example, had three thousand members by 1948.[62] The sale of liquor at public venues remained illegal, however, and the cost of liquor at private clubs could be prohibitive.

Although neighbouring Washington State had allowed the sale of beer and wine in restaurants since 1934, and the establishment of cocktail lounges in 1948, such bastions of "middle class respectability" as the Commodore Ballroom, Palomar Supper Club, Cave, and Hotel Vancouver existed, like their East End counterparts, as "bottle clubs." In a hallmark of Vancouver life until the mid-1960s, residents out for an evening at venues across the city were required to smuggle in their own alcohol and slip it into overpriced setups of glass, mixer, and ice provided by the establishment. Patrons had to be able to stash their bottles quickly in the event of a raid, and places to hide one's illegal alcohol were common innovations: tablecloths at the Commodore Ballroom on Granville Street had pockets sewn into the underside hem for patron's liquor bottles, and at least one well-known bass player had a trap door on the back of his instrument for the purpose.[63] At the Hotel Vancouver, the well-to-do patrons at the Panorama Roof would be alerted to an impending liquor raid, recalled bandleader Dal Richards. When the police arrived at the hotel, the bell captain would phone the Panorama Roof and the band would play "Roll Out the Barrel," so that patrons could hide their bottles before the liquor squad made it out of the elevator.[64] Likewise, the Penthouse Cabaret on Seymour Street employed a rooftop spotter to keep an eye out for police cars descending en masse, a backup system just in case another club hadn't phoned to warn that the liquor squad was on its way.[65]

Vancouver did not receive further significant changes to its liquor regulations until 1954, when the Sylvia Hotel was granted the first licence to operate a cocktail lounge, an attempt to enable "respectable drinking in respectable places," according to the *Vancouver Sun*.[66] The cocktail lounge was still a heavily proscribed space, however, and while bar service was available for the first time in some thirty years, standing at the bar was prohibited (patrons were required to sit on bar stools), unaccompanied women had to receive service at tables rather than at the bar, booths were not permitted, clear sight lines were required throughout the room, and the venue had to be "as brightly lit as the average kitchen." Cocktail lounges were also prohibited from selling draught beer, and the consequent emphasis on more expensive mixed drinks limited the broad social appeal of cocktail lounges.[67]

The legislation that allowed for the landmark opening of the cocktail lounge at the Sylvia created four new categories of liquor licence: a dining room licence that permitted the serving of wine and beer with meals; a dining lounge licence that allowed the serving of all liquors and was reserved for cabarets and select restaurants; a lounge licence that permitted the sale of all types of alcohol without meals; and a public house licence, which replaced the beer parlour licence and allowed establishments not attached to hotels to sell beer.[68] Despite these new categories, most nightclubs and dance halls remained unlicensed because the government granted the overwhelming bulk of the new permits to businesses housed in hotels. Until 1965, only three Vancouver cabarets operating outside hotels had dining lounge licences. In 1955, the Cave Supper Club was one of those granted an early licence, but restrictive operating hours, the requirement to provide meal service, regulations regarding club layout, and the need to implement a mandatory cover charge all hampered the success of the Cave following its licensing. In addition, the new licence prevented the club from being rented out by private parties who wished to bring in their own liquor. Though they faced the threat of police raids, unlicensed bottle clubs could operate more freely and with a higher profit margin than those that successfully applied for legal status, and as a result the bottle club remained firmly entrenched in Vancouver's nightlife until as late as 1968.[69] In no small measure, the freedom that co-operative jazz clubs such as the Cellar extended to patrons seeking entertainment, mixed company, and adult beverages was a large part of their wider appeal.

Jazz in the 1940s and 1950s

Britain's declaration of war on September 3, 1939, was followed quickly by Canada's own declaration on September 10, prompting many musicians to abandon their nightclub and orchestra positions in order to enlist. At the same time, hundreds of new jobs sprang up across the country to entertain the thousands of servicemen and -women shipping out, returning home, or spending leave. Many young musicians who would ordinarily have had to wait years to work in a professional setting suddenly found themselves in demand.[70] Additionally, many older musicians who declined enlistment or were excluded on the basis of age had their careers extended, bringing valuable and steadying experience to orchestras that played on with the bulk of their regular musicians away in uniform. Dal Richards, rendered ineligible for service due to his eyesight, recalled, "It was a farce. You'd have some sixteen-year-old kid sitting in the section next to a sixty-year-old."[71] Some who enlisted were posted to military bands, service that provided valuable training and prepared a generation of players for postwar orchestras and studio work.

Following the war, these young players found an atmosphere in which painting, dance, literature, and music all seemed to be in upheaval, and the absence of a venue that reflected these attitudes was stifling. While there were myriad musical offerings on a given evening in Vancouver during the late 1940s and early 1950s, none reflected the developments in jazz that had occurred in the wake of Charlie Parker, Dizzy Gillespie, Thelonious Monk, and the rest of the beboppers.

Although established mainstream jazz artists such as Duke Ellington and Louis Armstrong played with some frequency at venues such as the Cave and Isy's during the 1940s and 1950s, modern jazz in Vancouver was limited to the infrequent visits of American touring acts such as Norman Granz's Jazz at the Philharmonic. These touring jazz groups were usually presented by the Vancouver New Jazz Society, co-founded by radio personality Bob Smith, which presented regular concerts at the Denman (later Georgia) Auditorium. When not presenting touring artists, these Sunday afternoon concerts drew heavily on musicians regularly employed by the CBC and major downtown nightclubs, such as the Chris Gage Trio, vocalist Eleanor Collins, and guitarist Ray Norris. These concerts reinforced the musical hierarchy in Vancouver, providing repeated employment and exposure to a handful of musicians. As drummer Terry Clarke put it,

> [The] Chris Gage trio, Jimmy Wightman and Cuddles Johnson – Stan Johnson – were everywhere. And when I was a kid, my mom used to take me down to the Orpheum Theatre, to the Eaton's Good Deed club, which was like a Saturday morning, you'd go down for cartoons ... and serials,

> and a big show, which always featured the Chris Gage Trio. You know, who looked like they'd just gotten out of a coffin, who were probably up all night and then did this gig. And this same trio would show up everywhere. Chris seemed to be everywhere. And he'd also back up ... like Lennie Niehaus would come up and ... the Vancouver New Jazz Society would bring up people from LA, and that was the first working unit. And it was, gosh, you know, oh no, here we go again with the Chris Gage Trio.[72]

For those young musicians, like Tony Clitheroe, captivated by the recent developments detailed in *Downbeat* and heard on albums ordered into Vancouver record stores, the music left something to be desired.

> They used to have jazz concerts at the Georgia Auditorium, or the Denman Auditorium. It was the same building, but someone kept changing the names. It was at the corner of Georgia and Denman, right? And every now and again there'd be a jazz concert held there by an organization called the Vancouver New Jazz Society. So, I'd only been here a very short length of time and I used to go down there to see what was going on, and I just thought it stank ... I mean, the playing was excellent. It was absolutely immaculate. And that was the trouble, you know? Four-bar solos for everybody and nobody made a mistake, ever. And the arrangements ... they kept churning out the same charts every time.[73]

Faced with this musical climate and inspired by postwar developments in jazz as exemplified by Charlie Parker and Miles Davis, a group of young jazz musicians in Vancouver came together to establish a space where they could enact jazz in ways that were not otherwise possible.

The Wailhouse

In the years following the Second World War, a group of young musicians in Vancouver gradually came together, bound by their

2 John Dawe, ca. 1959 | *Photographer unknown; courtesy John Dawe*

interest in bebop and modern jazz, their exclusion from employment in the established studio and nightclub scenes, an affinity for the emerging counterculture, and above all, the need for a place to practise and rehearse. Most of these players were from British Columbia and had either grown up in Vancouver or drifted there from the island or the interior following high school. Pianist Al Neil, the oldest of the group, had returned from service in Europe, where he had survived the beaches of Normandy, and guitarist (later bassist) Tony Clitheroe had emigrated from England following his service in a Royal Air Force band during the war.

The popularity of bebop in Vancouver was, from all accounts, quite low through the early 1950s. While magazines such as *Downbeat* and *Metronome* were reasonably accessible, the records they advertised and reviewed had to be special-ordered into the local record stores. Both Al Neil and saxophonist Jim Johnson credited the record store Western Music with making many of the initial connections between the musicians who would eventually establish the Cellar. Al Neil said,

> We started from nothing. We just had this record store. We met there. It didn't have that many customers, either, come to think of it. But John [Dawe], myself, Jimmy Johnson ... it took a few trips to the record store before we kind of realized that from what the clerk was saying, he'd say, "Hey, there was another guy ordering that record," and so we figured it out, and it basically ended up about four or five guys, and they were the guys that more or less started the Cellar.[74]

The store stocked records, sheet music, and instruments, and ended up providing a long-running day job for Johnson: "Oh, well, I worked at Western Music. That was one of the day jobs that I got. I was there for several years, and yeah ... I guess I met [Al Neil] at Western Music, though I more associate him with later things at the Cellar club."[75] John Dawe, a trumpet and valve trombone player, had moved from Victoria with his family in 1943. Dawe, who first met Neil around 1949, would form particularly close friendships with drummer Bill Boyle, Johnson, and Clitheroe, and would be an influential member of the group that eventually formed and operated the Cellar (see Figure 2).

Entrepreneur and multi-instrumentalist Ken Hole moved to Vancouver from Nanaimo in 1952, enrolling at the University of British Columbia, where he met saxophonist and law student Walley Lightbody. The ensuing friendship would prove essential to the formation of the Cellar in Vancouver (and the later Scene Club in Victoria), as Ken's entrepreneurial energies got the project started, while Lightbody's legal acuity navigated the red tape at City Hall to obtain the requisite permits and licences. While still in high school on Vancouver Island, Hole had been active in a variety of orchestras and dance bands, often working with players, such as trumpeter Carse Sneddon, who went on to significant careers in Vancouver's studio and club scene. Unsatisfied with the musical opportunities he found as a student at UBC, Hole began to organize his own ensembles and make what contacts he could with like-minded young players. These efforts connected other members of what was to become the Cellar.

Tony Clitheroe, who although now known as a bassist was playing guitar at the time, was introduced to the scene through Ken Hole.

> I met Ken pretty early when I came here. I can't quite remember how that happened. I think he knew the people ... I rented a suite in a house up on Dunbar somewhere, and they knew him, I think. I guess they heard me practising on the guitar, and I guess they told Ken or something, and he came up some time and we played for a while. I think that's what happened. And so I started doing these strange gigs with Ken, and then he set up the big band and everything.[76]

Through Hole, Clitheroe also found a day job at a car insurance office operated by Hole's father. It was the last day job Clitheroe would take for several decades, as around 1956 he became able to support himself from his musical pursuits.[77]

Dubbed the Ken Hole Big Band, the ensemble played engagements at UBC, where it was known as the Varsity Dance Band (despite few of its members being enrolled as students), and took work wherever it could find it. Eventually, Hole booked the band on several tours to Vancouver Island, where they worked from as far north as Campbell River to Victoria in the south.

> I [managed] a restaurant in Kerrisdale called the Kerry Dale Caterers. It had a big convention hall in the back, so I said by god I'm going to put together a band, so I started with these guys here [*points at photo*] and that's the start of it [the Ken Hole Big Band]. And we started rehearsing during the week, and I bought up an old library, from a guy that had quit. Had about fifty tunes. And then a lot of the good musicians that we had in our group had made arrangements. And they gave me the arrangements if I would use them. So we started rehearsing those arrangements. So we had our own sound. We weren't copying Harry James or Duke Ellington or anybody else ... That's how that band started, and then we took that to the university and it became the Varsity Dance

> Band. It was the first dance band at UBC. And we played all the big dances and everything out there. And we went on tour. I organized a tour up and down Vancouver Island. We did it about two or three times.[78]

However successful, the Ken Hole Big Band did not fully satisfy the desire for a sense of camaraderie among the younger musicians in the area – it gave little opportunity for either personal practice time or for musical expression in a small group format, and its limited number of positions could not employ the number of musicians hoping to play.

In the mid-1950s, there were few places for musicians to play jazz in Vancouver. Clubs such as Isy's and the Cave tended toward floor shows and dance band music, where jazz expression was usually limited to a few bars worth of soloing on some of the more spirited charts. The Commodore, Panorama Roof, and Palomar Supper Club specialized in music for dancing, which was generally quite removed from the bebop these younger players focused on. After hours, the main venue for informal jam sessions was the infamous Penthouse on Seymour Street, run by the Philliponi (or Filippone) brothers. Part athletic club, taxi stand, private bar, cabaret, and supper club, the Penthouse kept notoriously late hours. Despite, or perhaps because of its colourful reputation, the Penthouse became *the* spot in Vancouver during the 1950s for club owners, musicians, waitresses, bartenders, cab drivers, reporters, actors, off-duty policemen, dancers, and anyone who wanted a drink late at night to congregate.[79] Trumpeter Jim Carney was among them:

> It was a sort of drinking, and bring your own bottle in a paper bag, and it was a ... I would describe it as a kind of social instrument for people to get together in the wee hours, to get together and drink and talk and listen to jazz when there were, there was no ... that was otherwise not accessible. In other words, the classy joints like the Palomar and the Cave and Isy's and the Arctic Club ... they shut down at 1 a.m., and they were also very expensive for most of us. But the Penthouse was very informal. As I recall there were like three storeys or two storeys, and there was a hangout for

> prostitutes. It certainly wasn't a brothel, but it was well known that if you wanted to connect, the place to be would be the Penthouse. It was a hangout for taxi drivers. And, you know, it did really have a social niche.[80]

At the Penthouse, Vancouver's working musicians could play informally on jazz repertoires that were unsuitable for their paid gigs earlier in the evening. The sessions weren't open to any who cared to play, operating instead as something of an offshoot from the nightclub scene for which the Penthouse operated as an unofficial clubhouse.

> It was strictly jam session. I don't think they ever paid the musicians; the musicians would just go there and play whatever they wanted to. The reason the uptown [younger] guys never got a look-in was that they really weren't as good musicians as the Fraser MacPhersons ... It was quite cliquey ... the guys who worked the commercial clubs, a lot of them were excellent jazz players, and they sort of had first dibs. And the customers didn't mind that at all. Nobody was screaming for Jim Carney to come up and play, you know.[81]

Given few opportunities to develop their musicianship and indulge their interest in jazz, in the fall of 1955 approximately seven young jazz musicians pooled their resources to rent a house just beneath the Fraser Street Bridge in Richmond. The mix of farmland and light industrial areas along the stretch of River Road near Mitchell Island yielded 999 River Road, on the northwest corner of what is now the intersection with No. 5 Road. Long unoccupied, the building's closest neighbour was the Dr. Ballard's dog food factory, which created a stench but led to the type of sparsely populated area perfect for late-night sessions.[82]

The building had ample parking, and soon housed a scrounged piano, a set of drums, and an acoustic bass. Entrepreneur and bassist Ken Hole was chiefly responsible for the organization of the effort, collecting postdated cheques from the others involved to cover rent and expenses. Other key players in the establishment of the jam space – quickly dubbed the Wailhouse – were pianists Al

Neil and Fred Massey, saxophonist Dave Quarin, trumpeter Jim Carney, guitarist (later bassist) Tony Clitheroe, saxophonist Jim Johnson, guitarist Jim Kilburn, and saxophonist Walley Lightbody (see Figures 3 and 4).

> I give Kenny Hole a lot of credit for a lot of these ideas. He was one of these guys that always had a smile on his face and was enthusiastic ... and could get that enthusiasm transmitted, and it became contagious, and so, I think he probably found this place, and everybody said, "Yeah, that's a great idea," and it was ... one of those things where you'd go down there with your horn at midnight, or ten o'clock at night or whatever, and everybody would have a jam session.[83]

Though the experiment would be short-lived, lasting only six months, the Wailhouse provided the essential framework upon which the Cellar would be built. The project identified a core group of young players who were both musically competent and dedicated to the creation of a space within which to practise their art and foster a sense of musical community. Though the Wailhouse was primarily used by practising musicians, many brought friends, girlfriends, and family members to sessions, and the space soon became known as a place to drink and socialize as well as a place to make music. Given Vancouver's restrictive liquor laws, a social space in which to mix drinking and community with musical activity became instantly popular.[84]

The Wailhouse also served as an invaluable place for young musicians to practise and experiment within a generally supportive community and without the performative expectations imposed by the presence of an audience who were not active participants in the scene. Tony Clitheroe, for example, was able to transition from guitar to acoustic bass during the period of the Wailhouse's existence:

> I was getting really fed up with the electronic problems [on guitar], and Ken Hole used to usually play bass, if he was there ... Hole very often was not there, but he used to leave his bass there. An old plywood bass. I think what actually started the thing [becoming a bass player], with him not

3 Jim Carney at the Wailhouse, ca. 1955 | *Photo by George Sedawie; courtesy Jim Carney*

4 Jim Johnson (saxophone) and Bill Boyle (drums) at the Wailhouse, ca. 1955 | *Photo by George Sedawie; courtesy Jim Carney*

> being there, I used to play bass lines on the guitar, right? Because the four bottom strings on the guitar are the same tuning as the bass. So I'd play bass lines if nobody was there playing bass, and then one time his bass was there and one time I thought let's see what this thing feels like, and I picked it up, and of course everything was more or less in the same place, just further away ... greater distances to travel, as it were. And I thought, you know, it's not much of a bass, but it was such a treat to play a purely acoustic instrument after all the battles I was having with the guitar.[85]

Clitheroe's switch from guitar to bass proved to be an essential element in the later success of the Cellar (see Figure 5). At the time there were few competent jazz bass players in Vancouver, and Clitheroe's adoption of the instrument allowed for regular jam sessions and regular ensembles to be formed. He recalled, "I figured that, well, I'd sort of take one for the team, as it were, and play bass at the Cellar, because I was pretty well available, but I figured sooner or later a bass player's probably going to show up and I'd be off the hook."[86] A multi-instrumentalist who had played clarinet and saxophone with an RAF band, Clitheroe took no formal lessons on bass yet nonetheless went on to a highly regarded career on that instrument.

> When I started playing bass, I had an ear-opening experience one night. As a matter of fact I was with John [Dawe]. We were up at his apartment. And I hadn't even thought about playing bass at this point ... I didn't want to play bass, I didn't even know what bass players really did ... Any gigs that I had after I came here, there was either no bass player in the band at all, or if there was I couldn't hear him, or if I could hear him, I didn't want to hear him. That's what it was like. So one night we were over at John's apartment, there were three or four of us over there, and John put on this record called *Bags Groove*.[87] You know the one? It was Thelonious Monk on it and Miles, Percy Heath, and I think Kenny Clarke, and I think Sonny Rollins is on one side or something. You probably know that Miles wasn't fond of

5 Tony Clitheroe, ca. 1960 | *Photographer unknown; courtesy Jim Carney*

Thelonious comping behind him, right? So, there was a long solo on one of the tunes where Thelonious laid out and it was just whoever was playing drums, and Percy Heath, and Miles playing. And I'm listening to this, and it was like an epiphany of some kind, right? I thought, "My god, is that what bass players do?" You know? The time feel that Percy Heath [had] – because he played right on top of the beat. And in fact, if anything, slightly ahead of it, and I was taking all of this in, right, and it was an amazing experience. It was like a music lesson during the course of one tune. And then when the thing started to look as though maybe I should play bass to sort of fill out the house rhythm section that we needed, I thought, I think I know what I have to do, and know how to do it, now, and I can do it.[88]

Renowned bassist and pianist Don Thompson,[89] who was a colleague of Clitheroe's in Vancouver for several years, confirms the influence, if not the process.

> Tony as a bass player? He had a magic sound. I don't know how he did it, nobody knew how he did it, but he sounded as though he was playing with an amplifier, but he wasn't. He had a sound that was so strong, and this unbelievably perfect time feel. He didn't seem to want to play solos, I don't know why. I don't remember hearing him play very many solos. He didn't seem to want to play solos, but he could play time and he could out-swing anybody around. He was an amazingly good bass player. He reminded me, if anybody, of Percy Heath. That's who he made me think of when I heard him play. That perfect time and perfect notes and perfect intonation and ... he really knew how to play the bass and make it work. Nobody else had a sound like him, either. And it wasn't just the bass. I mean, he had a nice bass, but it wasn't the bass, it was him. His left hand was really together, and he just never seemed to be working hard at it. But he just knew what to do to make it work. He was really, really good.[90]

In no small way, the unfettered opportunity to practice, rehearse, and play at the Wailhouse enabled Clitheroe to make this shift from guitar to bass. Rent-paying members all had keys to the space and were free to practise and rehearse whenever their schedules allowed. Such personal practice was then tested in late-night jam sessions, most of which occurred on Friday and Saturday nights and frequently had small groups of friends in attendance. Thus the Wailhouse enabled the scene to coalesce in a space that provided regular contact and a developing community for players and fans.

By early 1956, however, the Wailhouse was no longer meeting the needs of its members, and the venue had already been outgrown when a tree toppled in a windstorm and crushed the house. The location, while perfect for producing noise without the worry of neighbour complaints, was relatively far from the action of downtown Vancouver. It also lacked regular public transportation, and was therefore out of reach for the many musicians and fans who didn't have access to a car. Ken Hole recalled, "We weren't comfortable there. Number one, it was too noisy. Every time a big truck went over [the bridge] it was [*makes shaking noises*] ... and it was, the young guys that didn't have any transportation were out of luck, because it was too far out."[91] The quick success of the Wailhouse as a gathering place for those interested in bebop and other forms of modern jazz buoyed the ambitions of its founding members, and a move to a more central location was agreed upon. In April 1956, the musicians behind the Wailhouse collaborated with a few additional key members to open the Cellar.

part two

The Vancouver Scene

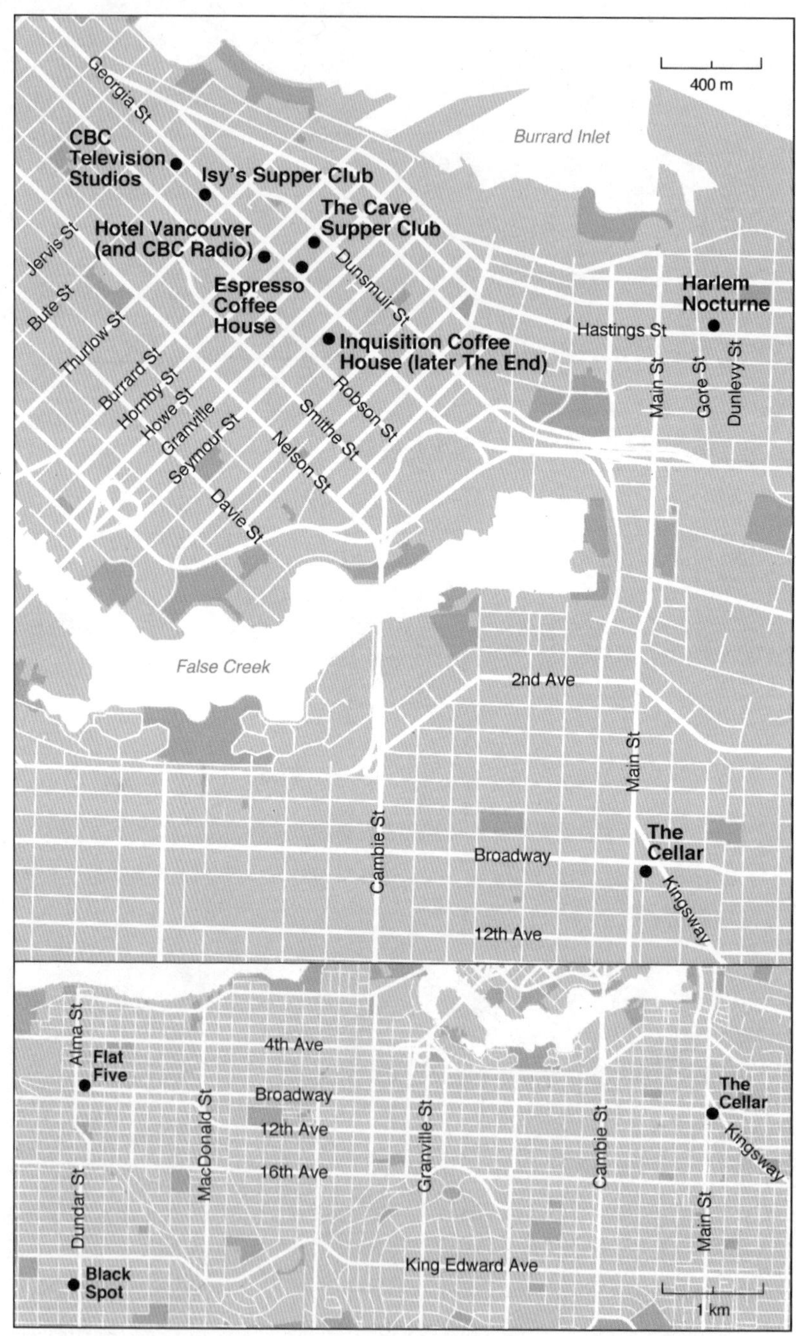

6 Location of the Cellar and other important venues in Vancouver during the period

3

The Making of a Jazz Scene

Vancouver's Cellar Club

The place just took off like that because there was no other place.

– John Dawe

Having outgrown the informal Wailhouse in Richmond, the players involved moved quickly to find a new venue for their jazz activities, and located space at 2514 Watson Street in the basement of a building that fronted onto East Broadway, between Main Street and Kingsway (see Figure 7). Though the Watson Street address is the one most often associated with the Cellar, it was also at times referred to as being at 222 East Broadway.[1] Detached on three sides, the Cellar building was bounded by Broadway in front and Watson Street on the western side, with the entrance and a small parking lot at the rear. The remainder of the two-storey building had commercial tenants, and the only adjacent building was also commercial rather than residential, with the happy result that the location provided both easy access to the city centre and the physical separation needed for late-night noise.[2]

The building was brand new, and the club was the first basement tenant. Initially hesitant about renting to musicians, the landlord was swayed by the fact that the Cellar would operate as a private club, and that steps had been taken to incorporate the organization and to acquire the necessary permits and insurance. As trumpeter John Dawe recalled,

7 The corner of Broadway and Kingsway, just a few steps east of the Cellar building, in the late 1950s | *Photograph by Alvin Armstrong; courtesy CBC Still Photo Collection*

> Ken and Walley set that up [not-for-profit status], you know, with Walley being a lawyer. We couldn't operate the way we were without it all being done properly ... the health inspectors and everything having to go down there and check everything out, and even to have a licence to open the place up we had to be registered.[3]

Formally incorporated and registered by law student Walley Lightbody as the not-for-profit Cellar Musicians and Artists Society, the club initially continued much as the Wailhouse had, with entrepreneur Ken Hole as the guiding organizational force.

Most of those who had been part of the Wailhouse remained involved, and other musicians quickly associated themselves with the new project, such as drummer Bill Boyle and John Dawe (both of whom had been in Toronto during the Wailhouse period), along with trumpeter Ed Roop and drummer Don Cumming. From its very beginnings, the Cellar welcomed like-minded artists from other disciplines, and its founding members included several non-musicians:

8 *The Trio* (1954), by Harry Webb. This painting hung over the bar in the Cellar. | *Courtesy Adrienne Brown*

dramatist, producer, and jazz enthusiast Barry Cramer, who eventually would be involved in the staging of avant-garde theatre at the Cellar; and artist, designer, and jazz enthusiast Harry Webb, who provided some of the artwork hung in the club, most notably *The Trio,* which was displayed over the bar (see Figure 8). In later years Webb would design numerous promotional posters for concert and theatrical presentations at the Cellar.[4] Painter and muralist Frank Lewis also contributed art to the new space, most notably a large, red-hued mural that hung over the stairs leading down from the parking lot to the club. Though no images of the complete work seem to remain and its whereabouts is unknown, the painting was by all accounts quite striking, and a key element of the club's decor.[5] Along with Harry Webb, pianist Al Neil, and guitarist Jim Kilburn, designer John Grinnell also assisted with the club's interior design, and may well have had a hand in the production of club advertisements and associated paraphernalia such as membership cards and matchbooks (see Figure 9).

Operating as a private members' club, the Cellar had a two-tier membership structure. A small group formed the inner circle of "charter members" who were required to make a monthly contribution

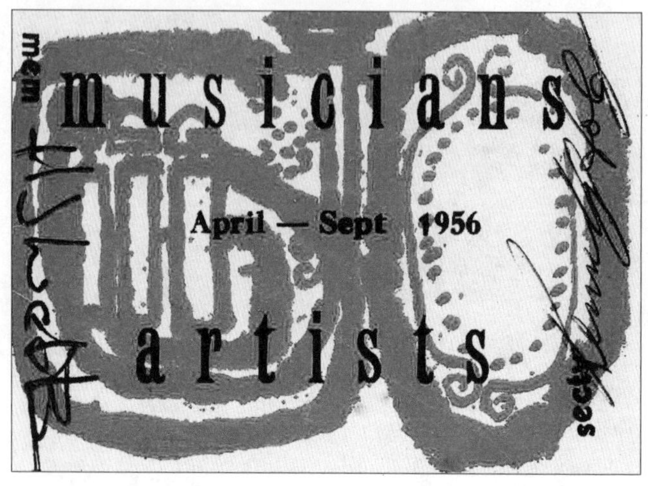

9 Cellar membership cards: [*top*] membership card belonging to Harry Webb, 1956; [*middle*] membership card belonging to John Dawe, 1958 (note indication of charter membership); [*bottom*] front and back of an unused social membership card, ca. 1960 | *Courtesy Adrienne Brown and Gregg Simpson*

toward the rent, while more casual participants held social memberships. Charter members were often referred to as "core" members, and were generally, though not always, practising musicians. These members were responsible for the payment of the rent and other operating expenses, organized club operations, cleaned the facility, and accomplished all the other tasks associated with keeping the Cellar functioning. Ken Hole recalled the early financing:

> So we all got together and Walley Lightbody incorporated it, and I was the president and he was the secretary and treasurer. The rest of the guys were members. Then we set up a program, in order to pay the rent, that everyone gave us postdated cheques ... We would just put them through every month to help pay for the rent until it got going, and that way ... we knew we had some capital coming in, and then of course we built the bandstand and so forth, and we got some tables and chairs donated to us, and we started opening up with jam sessions ... [The audience] would come in and the money would go to the electricity, and to pay the rent.[6]

While some, like Lightbody and Hole, bore titles such as president, vice-president, or treasurer, most charter members, like John Dawe, simply understood that it was their obligation to help out beyond their rent payment, and that it was only through their efforts that the Cellar would remain open.

> We did everything down there. We cleaned the place, we did every damn thing. Each of us took turns. On certain weekends it was so-and-so's job to clean the place and then somebody else took a turn the next weekend, so ... the place had to be cleaned, the next afternoon you know, to get it ready for the next night. We did all of that stuff. A lot of the people who were social members, and other musicians, they just walked through the door and they did nothing ... they were the customers. We did everything down there to keep that place running. And a lot of the other musicians weren't aware that we were doing everything in that place ... that

> the members were taking care of everything down there. They don't realize how much work we put into the place.[7]

Being a charter member brought not just extra work but extra privileges, as charter members received keys to the club and access to the space for practice and rehearsal purposes whenever it was not in use. This ability to practise and rehearse freely would prove vital to the development of many Cellar musicians and groups. As bassist Tony Clitheroe and John Dawe described:

> The place was available to us. There were about ... well, when it started out, the membership ... we had charter members and associate members, right? The associate members were people who could just walk in off the street, pay two dollars and get an associate membership. But the group that was known as charter members sort of ran the place, and the number fluctuated quite a bit. Sometimes as many as twenty, sometimes maybe only ten or eleven.[8]

> There must have been a core group of probably about fifteen people, I would think. Hard to say now after all these years, and a lot of the names I actually forget now. We paid a yearly fee, forty or fifty or sixty dollars – as time went by it changed as the rent increased – and that kind of insured that at least the rent was going to be paid, and the light bill was going to be paid, you know? The rest [of the income] was kind of the fees that came in through the door.[9]

Associate or social members (both terms were used) were initially required to be nominated by charter members, and were then able to purchase a yearly membership that granted them access to the club as listeners provided they paid a cover charge. Members were free to bring guests to the club, but were responsible for ensuring that their guests were not disruptive to the music. The cover charges collected from associate members and their guests formed the bulk of the Cellar's revenue, and enabled a small financial cushion to build up in the society's accounts.

Though the rules governing social members eased over the years, the early concern was to ensure that the space remained focused on the presentation of jazz in a serious and supportive atmosphere, and that the Cellar did not become merely another casual social club. Ken Hole noted that becoming a member

> wasn't that difficult, once we got to know you. Then we would allow you in. Because we wanted to make sure that this was a very close resemblance to a musician's club and an artist's club, and if you were a good artist and recommended by one of the musicians or local people and you seemed like a nice person, we'd let you join in. But we were very careful about that. We weren't in it to make money, we were in it to further jazz and the talents of the local musicians and artists.
>
> We kept a very big handle on it, and we had someone on the door all the time. No one could just walk down there and come in unless they had proper identification, and we kept this a very exclusive place to go for the people that supported what we were doing, and that was it. Period. Now if a member brought down a couple of people, he was responsible for those people, and he had to make sure that they were supporting the type of music we were doing and the camaraderie that we had going. Because everyone knew everyone by their first name, you know. And then if someone was really interested in jazz, interested in musicians or artistry, then we would arrange to have them admitted into the club [as a member]. It was very exclusive, but it sure worked out well, because we never had any problems there that I can recall.[10]

That the Cellar operated peacefully to a crowd who were there first and foremost for the music is confirmed by Cellar regular Lyvia Brooks, who at the age of seventeen or eighteen worked Friday nights and Saturdays upstairs from the Cellar in her family's shirt shop.

> It was very calming. It was the kind of jazz I liked. I'm not crazy about Dixieland, I must say, because I just loved to be a bit calmed down after a day's work. And it was beautiful.

> Absolutely beautiful music. And very well respected. I think there were all types of people in the audience. All age groups. People that may have acted very differently at another place, perhaps, but everyone was very well behaved here [at the Cellar]. It was like a ... a refuge, sort of. It was sort of a rough and tumble neighborhood, and this was a calm peaceful refuge in the heart of the neighbourhood. I'd never seen anybody cause a problem there [at the Cellar]. As I say, some of these same people might cause problems somewhere else, but not there. People were definitely there to enjoy the music ... the Cellar was, again, like a sanctuary. There was peace and calm, and you were accepted no matter who you were, and you sat and enjoyed the music, and as long as you respected that you were fine there.[11]

The entrance off the parking lot opened to a set of stairs that led down to another door opening into the performance space itself (see Figure 10). At the foot of these stairs a pay window was installed, much like the ticket booth of a movie theatre. Once a patron had produced a membership card and paid the cover charge, the door person pressed a button that released the inner door and allowed entrance to the club. As the club developed, well-known local musicians were generally allowed entry to the club at no charge, whether they had a membership or not. Bassist Paul Ruhland recalled benefitting from this arrangement: "Before you opened the door to the Cellar there was a little window, almost like a cashier window on the left-hand side, where you paid whatever ... if you weren't a musician, you gave something. [Musicians] were members by acclaim."[12] In the early years the door was usually staffed by Bill Schlossmacher, an employee of Ken Hole's restaurant businesses, who was paid a small fee to manage the door. After 1958 this role was filled most often by Ricci Quarin, wife of saxophonist, charter member, and eventual club manager Dave Quarin.

Initially, the Cellar Musicians and Artists Society rented just half of the large basement room, stringing a curtain across to hide the unused portion from view. Tables and chairs were donated to the group through Ken Hole's connections in the restaurant industry, and guitarist Jim Kilburn, who was employed as an electrician for

10 [*L-R*] Dave Pike, unknown man, Carla Bley, Paul Bley, Don Francks (with trash lid), Ken Hole, and Dave Quarin in parking lot behind the Cellar, October 1957. The Frank Lewis mural is visible just to the left of the open doorway. | *Photographer unknown; courtesy Jim Carney*

the city of Vancouver, did the required electrical work. Others chipped in labour to construct the bandstand, bar area, and ticket window, and to decorate the space. Initially, the club operated as a public venue only on the weekends, with performances on Friday and Saturday nights (and occasionally Sundays). Otherwise, the club was available to charter members to rehearse and hang out.

As a non-profit owned and operated by musicians, the Cellar Musicians and Artists Society was able to strike a deal with the local Vancouver chapter of the American Federation of Musicians to avoid paying union scale to the bands that performed there. Although the 1954 amendments to the BC Liquor Act made it technically possible for the Cellar to apply for a liquor licence, it, like the vast majority of clubs in the city, remained a bottle club, serving soft drinks and ice and subject to infrequent inspections by the liquor squad. Vancouver's archaic liquor laws may indeed have contributed in no small way to the almost instantaneous success of the Cellar, as suggested by saxophonist Jim Johnson:

> Yeah, there were a lot of people that started coming down there. And at that time in Vancouver, we didn't have very liberal liquor laws, or drinking. If you wanted to have a beer you could go to a hotel beer parlour, which was sectioned off into the men's side and the women's side. And you could only sit on the women's side if you had a woman with you, you know? Men had to go – single men, had to sit on the men's side. And that went on for years, as far as I remember. So people, after they went and saw something downtown in regular hours, wanted another place to go. So I guess the Cellar became kind of a bottle club, that is, people certainly brought their own drinks, because we couldn't sell drinks.[13]

In later years, as the Cellar began both to advertise and to bring in more widely known musicians from the United States, the club sometimes applied for special-occasion permits that allowed the sale of alcohol for a limited time, on a case-by-case basis. Tony Clitheroe recalled that this was rather an effort:

> [The Cellar was popular with students] because it was a place they could bring their girlfriends, and bring a bottle, and that kind of thing ... we had no liquor licence. Matter of fact, at that time around Vancouver there were some really archaic laws to do with liquor, and once in a while we used to, if we had something special happening down there, we'd get a liquor licence. We'd go to the police department and get it all set up and then somebody would bring in one of these portable bar outfits, you know, and we'd do it that way. It was a pain in the neck, having to do it like that.[14]

Many of the musicians involved with the Cellar were attending university or worked day jobs during the week. Walley Lightbody was studying law at UBC, Ken Hole was kept busy both by his father's insurance company and his restaurant businesses, Dave Quarin worked as a bookkeeper for a shipping company, Jim Carney was studying at UBC, and Jim Kilburn worked for the city of Vancouver. Others purposefully kept their non-musical activities to a minimum, taking part-time employment in order to maximize the amount of time and energy they could invest in rehearsing, playing, and thinking about music. Jim Johnson, for example, worked at Western Music, while John Dawe and Al Neil took part-time work at the post office.

> Sometimes I worked part-time over at the post office, which a lot of us did, four hours a day or something, you know, from four or five in the afternoon until around nine at night, and that gave us an amount of free time and pocket money. Booze money and cigarette money. Walking-around money ... most of the rest of us had no responsibilities [i.e., families]. We were irresponsible people in every way that you could imagine.[15]

As charter members, these young players took advantage of the ability to use the space during the week to practise and rehearse. The Cellar quickly became a central focus point in the lives of many of the musicians involved, and John Dawe and several others rented a house near the club.

> For a few years, myself and some other musicians lived in a house, we called it the bebop house, which was about three or four blocks away from the Cellar. So we didn't annoy the neighbours I would wander over to the Cellar during the week, when it wasn't open, and use it as a practice place ... Ray Sikora's big band rehearsed down there every Sunday morning, or whenever most of us could get up. And uh, all the groups ... all the members were down there rehearsing, and practising. We used it to practise. I was practically at the place seven days a week.[16]

As the Cellar evolved and began to bring in musicians from the United States, visiting players would often stay at the "bebop house," particularly those, like the Montgomery Brothers, who were repeat visitors to the Cellar and developed friendships with many of its members.[17]

Despite his full schedule outside the Cellar, Ken Hole acted for the first few years as the de facto manager of the club, with Dave Quarin helping with the accounting and bookkeeping.

> I would be there on the weekends most of the time. Walley was in and out, though of course he wasn't going to university on the weekends, so he would be there quite often. But I was there on a regular basis, because someone had to manage the place, you know. And I did the hiring of all the groups, and making sure that they were billeted out okay and so on.[18]

Recognizing the conflict of interest inherent in participating as a musician while simultaneously controlling the performance schedule, Hole refrained from performing on weekend evenings, limiting his musical participation to the Ken Hole Big Band and to jam sessions.

> I did not, on purpose, get in the front of anything. I was a backup. If someone didn't get there, I'd pick up the bass and play the bass, just to fill in. Because I stayed away and did the organizing, and let the other people get featured. All the musicians. And that meant that they couldn't ridicule me for trying to be a big shot. So I just stayed back and did what I had to.[19]

Though weekday activities and after-hours jam sessions were left to develop organically, Ken Hole attempted to program the weekend evenings in a manner that met contemporary expectations for club performances: a named band as attraction, and two or three professionally presented sets. The musicians involved with the Cellar were encouraged to form their own groups and develop material sufficient to carry a weekend performance. In rotating fashion, they were granted the opportunity to play Friday and Saturday nights to an audience of colleagues, club members, and guests, after which more informal sessions routinely lasted until morning.

> I wanted to have a group every week that played for that Friday, Saturday ... you know, so that they could write their own charts and do what they want and give them something to work toward, and then they'd want to come and hear the next group that was playing and I'd just keep revolving them around. And we ended up with ... I can't remember the exact amount of musicians we had. It was, you know, close to a hundred. Probably seventy-five to a hundred. A lot of them weren't qualified, but they just wanted to be part of it. And the essence of it [was], a lot of them got [musical] jobs elsewhere.[20]

Starting Out, 1956–58

The Cellar opened in April 1956 (the exact date remains hazy) with an informal weekend of sessions, ad hoc groups, and late-night jamming. The bandstand and eight or nine tables filled the half of the basement leased by the group to accommodate a small audience of about twenty members and guests. However, word of the club's opening had spread quickly, and demand far exceeded capacity, causing a line to form up the stairs and out into the parking lot. A letter issued to the Cellar membership on May 3, 1956, described the situation as well as the initial steps taken by the executive in response:

> First, our apologies if any of your friends were turned away on the opening night of "jazz in the Cellar." If you were present you will no doubt realize that with the facilities we have available, it is impossible to accommodate a crowd anywhere near the size that appeared on Saturday night. It is our regret that we have found it advisable to limit the number of guests to ONE PER MEMBER on Saturday nights, and that persons desiring memberships will have to make application through a member. It is also required that members present their cards at the door and sign in their guests.

This early popularity continued beyond the club's official opening weekend, prompting a hasty expansion. Trumpeter John Dawe said,

> It was just fantastic, and it caught on so strongly that it overwhelmed us. When it had been open a month maybe, or less, people were lined up around the block to get into the place. We didn't know what to do, because we were only renting half of the basement, and we had a curtain stretched across it. So we had to rent the other half, and we had to start painting the walls and build more tables. The place just took off like that because there was no other place [like it in the city].[21]

After renting the remaining half of the basement, Cellar organizers undertook further renovations, relocating the stage to suit the larger space and adding more tables. Like most jazz clubs of the period, even the expanded Cellar was small, with most estimates suggesting that the low-ceilinged room held between sixty and seventy people when operating at capacity (see Figure 11).[22]

Neighbourhood resident Lyvia Brooks, who worked upstairs, recalled:

> On Friday nights I would usually have a date that would come and pick me up, well they'd come to the store, and when the store would close at 9 p.m. we would go downstairs to the Cellar and enjoy the music. And quite often on Saturday night too ... I don't know if I had a membership card or what I had. Because I was one of the neighbourhood people, at that point, I don't remember if I really required anything. They just seemed to always let me in there. Ken Hole and Walley Lightbody were the two people that were the main guys there. And it was very dark. Always. And all these people were very well behaved, and all listening to the music. All appreciating the music. Nobody talked when the music was on.[23]

The Cellar was not yet advertising in Vancouver-area newspapers, but John Dawe noted that news of its existence spread anyway: "The first three years I found there was hardly any newspaper advertising done, so we must have done it mostly through word of mouth and other organizations, local DJs [that] we would get in touch with and keep the name out there."[24]

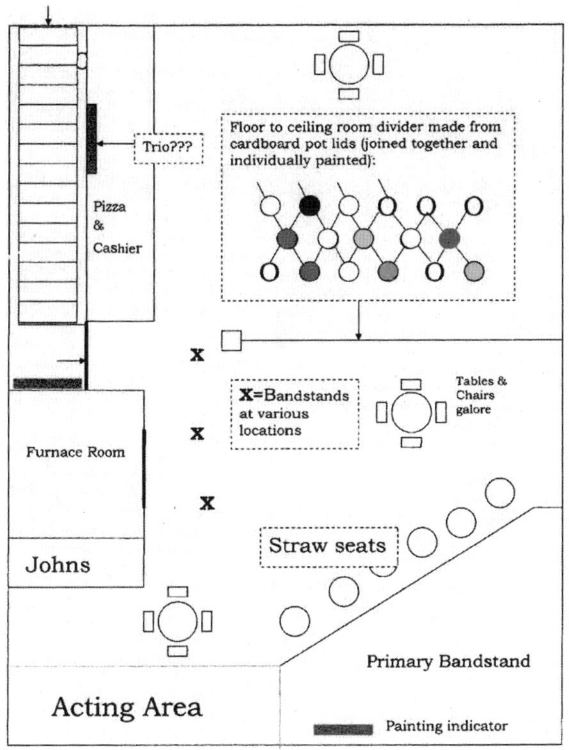

11 Cellar floor plan | *Courtesy Jim Kilburn*

Though the small core of charter members were pledged to help pay the rent and utilities, the hope was that the Cellar could become self-sustaining and pay its operating expenses through the cover charge paid by the crowds drawn to the weekend performances. In addition to the small one- or two-dollar door fee, the club sold 7-Up, ginger ale, Coca-Cola, and ice at a modest markup, as well as premade, wrapped sandwiches that were picked up before each evening's performances. John Dawe recalled that the environment was "very rustic. That's my best description of it. It was a great place to come and you didn't have to spend any money. Everything was real basic" (see Figure 12).[25] Drummer Terry Clarke agreed:

> The Cellar was almost the classic *cinema verité* version of a jazz club. Because it was people smoking and you know, little

12 [*L-R*] Jim Johnson, John Dawe, Bob Miller, and Vivian Cook in the Cellar, ca. 1959 | *Photo by Carol Hunter; courtesy John Dawe*

> candles on the tables, and round tables, and it was really classic. I didn't know that [at the time]. Maybe it was the very first time I'd ever been at the Cellar, but ... my eyes started watering. And I didn't know what that was all about, but my eyes were stinging me and I was tearing up and I had to leave the club. Well it was [all] the smoking and no ventilation. I'd never been in a smoke-filled room in my life. I mean, my dad smoked a bit, but to be in a closed room with no ventilation ... It really was a cellar, and everybody smoked, constant smoke, and I was a virgin [to that kind of atmosphere], and I remember I was practically in pain, and had to leave the club and just air it out. And of course I reeked when I got home, just like we did for twenty-five years [as working jazz musicians].[26]

In an attempt to both increase the meagre cash flow and make the Cellar a more hospitable place, Ken Hole approached his contacts in the restaurant world, a move that inadvertently resulted in the Cellar becoming one of the first establishments in Vancouver to sell pizza by the slice. Local restaurant supplier Tevie Smith had begun to import pizza-making equipment from his native Italy, and provided the supplies needed to create pizza in-house at the Cellar, including an electric pizza oven.

> And a lot of people came down just to try it. And we used to have the little wedges, you know, and sell them for fifty cents or whatever it was, and it was so easy for us to administrate that, especially at two or three in the morning. And then when once we were finished we just put everything in the fridge and went home. That was a first for the Cellar, introducing pizza to Vancouver.[27]

Though the general consensus appears to be that the pizza itself was quite forgettable, its presence at the Cellar, including its pervasive smell, is one of the most commonly recalled aspects of the club by those who were frequent visitors.

> We usually had some food. I guess you could describe it as food. Bad pizza, mostly. Really bad pizza. I never touched pizza for years after that. I figured all pizza had to be that bad, right?[28]

> We sold mixer, we sold 7-Up and Coke. We had the worst pizza in the world. It tasted like old shoe leather. It was just awful. It was hardly edible. In fact, today you wouldn't call it pizza.[29]

> You had to go downstairs [to get into the club]. And you could smell the pizza [coming up the stairs].[30]

While selling pizza at the Cellar may have augmented the club's cash flow in some small way, the main advantage of the in-house food service was that it eliminated the need to leave the club to eat, thereby prolonging late-night sessions.

By the end of 1956, the club was firmly established and had become both the vital centre of Vancouver's modern jazz scene and a viable entertainment alternative to the more mainstream offerings at downtown clubs such as Isy's and the Cave. While there were

13 Al Neil, Bob Frogge, Freddie Schreiber, Bill Boyle, and John Dawe, ca. 1958 | *Photographer unknown; courtesy Jim Carney*

apparently several hundred social members by year's end,[31] the most regular contributors to the club as performers and organizers were musicians Ken Hole, Walley Lightbody, Dave Quarin, Fred Massey, Tony Clitheroe, Jim Carney, John Dawe, Bill Boyle, Jim Johnson, Ed Roop, Al Neil, and Jim Kilburn (see Figure 13); artists Harry Webb, John Grinnell, and Frank Lewis; filmmaker and drummer Don Cumming; emcee Barry Cramer; comedian and vocalist Don Francks; and vocalist Doreen Williams. Late 1956 also saw the arrival of vibraphonist Bob Frogge from Kansas City, bassist Freddie Schreiber from Seattle, and drummer Chuck Logan from California, all of whom would be important figures in the next stage of the Cellar's development.

Imports: American Jazz Artists at the Cellar

As soon as it became clear that the Cellar was drawing enough regular business to remain solvent, several charter members began to consider bringing in some of the American artists they heard on records and radio, but who rarely made it north of the border to Vancouver. Though there were infrequent presentations by the Vancouver New Jazz Society and occasional visits to the downtown supper clubs by such established artists as Duke Ellington and Louis Armstrong, little small group modern jazz was on offer in Vancouver at the time, particularly by the famous American artists of the day. By banking whatever profits the Cellar made, the charter members hoped to import some of the musicians who inspired them – in order to listen, and also to learn. Pianist Al Neil recalled their reliance on imported recordings:

> At any given time, our repertoire would be stuff that we'd taken off the most recent record that somebody would get. None of us had much money, and there was only one record store ... Between [Tony] Clitheroe and Bill Boyle, we could take all the stuff off by ear ... John Dawe was good with the basic harmony and I could do the extended chords, and Clitheroe would just hear the bass and play it. Same with Boyle. But we were basically learners. You know. So whatever you heard there, even in 1957, we weren't playing that stuff as well as New York [musicians were].[32]

Initially, Ken Hole hoped to form an alliance of sorts with Seattle (the closest US city of any size) and attempted to work out an informal exchange program whereby Seattle-based groups would be featured for a weekend at the Cellar while a group of Vancouver musicians played in a Seattle-area club. However, Seattle lacked a jazz club or jazz society with the same sort of organizing principle as the Cellar, and the experiment was short-lived. While the Seattle musicians by all accounts enjoyed their performances at the Cellar, the Canadian musicians, such as John Dawe, were less impressed with the venues and conditions they found following the lengthy drive south.

> When the Cellar first opened up, Ken thought it would be great if we could get a thing going between Seattle and Vancouver, and use some Seattle musicians ... an exchange kind of thing, you know. One of Al's group or somebody's

> group would go down and play in Seattle, and Ken would line up a group from Seattle to come up and play at the Cellar. So we did a few things sort of like that. It didn't work out very well. We played at a place called Birdland there, which really wasn't a jazz place, it was an R&B place mostly. Dancing and a great big barn [of a place]. It wasn't an intimate jazz club. But I'm sure there were clubs around Seattle where there was some jazz going on. I can't think of the names of what they might be though, in that particular period. You know what jazz clubs are like, they open up for six months and then they're gone and you never hear of them again.[33]

Undaunted by this initial failure to expand the club's musical horizons, the Cellar began to look at hiring well-known American artists to play short engagements. Through a combination of in-person requests made to touring musicians in Seattle and Portland, and the connections of expatriates Freddie Schreiber, Bob Frogge, and Chuck Logan, in 1957 the Cellar hosted a handful of significant American artists, many of whom worked with the local Vancouver players formally as well as in informal sessions. Logan recalled, "Basically, with the contacts that I had in LA, from working [in that city] ... they wanted to start bringing artists up from there. Harold Land and I got in touch with Monk Montgomery and he brought up his brothers, Don Cherry, Ornette Coleman."[34]

Between spring and December of 1957, the Cellar featured saxophonist Art Pepper with Al Neil (piano), Tony Clitheroe (bass), and Bill Boyle (drums); the Mastersounds featuring Buddy and Monk Montgomery (see Figure 14); trumpeter Don Cherry's Jazz Messiahs featuring James Clay (tenor), Don Payne (bass), and Billy Higgins (drums); saxophonist Sonny Red with a local rhythm section of Tony Clitheroe, Fred Massey (piano), and Bill Boyle; the Paul Bley Quartet featuring Dave Pike (vibes), Charlie Haden (bass), and Lennie McBrowne (drums); Lou Levy with Ted Owens (drums) and Paul Ruhland (bass); and Don Cherry and saxophonist Ornette Coleman with Ben Tucker (bass) and Billy Higgins (drums). An additional highlight of the Cellar's 1957 season was an epic late-night jam session attended by the majority of the artists featured on 1957's Jazz à la Carte tour.

14 Monk Montgomery, unknown person, Vivian Cook, and Bob Frogge at the Cellar, ca. 1957. Notice the Cellar renovations in progress. The door at the far left was the entrance from the stairs. | *Photo by Carol Hunter; courtesy Jim Carney*

These engagements by high-profile American jazz artists further solidified the Cellar's place on the Vancouver entertainment scene, drawing a wider audience than would usually attend the weekend showcases for local groups. Whenever possible, the Cellar arranged for visiting American artists to work extended engagements rather than single evenings, and out-of-town musicians were often in the city for anywhere between a week and a month.[35] The experience of playing with visiting artists helped the Cellar-based musicians by boosting their confidence and providing a sense of membership in the larger jazz community outside the relatively insular and isolated Vancouver scene, as Ken Hole recalled:

> We made a little money, and we had some contacts in the States, and then all of a sudden we had musicians wanting to come and play in the jazz club ... They'd come up and play for the weekends and play with the local guys, and be featured ... They started to come in with the understanding that the boys could sit in with them, jam with them. And

> it caught on like you wouldn't believe. And soon we didn't have enough room there for everybody on a Saturday night or a Friday night ... I mean it was camaraderie, and everybody talked shop, and everybody was learning from these musicians coming up from California. They'd learn a new method of playing jazz, and some phrasing that we'd never heard before, and the next thing you'd know, the local guys would be doing it. And that's how the jazz word spread amongst musicians because we all got to listen to one another and [to] people from other jurisdictions that had other styles and so forth. And that was really good for the young [musicians] in the BC, Lower Mainland area.[36]

John Dawe, for example, recalled that Sonny Red's appearance at the Cellar introduced the musicians there to "On Green Dolphin Street," a mid-1940s' movie tune that would go on to become a jazz standard but had not yet found its way to Vancouver as a meaningful part of the jazz repertoire.[37]

The Cellar's charter members were responsible for all aspects of these engagements. Initial contact and booking most often fell to Ken Hole and Dave Quarin, often with the assistance of Logan, Frogge, or Schreiber, who had numerous contacts in the west coast scene. Other members were tasked with picking up the musicians from the airport, providing transportation around town, locating instruments, providing lodging, and arranging formal rehearsals when required. Though most imported players were housed at the nearby City Centre Motor Inn, just around the corner from the Cellar on Main Street between East Fifth and Sixth,[38] some were housed in the homes of Cellar musicians. Initially, home-stay arrangements were largely an attempt to save money, but friendships quickly developed between many of the Cellar members and their American colleagues, which often resulted in repeat visits to the Cellar over the years. Dave Quarin and Jim Kilburn in particular developed a reputation for hosting American players, as did the nearby "bebop house" shared by several younger, unmarried musicians.

One of the first major American stars to visit the Cellar was Art Pepper, who arrived in Vancouver in May 1957 fresh from both a stint in prison and the January 1957 recording of what would become his most famous record, *Art Pepper Meets the Rhythm Section*.[39] Walley Lightbody and Al Neil went to meet Pepper when he arrived:

> I remember going to the airport to pick up Art Pepper. And I had to wait and wait, and he was held up at customs, and I thought, "Oh my god, he's not going to get in." And the next thing I knew he came through, he had a suitcase under his arm, and I said, "Gee, what was the holdup?" and he said, "Well you know, I've got a new album out, and I brought up eight copies of my new album," and that was the thing that bothered them. "I also had about six bottles of cough medicine which is about eighty percent morphine," he said. "They didn't pay any attention to that at all."[40]

> Art Pepper had a lot of trouble getting in [to the country]. We waited around the airport for [a long time] ... we told him we'd pick him up at the airport. Dave Quarin and me and maybe one other person. And we got in a position where we could see everybody coming out of the proper gate that was coming, and it looked like it got to the last person and then we saw this guy, I guess it was winter, and he had this big coat with his collar up, and it was long ... I don't know if it was stylish at the time or what. Must've been. He seemed to be straggling, and he had one last person to go through and he was carrying a bottle in his hand, and the guy [customs official] kind of looked at it, and Art Pepper explained it to him, and it turned out it was cough syrup, but I guess the guy didn't know that – this was the time before they banned it – [the cough syrup contained] laudanum. It was the next best thing for a junkie. It took the drug enforcement [people] several years to realize. I think there was a time when you didn't even need a prescription. Just cough syrup. [Laudanum was] just listed as an ingredient.[41]

To avoid trouble with Customs and Immigration over work visas, Pepper had travelled from California without a saxophone.[42] As Pepper was both fond of Martin saxophones and an official endorser of the brand, Jim Johnson was tasked with locating a suitable instrument upon his arrival.

> I was involved with Art Pepper, because I was working at [the] Western Music store, and Art Pepper was coming to town to play at the Cellar. But because of his record I guess, he had a narcotics record, and he had to cross the border, so he didn't want to bring his horn. So I was commissioned at Western Music to bring him a Martin alto saxophone. But we didn't have a Martin alto saxophone. But I managed to bring every alto in the store out for Art Pepper and he turned them thumbs down. He must've had a contract with Martin ... even then, I guess. So, I flunked out. I had all these saxophones, and he said, "Naw, I don't want to play those." So somebody managed to get hold of Cliff Binyon, who was an alto player for Dal [Richards] and all the downtown guys, and Cliff Binyon agreed to let him use his Martin saxophone. The only Martin in town, as far as we know. So Art Pepper got a Martin alto saxophone, and he got my necktie and tie pin, which he borrowed from me and never gave back.[43]

Several of these early experiments in bringing in American jazz artists to perform at the Cellar turned out to be meaningful engagements for the American musicians as well as for their Canadian hosts. Though now widely regarded as significant and influential players, in the mid-1950s Paul Bley, Charlie Haden, Don Cherry, and Ornette Coleman were in the early stages of their careers and eager to find opportunities to play. In August 1957, trumpeter Don Cherry played the Cellar with a group that included bassist Don Payne, drummer Billy Higgins, and tenor saxophonist James Clay. Most notably, the engagement included numerous compositions by Ornette Coleman, who at the time was finding limited outlets for his unorthodox style in Los Angeles. Cherry's group was impressed by the collegial, non-commercial atmosphere of the club, and Cherry, in addition to beginning what would be a long-lasting friendship with Jim Kilburn, impressed upon manager Ken Hole the merits of hiring Coleman's group in the future.[44] In October 1957, Paul Bley appeared at the Cellar soon after the debut recording sessions of both Charlie Haden (bass) and Dave Pike (vibes) on Paul Bley's *Solemn Meditation,* and with Lennie McBrowne (drums) presented the complete ensemble from that session (see Figure 10).[45]

In November 1957, Ornette Coleman himself played the Cellar, an engagement with early career significance as these Cellar dates are reportedly one of the first opportunities Coleman had been given to play his own compositions as a leader (see Figure 15).[46]

> In the fall of [19]57 Don Cherry was back again ... this time with a very startling group ... this was the first time that these guys had worked together as a group publicly and Ornette Coleman was more than a bit of a shocker! ... They did a lot of Ornette's tunes, which at that time were still fairly conventional, but Ornette's solo style was extremely "unorthodox" ... you either dug them or you hated them, but after the 3rd nite [sic] most of us were starting to dig what they were putting down.[47]

According to Ken Hole, Coleman told him that the Cellar engagement represented a then-rare opportunity for him to play his compositions and unique musical style for an audience that was supportive of his experimentation, if at times a bit perplexed by it.

> You know something that I'm so proud of? When Ornette Coleman finished his playing there, because he was there for about a month, with Don Cherry, and when it was all over he came over and he started crying. And he said, "Ken, you are the first person ... who has ever asked me to play [my own material] and offer[ed] me a job, and I'll never forget it. You're the first person that's ever had enough guts to hire me to play. And Ken, no matter where I am, if you ever need me, you've got me for nothing to play a concert." And he left here and went back to California, and the next thing you knew he'd gone to New York and become a real celebrity. That was one of the best jazz moments I ever had. When he cried on my shoulder and thanked me for being the first person to take a risk on h[im] and his plastic saxophone.[48]

> I remember that just like that. [Ornette] was so ... just so happy that he'd had a chance to play. And of course play with people who understood music. And he did a good job.[49]

Significantly for Coleman's career, Cherry recorded the Cellar engagement and upon returning to Los Angeles called the local *Downbeat* office to say, "Look, we made some tapes up there. I'd like you to hear them because I really think you'll dig the charts. Some of them are by Ornette Coleman, and ... they're just too much." These

[*a*]

[*b*]

[*c*]

[*d*]

15 Ornette Coleman (saxophone), Don Cherry (trumpet), and various musicians play the Cellar in November 1957: [*a*] Ornette Coleman (centre), Ben Tucker (bass), and Billy Higgins (drums); [*b*] Ornette Coleman (right), Don Cherry (second from right), Ben Tucker (bass), Billy Higgins (drums), and Don Friedman (piano); [*c*] Don Cherry (right), unknown bass player, and Chuck Logan (drums); [*d*] Don Cherry (left), Chuck Logan (drums), and Dave Quarin (saxophone) | *Photographers unknown; Coleman photos courtesy Walley Lightbody; Cherry photos courtesy Jim Carney*

Cellar recordings were west coast *Downbeat* editor John Tynan's introduction to the music of Ornette Coleman.[50]

Though several of the musicians who were involved in the organization of the Cellar were already being heard on Vancouver radio by 1957, the visiting American jazz stars helped to boost the profiles of both the club and the musicians who most often played there.[51] The publicity that surrounded pianist Lou Levy's 1957 performance, for example, led to an invitation for Levy to perform a short solo set on a local television program, an engagement that Levy split with Cellar regulars in the Fred Massey Quintet – Massey (piano), Paul Perry (saxophone), John Dawe (trumpet), Tony Clitheroe (bass), and Bill Boyle (drums).[52] Though Levy did not use this precise group for his Cellar performances, he did employ local bassist Paul Ruhland and drummer Ted Owens. Art Pepper's 1957 appearance also led to television exposure for Cellar musicians as Pepper, backed by Al Neil (piano), Tony Clitheroe (bass), and Bill Boyle (drums), performed live on a local half-hour television program, *The Cool Pepper Show*.[53]

Playing with seasoned American jazz artists was at times rather stressful, and not all of the experiences were positive ones for the Cellar's musicians. They had to negotiate not only the pressures and insecurities inherent in performing improvised music, but the at times challenging personality traits and personal problems of their visiting guests. Art Pepper's engagement, for example, presented particular problems for pianist Al Neil. Bassist Tony Clitheroe recalled:

> That was not a fun gig. Well, Al didn't seem to know what to do. And of course Art was in one of his altered states most of the time. I got along fine with him, had no problems at all. I enjoyed playing with him. But Bill Boyle, I think, was playing drums, if I'm not mistaken. It was Bill Boyle, Al Neil, and myself. And Art.[54]

Clitheroe's recollections are confirmed by Al Neil, who was remarkably candid about his struggles, recounting the stress of dealing with a musical job for which he felt unqualified, as well as Pepper's brusque and at times erratic behaviour.

That was one of the toughest gigs I ever played, with that guy ... Total junkies like him like to play with other junkies, and I wasn't at that time. That would be one reason. I put that together. And the other reason ... I knew all the people he'd played with, and had all of his records, Pepper's records. And I knew I could comp, and I learned all them off the records, all the standards that he played, and I wrote them out, and handed it to him before we started playing at the Cellar. I thought the first set went pretty good.

The second [set] ... he took a long intermission and he came back up and the very first tune he got ready to play, and I thought he was just going to ... I'd listed about twenty really good standards and he'd recorded them all. I was beginning to relax a bit, like this was going to be good enough for him, you know, and he put his horn up to his mouth and he just [*mumbles incoherently*] and I ... if he named a tune, I don't know what it was, and then he started playing and indeed, it was a tune I didn't know. And it was slightly offbeat, like "Begin the Beguine" or something. So I foolishly ... I thought, there's not much chord changes in this, I'll give it a try, and I tried for a few bars and then realized that [it was hopeless]. Clitheroe got it right, because he used to play all kinds of stuff when he wasn't playing at the Cellar.

And then there was a long intermission again, and he didn't seem to want to come back to play, and he was sort of booked to play one more set, a later set. And then what happened was Chris Gage came in.[55] Chris and I were good friends. Chris came in, and somehow or other ... I was just sitting forlorn at a table, waiting to get the call back, and the first thing I notice Chris came over to me, and said, "Art wants me to sit in." And I said, "OK." And Chris did the rest of the gig. I played the first part of it, and as soon as Chris came in ... it was way better than what I was doing.

Chris played beautiful standards and beautiful harmony, and he knew it wasn't bebop, but he was getting close to it by that time. He was a really good accompanist for Art. And then we still had this half-hour TV show, and we'd rehearsed for only twenty minutes or something, a certain number that

> we'd already played at the Cellar, and live, halfway through ... No, it must have been ten minutes before we went on the air, he came out, and we'd already rehearsed and he came over with a slip of [music] paper and I looked at it, and I could read a little bit, but it wasn't hard for me to grasp that there was a lot of off-beat stuff and his notation wasn't all that legible. We got through it, but it wasn't ... I think he was a bit disgusted. And he was a guy that never used your name. He never used my name. And he never spoke to us.[56]

Pepper's displeasure with Al Neil's playing shouldn't be taken as a statement on Neil's musical talents. Neil was at the time a well-known and well-respected jazz player in Vancouver, and one of the most frequent Cellar collaborators. Though Neil would eventually move away from mainstream jazz expression toward free improvisation, mixed media, writing, and performance art to become a significant force in Vancouver's artistic avant-garde, in 1957 he was still very much enamoured with and proficient in mainstream jazz expression. As John Dawe saw it,

> Art's a hard guy to work with anyway – very demanding, and on top of that he's a junkie, which doesn't put him in a good mood. And he had a few words with Al. I think he talked to Al and said, "Al it's musical, not personal." Which is worse! Al wished it had been personal. He just didn't like the way Al was laying the chords down. He was very particular about that. He brought some music with him too, some originals that he had, and Al wasn't playing those tunes the way he wanted him to lay the chords down in a certain way. It's touchy stuff.[57]

After Hours

Beyond its function as a formal venue for performances by local and visiting groups, the Cellar was a key site for informal gatherings of the Vancouver jazz community.[58] These sessions, which began after the last scheduled set on weekends and at impromptu hours during the rest of the week, were in many ways the most important element of the Cellar for its charter members and most earnest fans. While much of the Cellar's audience was understandably focused on the formal performances and special presentations, for scene insiders the late-night sessions were often the main draw. Staged after most musical jobs had ended, the sessions enabled working musicians to participate in the Cellar scene and to develop their jazz chops outside their professional duties. These after-hours sessions (attended generally only by players and the very closest fans and friends) facilitated the exchange of ideas and material, encouraged collaboration between players who might not usually play with one another in formal groups, and were the site of "the hang" – the gossip, conversation, networking, and community building that form the vital basis of any scene.

Through word of mouth, the existence of the Cellar as a welcoming space for jazz musicians until the early hours of the morning became well known, and the Cellar became a post-gig destination for American musicians booked at larger venues such as the Georgia Auditorium, Isy's, and the Cave Supper Club. As drummer Chuck Logan recollected:

> Yeah, they'd be someplace else, and then it would be like, "So where's the place to go?" "Oh man, the Cellar!" And as soon as they got off, as soon as someone would say the Cellar, and they'd ask where it was, we'd get a phone call – so-and-so is on his way. And it would be like a welcome mat by the time they got here.[59]

One of the most memorable of these late-night jam sessions occurred in the fall of 1957, during what most of those interviewed recalled as the last visit to Vancouver by Norman Granz's touring all-star show Jazz at the Philharmonic. It seems, however, that the travelling jazz show in question was not the famous Jazz at the Philharmonic, but rather one of the concert tours staged by Norman Granz's brother Irving, known as Jazz à la Carte.[60] The Granz production was performing at the Georgia Auditorium, and numerous members of the show made their way to the Cellar afterwards. Ken Hole related:

> That was a great night. That's the best night we ever had there. That's the last time that the JATP [Jazz at the Philharmonic] came to Vancouver, and the fella that did it ... Norman Granz, he packed it in after that. And we had everybody there, the whole gang. Chuck Logan ... we went in after [the performance] and talked to everybody, in the dressing room. And they got taxis and they all came up. And there was the MJQ ... what's his name, good player, the Modern Jazz [Quartet] guy [Percy Heath] came out, and he brought his own bass with the little wheel on it and brought it down the stairs [into the Cellar]. Ella Fitzgerald was there, but she didn't sing that night. We all jammed, and everybody got in and played with our local guys and they played with the top guys, and then at the end of it we had just Percy Heath and Ray Brown. And Ray Brown played my bass. He liked it too. And this was about three o'clock in the morning, and they started a fugue going and they both played opposite each other for over two hours. It was daylight when we walked out. And it was just fabulous. Musically, with our group playing with the top musicians in the world, [it] just blended in beautifully ... there was no pressure because we were all musicians, and we all belonged to the unions and all the rest of it. So it wasn't a matter of outflanking anybody. We were just there because ... all these top people coming in realized that this was a jazz club for registered musicians, and it was in-house, it wasn't anything to do with the outside world. Oh, what a great night that was. Just blew me right away. And I didn't play at all.[61]

"It was great," said singer, comedian, actor, and frequent Cellar master of ceremonies Don Francks, "because if I was doing a late gig somewhere, I could drive [over] and go to the Cellar, and hang out."

> One of the beautiful times was about three in the morning, and I think Jazz at the Phil[harmonic] was in town, they were playing at the Georgia Auditorium. And I didn't go ... I think I had to work or something, and then I went there

[to the Cellar] and it was getting late. I don't know what time. Two o'clock in the morning. And in walked these two – I wouldn't say elderly, but they were older – black cats walked in carrying instrument cases. And [we] looked, and looked again, and it was Roy Eldridge and Coleman Hawkins. Because at the Cellar you didn't know who was going to drop in. It could be some heavies. This was pretty heavy. So naturally we waited, and they got up and blew, I don't know who was blowing with them ... local cats but [they could] play.

And then everybody split and they [Hawkins and Eldridge] say, "Well, guess we'd better get going. Maybe you could get us a cab." And I said, "No, no, wait. Where are you going?" And they said they were going to the Georgia Hotel, and I said, "I'd be glad to take you if you don't mind." And they said, "That would be very kind." And we opened the door [of the club] and I had just finished restoring a 1931 Packard Super Eight four-door sedan. Black cherry, like a dark cherry, with black fenders looking like it had just come out of the showroom. I opened the doors and Coleman got in and he moved over a little bit, and he said, "Come on, Jazz," because "Little Jazz," that was [Eldridge's] nickname, "You getting in here, Jazz?" and he said, "No, I'm sitting up here with my man. Ain't this [the car] something." And we got in and Little Jazz couldn't keep quiet. He was just saying, "Hawk, ain't this something. This is a bad joint." Because they used to call – sometimes a car was called a joint, not what you smoke. And Hawk's quiet. And [Eldridge] is looking at everything and asking what's this, and what's that, and then he said, "Dammit Hawk, you've got to tell me, ain't this the best ever [car]?"

And there was just this quiet moment, and he [Hawkins] suddenly said very quietly, "Fletcher wouldn't drive nothing else but a Packard." And it was quiet, and I looked in the rear-view mirror, and Hawk was just sitting there with his case in the back and you could see that he was back in 1931, 1932. Because Fletcher Henderson ... but he never said Henderson, he just said Fletcher, and I knew what he was

> talking about. And then we sort of had a quiet journey to the hotel. And that's probably one of the neatest times I had at the Cellar. Aside from some really good jamming.[62]

Is You Is, or Is You Ain't: The Pressures of Success

Throughout 1957, the Cellar remained fairly low key in terms of its advertising, even when hosting American artists,[63] preferring that news spread via word of mouth in the musical community and on the University of British Columbia campus. Some students had found their way to Jack Kerouac, the beats, and jazz music, and Cellar members Jim Carney, Walley Lightbody, and Gavin Walker (among others) were active members of the UBC Jazz Society. In later years this relationship would extend to include campus presentations of Cellar-based jazz groups, and concerts and workshops featuring visiting American artists brought in by the Cellar. Indeed, the only exception to the lack of formal advertising in the Cellar's initial years seems to have been the UBC campus, where the club enjoyed a significant presence in campus publications. The Fall 1957 issue of the student-run magazine *Pique,* for example, featured a full-page glossy advertisement for the Cellar on its back cover (see Figure 16), and UBC law student and acting Cellar president Walley Lightbody wrote a regular jazz column for the magazine entitled "The Jazz Scene." In addition to general commentary on current events in jazz (Dave Brubeck, Miles Davis, etc.), Lightbody had this to say about the scene in Vancouver:

> In closing I wish to mention that the jazz scene in Vancouver is far from stagnant. The local jazz club known as THE CELLAR and located beneath the traffic at 222 East Broadway will start swinging six nights a week as of October 4 and will at this time present from the Hillcrest in L.A. the Paul Bley Quartet for ten days. Other artists appearing in the near future will be Buddy DeFranco, Conte Candoli, Bob Cooper and Cal Tjader. Anyone interested in more information can usually find me drinking coffee or sleeping somewhere in the Brock.[64]

16 Ad for the Cellar on the back cover of the Fall 1957 issue of the UBC campus magazine *Pique* | *Courtesy Walley Lightbody*

By the end of 1957, the Cellar had been operating for twenty months and had evolved from its roots as private house sessions in the Richmond Wailhouse to be a vital and popular part of an emerging Vancouver jazz scene. Initially open only on weekends, the Cellar was now operating as many as six nights per week, hosting well-known American jazz stars as well as locally based groups, and was a popular enough draw to be financially stable.

As it became clear that the club was not destined for immediate failure but rather could be a successful enterprise, tensions rose within the Cellar's organizational core as to the purpose and future development of the club. On one side of the ideological divide were musicians Al Neil, Tony Clitheroe, and other players who were focused upon the Cellar as a laboratory and presentation space solely for jazz. The Cellar had sprung from the need for a place in which the city's younger, less established jazz musicians could network, practise, and perform, and the majority of the voting membership of the Cellar Musicians and Artists Society, including John Dawe, continued to see that as the club's main purpose.

> You got to remember that we weren't trying to run a business, we were just trying to keep the place afloat. All we were really after was to get enough people into the place to pay the rent and build up a bit of a bank account so that we could bring some out-of-town guys in. That was the main idea of the place ... As far as publicity and advertising ... we weren't really very heavy on it. We weren't trying to make money, we just wanted to keep it going.
>
> None of us hardly were interested in money, in making money. If it happened, that was okay, but none of us had that drive to want to be studio musicians ... none of us had that intention. We had absolutely no ambition to make money out of music. If the money came, that's cool, or if a studio job came that was to our liking, or that we were able to handle ... we weren't against it, but we weren't particularly aimed in that direction.[65]

On the other side were those, such as Ken Hole and Walley Lightbody, who sought to broaden the club's programming to increase its popularity and profitability. Hole believed that the Cellar could increase its audience by expanding its musical offerings slightly to include some vocalists and popular music that, while being jazz-influenced, fell somewhat short of the bebop-focused music the Cellar musicians were interested in playing. His ambition was to increase door revenues enough to book top-tier jazz artists such as Miles Davis and Stan Getz, an interest born from his busy career as an entrepreneur in the restaurant business.

In January 1958, the voting members of the Cellar Musicians and Artists Society convened to discuss the future of the club. Though the issues were not personal and the meeting remained civil, the divide between the two sides proved too wide to bridge and resulted in the resignations of both Ken Hole and Walley Lightbody. Al Neil recalled:

> There was a really early meeting, we must have rented an office building or something. We did that in those days. And we had a meeting with everybody that played, and a couple of others, I guess you'd call them hangers-on, at the time. Lightbody was a player, but he already seemed [more focused on his legal career] ... and Ken Hole. They seemed to have formed an idea that this could go somewhere, could be a commercial success. And none of us players ... we were all too busy learning how to play, and we all had day jobs. So it might have flown through somebody's mind, but it wasn't talked about as far as I can figure out. And Hole particularly went on and on about it, his plans. And it finally dawned on us that he was an entrepreneur ... So I guess the meeting must have ended kind of ... not totally disruptive, but verging on that. Because we could feel the split ... and the people that wanted to take it one way, and we just wanted to carry on, at least for the time being. With local groups, and the odd group from LA.[66]

Walley Lightbody was not persuaded:

> I remember it well, the meeting we had there. Al Neil was a big spokesman for the, if you want to call it "the other side." I remember saying, "Well, you know, if that's the way you feel about it, I'm out of here, and I'm tendering my resignation and I'm gone." And Ken said, and surprised me, as soon as I resigned he said, "I'm resigning too, and I'm out of here too." I remember that coming as a surprise, because I just made the decision on my own, that I have too many goddamn things to worry about rather than getting involved in a fracas here. I [was] a full-time student.[67]

Lightbody soon relocated to Vancouver Island to complete the articling necessary for his law degree, and he and Hole would team up again to open the Scene in Victoria, a jazz club that melded some of the Cellar's operating principles with Hole's commercial and entrepreneurial interests. Jim Johnson summed up the split thus:

> I think Kenny Hole would have turned the Cellar into a business, but we turned him down. At least those of us who were voting members of the society. And we just wanted a place to go after hours and, at the time, I guess none of us felt that we wanted to get involved with running a business. We just wanted to play. Dumb musicians just want to play, they don't want to make money. So we had a falling out with Kenny Hole and he went his way.[68]

Though the Wailhouse and Cellar operated primarily as local expressions of the jazz scene within Vancouver, they also intersected with the wider scene through an awareness of and eventual interaction with jazz activity in other areas. John Dawe and Bill Boyle, for example, travelled to Toronto during the Wailhouse period, returning with information related to jazz practices in that city; jazz radio and periodicals such as *Downbeat* and *Metronome* spread information related to scenic activity in American cities;[69] and the self-conscious desire for practical engagement with jazz scenes beyond Vancouver led members of the Cellar to import American artists to perform there. Participation in such activity, however sporadic, helped to foster a sense of community that was musically rather than geographically bounded, and that functioned despite distance and regional difference. This sense of wider connection and community then engendered a sense of confidence that was a bulwark against the tedious, unending, and at times divisive work of day-to-day club operations.

4

No Room for Squares

The Cellar as Artistic Hub

We just wanted to play. Dumb musicians just want to play, they don't want to make money.

– *Jim Johnson*

With Ken Hole's departure, a new manager was needed, and saxophonist Dave Quarin was voted into the position. Since the position was a more or less full-time responsibility, the club arranged to pay Quarin a small salary so that he could quit his day job as an accountant.

> Well, it was sort of an elective process. He was one of the charter members, so we had a meeting one night and had a vote as to who we'd like to have for the manager of the place.[1]

> Dave Quarin, when the place opened, Dave was an accountant for some company as his day gig. Which, when Ken Hole and Walley Lightbody decided to leave, uh, we made Dave the manager, and he quit his day gig. So we paid Dave a regular salary. Not very much, but it was a salary. So Dave lived on very little for a long time. And he was married then, couple of kids ... most of the rest of us had no responsibilities.[2]

Quarin's ex-wife, Ricci, who would herself play a key part in the club's operational success, recalls that Dave, upon returning home from the decisive 1958 Cellar board meeting, sat her down and asked if she would be all right "with eating hotdogs from then on," because he wanted to accept the manager job despite its low pay.[3] Ricci agreed, and Dave assumed managerial control of the Cellar in January 1958.

In addition to hiring Quarin as the club manager, the remaining Cellar members had to elect a new board of directors and re-register the not-for-profit Cellar Musicians and Artists Society with the appropriate authorities. Musicians Don Cumming and John Dawe remembered the paperwork:

> Then there was a political commotion about how [it was going to be run]. It ended up with twenty-seven of us in the society, and you had to form a board of directors ... The group of us didn't feel that it was, that they [Ken Hole and Walley Lightbody] could do a good enough job, I guess, for what we wanted as an artists and musicians club. Not just a commercial hangout, I guess ... Anyways we had to go to a lawyer and put it together, but we did it. So there was a bit of a ... hassle there to some extent, I guess.[4]

> We got together with a lawyer [and] got everything re-registered properly after [Ken Hole and Walley Lightbody] left. We went through the whole process of re-registering it. All kinds of wretched stuff that none of us wanted to do.[5]

The working arrangement with the local chapter of the American Federation of Musicians was also reconfirmed, and under Dave Quarin's management the Cellar began 1958 and the second phase of its eight-year history.

Quarin and the Cellar's board of directors worked quickly to professionalize the operation. An answering machine was added to the club's telephone to provide information on operating hours and the week's performances, and in the summer of 1958 the club ran its first advertisement in the *Vancouver Sun*.[6] Positioned in the entertainment section, the ad used the 2514 Watson Street address and advertised simply "Jazz in the Cellar" on Friday, Saturday, and Sunday evenings. This initial ad ran only in the Friday edition of the newspaper and shared space with movie listings and advertisements for plays, live theatre, major concerts, and the weekly entertainment available at the Cave and Isy's downtown. The musicians who enjoyed steady employment at these downtown clubs and at the nearby CBC studios represented an entirely different musical world from that of the Cellar.

> Vancouver was very, very strange in those days. It was divided into two places: the downtown core, which was tough to break into, and the rest of Vancouver or wherever. And all the rest of us young guys were in the whatever. We were out on the side.[7]

Though free of any overt animosity, a very real divide existed between the musicians who worked the downtown clubs and took the majority of Vancouver's studio work, and the younger players who focused almost exclusively on jazz, primarily at the Cellar. The split was based partially on ability – the (usually older) downtown players were generally better sight-readers and doublers[8] – and partially on musical ideology and lifestyle, as trumpeter John Dawe recalled:

> Then all of a sudden in 1955–1956, hard-core bebop came back again with a vengeance, and I think that struck some people as being a step backward, you know. I remember talking to Dave Robbins, who was a marvellous musician, trombone player ... He used to come into Western Music where we used to hang out on Saturdays and listen to records, and he'd open the door and say, "Hey man, we don't listen to that stuff [bebop] anymore, that's old-time stuff." We'd all laugh and say, "Yeah sure, Dave." And he [was] partly right, and partly full of crap. But anyway, [that was] the big difference between the guys that played at the Cellar and the guys that played downtown and did the studio work and that. That was the big difference ... [it] was stylistic. We were light years apart that way. Oh man, yeah. And now it doesn't

> make any difference, because everybody digs everything, pretty well. Things kind of evened out after that, but there was a big discrepancy between styles [at the time].[9]

The musicians who played the clubs and studios of the downtown core were referred to as "downtowners," and those who played the Cellar (and in later years the Black Spot and Flat Five) just minutes south across False Creek were called "uptowners." Uptowner John Dawe explained,

> We used to call them the "downtowners." That was Paul Ruhland, and the Chris Gage Trio, and the guys that played the Cave, the supper clubs downtown. I think there were a lot of put-downs on both sides. We were stone-ass beboppers who didn't give a damn about anything, making money or anything, and a lot of us were incapable of making money. You know, just, none of us were great readers or anything. So I don't think any of us had ambitions to become studio musicians or nightclub musicians.
>
> We were just ... we were jazz bums, you know, we didn't appreciate the kind of music they played for a living. Because they were just backing up bad, bad acts most of the time. And then occasionally they'd back up somebody good, some great singer or somebody would come into town. But those guys were real well-rounded musicians. They weren't real well-rounded jazz-wise, but boy, they could cut anything. You'd put them in the studios and they'd do it on sight! Great sight-readers and players like that. But they didn't appreciate us too much.[10]

Though the exclusion of Cellar musicians from well-paying downtown gigs was at least initially based upon a lack of professional skills such as sight-reading and doubling, the split deepened along musical lines, with the jazz-oriented Cellar players embracing their professional shortcomings as part of their identity as jazz musicians, and some of the downtown players avoiding a type of music and lifestyle they found disagreeable. Bassist Paul Ruhland, one of the few downtown musicians who had something of a regular presence at the Cellar, suggested that the exclusion might have worked both ways:

> It was a matter of ... the leaders that were working downtown, were a special group of leaders, and they hired always the same people. They didn't want to hire the Cellar guys because they couldn't read, or were poor readers. So ... I was lucky, I was a good reader, so I got hired for all the CBC shows, for instance ... But then you see, it developed to be a kind of a clique thing ... We were the downtown guys because we played downtown at the Cave, and we played downtown at the CBC, and it was always the same guys. Whether it was a ten-piece band or a fourteen-piece band it was always the same people that would be working around downtown. [But] those guys never got to work at the Cellar.[11]

Under the management of Ken Hole, the Cellar might well have begun to hire well-known local jazz-oriented groups such as those of Ray Norris, Fraser MacPherson, Dave Robbins, and vocalist Eleanor Collins, all of whom had large public profiles due to their regular appearances on CBC radio and television and at the major clubs and theatres in Vancouver. Indeed, the programming of Victoria's Scene Club, established by Lightbody and Hole in late 1958, reflected such choices. However, with the Cellar firmly dedicated to the needs and interests of its members, its programming remained centred on those who were regular participants in the scene, and on whichever American jazz artists they were able to bring in.

Beyond Ruhland and Ray Norris (who apparently became a Cellar member shortly before his move to Toronto and untimely death in 1958),[12] few of the downtown musicians frequented the Cellar. While these musicians were all working steadily and therefore unable to attend the scheduled public performances at the Cellar, the club was well known as an after-hours venue for musicians, and hosted jam sessions that routinely stretched into the daylight hours. For the most part, however, musicians employed in the downtown clubs opted instead for sessions at the Penthouse Cabaret and, in later years, at the Espresso Coffee House.

That said, photographs do show well-known downtown saxophonist Fraser MacPherson participating in a jam session with Cellar musicians and visiting American Bill Perkins (see Figure 23 in Chapter 5),[13] and ads in the *Vancouver Sun* show that the Chris Gage Trio and bandleader Ray Sikora were at times employed by the club.[14] Sikora in particular was something of a fixture at the Cellar, which was one of the few spaces that could accommodate his big band on a regular basis. In the Ray Sikora Band (of varying sizes) there was a considerable mingling of uptown and downtown players, though this generally did not extend to Sikora's work at Isy's or the Cave.

The Cellar was a place where bebop and youth were the predominant characteristics, and where some knowledge of the contemporary counterculture, be it in literature, art, drama, painting, or music, was required cultural currency. Likewise, the scene surrounding the downtown players was predicated upon its own culture and shared musical experiences. Nonetheless, musicians on both sides of the divide had much in common, and to think that such musicians as Fraser MacPherson, Chris Gage, and Dave Robbins were uninterested in modern jazz is patently absurd. The nuances, politics, and normative expectations of the scene, however, seem to have maintained and defined difference, as described by musicians Gavin Walker and Stan Perry:

> Some of these guys would come down [to the Cellar], not all the time, but it was almost ... there was almost a feeling of ... there was a bit of a division there too. Because these guys were club musicians, and some of them, you know, had attitudes. You know, like, "These guys are JUST jazz players, and we play jazz too, but we're able to do all this other stuff too." The readers, right? So there was a little bit of a push-pull thing, and that drove the jazz guys into sort of a "We're the real deal" sort of thing. You know. It wasn't like a horrible sort of situation, but there was that tension there. I detected it, and I'd talk to the jazz guys and they say, "Oh yeah, [the] downtowners were in and a couple of guys sat in and they're not as good as they think they are," et cetera, et cetera.[15]

> Wonderful players. But they seldom, in my time, anyway ... they're at least ten years older than I am, but they seldom, if ever, came to the Cellar when we were there ... We considered ourselves the lifeblood of jazz, right? You know? Other than the big-timers like Miles Davis and Charlie Parker and all the rest of it. But these guys were ... actually making a living playing. There were two major nightclubs in Vancouver, one was the Cave and the other was Isy's ... And they were great musicians, I don't have to say that, but they very rarely ... I can't ever remember them playing at the Cellar when [I] was there.[16]

Interestingly, a similar split existed in the contemporary visual arts and literary communities, according to poet Jamie Reid.

> There was a bit of antagonism between the downtowners and the university people. The university people were sort of above it, if you know what I'm saying, and the downtowners used to slight them in various ways. That was the bohemian art, and Al Neil and [poet] bill bissett are sort of the quintessential representatives of that type of artist in those days. For me, the two geniuses of the scene.[17]

Shared feelings of being marginalized by both society at large and the wider manifestations of their own art worlds may have been the catalyst for the unique and important relationship that developed between the Cellar and the non-musical arts community in Vancouver. Though the Cellar had always formally been known as the Cellar Musicians and Artists Society, this wider association was more fully realized only beginning in 1959. In large part, the increased presence of other arts at the Cellar was due to the influence of Al Neil.

Non-Musical Arts at the Cellar

The Cellar had long associated itself with jazz fans and supporters who came from different branches of the arts, functioning as something of a node where various complementary art worlds intersected. Visual artists such as Harry Webb, John Grinnell, and Frank Lewis had played important roles in the establishment of the Cellar space, while comedian and vocalist Don Francks and producer Barry Cramer were valuable assets to the club as emcees. On any given evening, the Cellar's audience was an eclectic mix of musicians, visual artists, writers, actors, and those drawn to the artistic counterculture of the time.

> That was the time of Jack Kerouac, you know? And the beat generation and all that kind of stuff, and everything was very cool and quiet.[18]
>
> I think they had all kind of audiences. All kind of early, what they called hippie and bohemian audiences.[19]
>
> The Cellar was the centre for people who wanted to listen to jazz, and the people who wanted to listen to jazz were, let's say, a bohemian minority, as it were. They'd read Jack Kerouac and they'd read Allen Ginsberg and jazz was the hip thing to listen to, and then they took it up seriously and learned something about it. And listened to it, and some of them learned to play it and so on and so forth. So they were the, I guess, the foundation ... [the] youthful jazz crowd here in Vancouver... [Artist] Fred Douglas and [poet] Curt Lang used to go there. This was even before I knew them, actually.[20]

Nonetheless, the Cellar was predominately a music club, and made few formal attempts to actively embrace other art forms before 1959.

> Well, it was known as ... the official name of the place was the Cellar Musicians and Artists Society, so there was no attempt to reject anyone who wasn't a musician, but mostly it was music that was going on down there, you know.[21]

From 1959 through the early 1960s, however, there was a concerted effort to more proactively engage with forms of art that were deemed complementary in spirit and aim to the bebop and modern jazz being performed, formalizing a hitherto tacit understanding that the Cellar was a main site of meeting and intersection for Vancouver's artistic counterculture writ large. Among the organizational core of the Cellar, the driving force toward artistic inclusivity and experimentation was pianist Al Neil, as drummer Gavin Walker noted:

> He was the personification of what the Cellar was all about. Artistic truth ... sort of alienation from regular society out there ... He saw [the Cellar] as a real oasis, a real cultural centre ... And that was a really interesting aspect ... [Barry Cramer] really wanted to do these plays at the Cellar, and ... it became a cultural centre. And Al Neil was really encouraging of that. Because some of the musicians were like [*dismissive hand gesture*], "Man, this is a jazz club, what has this got to do with jazz?" But Al Neil was right there, [saying,] "No, man, this is all part of it."[22]

One of the first major efforts toward this wider inclusivity was the monthly staging of plays at the Cellar.

Complete records of the theatrical events staged at the Cellar have been lost and the recollections of surviving participants are unclear, but it seems that between the spring of 1959 and at least the summer of 1960, a monthly series of plays was staged under the auspices of Barry Cramer, with the full support of Al Neil. For the most part, these plays were short, one-act productions, intended initially to precede the evening's musical content and, later on, to fit within the break between the first two sets. Promotional posters for the plays were designed by artist Harry Webb, and the surviving copies of these provide rare and useful evidence as to the evolution of the Cellar's marketing strategies. Al Neil remembered,

> Yeah, I was mostly responsible for that. But I didn't think it up ... I met this guy Barry Cramer. He was working at the very first TV station, I forget what it would be called. But he wasn't onscreen, he wasn't doing anything creative, and so he was pissed off with the job. He got the idea, I guess, and I backed him up on it ... And he started off with Samuel

> Beckett. And because he had been in broadcasting, without us having to pay any money, when we were ready to put it on, he got publicity ... He had friends that he knew in broadcasting. And [he] got a good turnout. Probably a hundred people would show up. And there w[ere] two Beckett plays, and a couple of others by current European [playwrights] ... I've forgotten them now. But they did go [over] very well.[23]

No one I interviewed could definitively identify the first play to be staged at the club, but one of the earliest productions was Samuel Beckett's *Endgame,* a work that was still relatively new and controversial.[24]

> The thing is, those plays were not really accepted at the time ... they were still pretty out there. Unlike today. They were, like, Beckett was very obscure, and Edward Albee was, like [out there] ... nowadays they're part of the mainstream of theatre, but back in those days that was avant-garde.[25]

Endgame was performed between May 24 and 28, 1959, and the 8:30 p.m. curtain time noted on the Harry Webb–designed poster confirms that that this production was offered before the first set of music. That no particular band was advertised on the poster suggests that this early dramatic experiment involved a local jazz group, very likely the Al Neil Quartet, given Neil's support for the project. This poster is also the first hard evidence of the Cellar's experiment with advance ticket sales for special events rather than a standard door charge (see Figure 17a). Over the years, advance tickets for Cellar special events would be available at the 711 Shop (a clothing store owned by Barry Cramer's family),[26] at Just Jazz Records, and, as this poster informs us, at H. Kaye Bookshop on Howe Street in the downtown core. The poster is unclear whether the $1.50 *Endgame* ticket would have also granted admission to the music that followed, though it is likely.

The title of the June production has been lost, but Cramer staged Eugène Ionesco's *The Lesson* between July 27 and 30, and *The Lesson* shared billing with Art Pepper, who performed at the Cellar from July 24 to August 2. Harry Webb's poster for this event uses the 222 East Broadway address, and advertises both *The Lesson* and the entire run of the Art Pepper Quartet (see Figure 17b). Advance tickets were once again available at H. Kaye Bookshop, this time for the price of $2, though it is once again unclear whether this price included admission to the Art Pepper performance. While some recall that cover charges for visiting American groups were usually higher than for local groups,[27] the appearance of Charles Mingus at the Cellar had an advertised price of just $2.25, so it is conceivable that the ticket price included both the play and Pepper's group.

Jean Giraudoux's *The Apollo of Bellac* was staged between November 9 and 12 (see Figure 17c), and the poster provides evidence that at least some of the plays performed at the Cellar were officially licensed.[28] *The Apollo of Bellac* was produced "by special arrangement with Samuel French," a New York–based publishing house specializing in plays, suggesting that theatrical performances were proving popular enough to sustain such an expense, and further, that some portion of the cover charge collected by the Cellar might have supported the club's theatrical efforts. This poster also indicates that the advance ticket sale location had moved, at least temporarily, to the Cramer family's clothing store on Granville Street in the downtown core. If the club kept to its monthly format, another four productions would have been staged between *The Apollo of Bellac* in November 1959 and the next play for which definitive proof exists – Saul Bellow's *The Wrecker,* between April 24 and 28, 1960 (see Figure 17d). A poster also survives for a February performance of Tennessee Williams's *I Rise in Flame, Cried the Phoenix;* the year of the performance cannot be determined but was probably 1960 (see Figure 17e).[29]

Samuel Beckett's *Krapp's Last Tape* was performed from Sunday, May 22, to Thursday, May 26, 1960, leaving Friday and Saturday solely to jazz performance. This scheduling suggests something of a shift in policy for the staging of plays at the Cellar, perhaps due to conflict between the jazz and theatrical factions at the club, or perhaps simply a response to increased popularity for the weekend concerts that made accommodating the plays more difficult. The poster uses the Cellar's 222 East Broadway address, and for the first time gives headline billing to a specific actor,

[a]

ENDGAME

A PLAY

BY SAMUEL BECKETT

ANOTHER EVENING OF
DRAMA AND JAZZ AT

THE CELLAR

MAY 24 TO 28 830 P.M.

TICKETS 1.50 AT H. KAYE BOOKSHOP 857 HOWE

[b]

THE CELLAR PRESENTS
JAZZ & DRAMA
REAR 222 EAST BROADWAY

THE LESSON
BY EUGENE IONESCO
STAGED BY BARRY CRAMER

THE ART PEPPER QUARTET
JULY 27th to JULY 30th

THE ART PEPPER QUARTET
JULY 24th TO AUG. 2nd

TICKETS 2.00 AT H. KAYE BOOKSHOP 857 HOWE

[c]

THE APOLLO
OF BELLAC
by Jean Giraudoux
BY SPECIAL ARRANGEMENT WITH SAMUEL FRENCH

NOV. 9.10.11.12. 8 P.
ADVANCE TICKETS ON SALE AT
THE 711 SHOP 783 GRANVILLE ST. $1.25
AT THE DOOR $1.50 REAR 222 E. BROADWAY

COMEDY AND JAZZ AT
THE CELLAR

STAGED BY
BARRY CRAMER

A WISE & WITTY
COMEDY ABOUT
LOVE

[d]

THE
WRECKER
A COMEDY IN
ONE ACT
BY SAUL BELLOW

APRIL 24th TO 28th 8:30 P.M.
STAGED by BARRY CRAMER

DRAMA AND JAZZ AT
THE CELLAR
AT THE REAR OF 222 EAST BROADWAY

ADVANCE TICKETS AT THE 711 SHOP
783 GRANVILLE MU. 5-6018

[e]

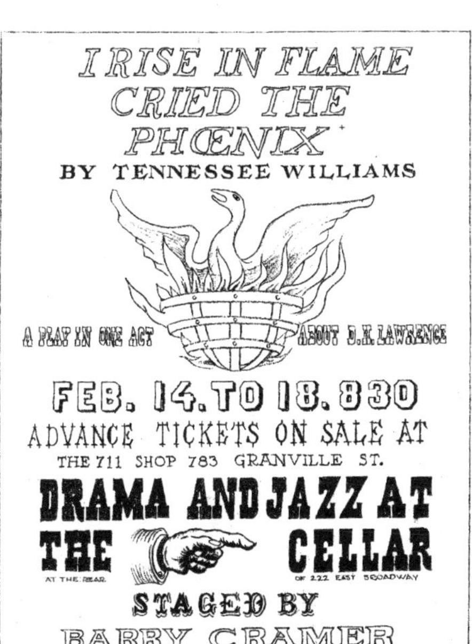

[f]

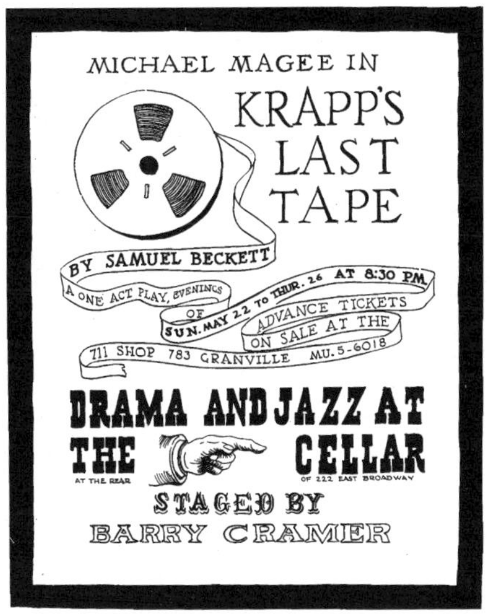

[g]

17 Posters for theatrical events staged at the Cellar between 1959 and 1960 | *Designed by Harry Webb; courtesy Adrienne Brown*

Michael Magee (see Figure 17f).[30] The final poster surviving from these early theatrical presentations is for an August 1960 staging of Brock Brower's *The Tender Edge* (see Figure 17g).[31] It is unclear whether the productions continued or *The Tender Edge* marked the club's final experiment with theatre until 1963.[32] Gavin Walker and Al Neil recalled that Edward Albee's *The Zoo Story* was staged during this period (1959–60) though no poster advertising its performance has been recovered.

Filmmaker Don Cumming recalled directing another production sometime between 1959 and 1961:

> It [the production of plays at the Cellar] was great. I even directed a play. The play was written by Patsy Southgate and was called *Freddy.* It was a metaphor. I actually had to get someone to build a horse. And the whole thing had to do with the horse, and of course horse was a metaphor for heroin. I got it out of the *Evergreen Review.*[33]

Despite these recollections, the only evidence for the dates of *The Zoo Story* and *Freddy* comes from *Vancouver Sun* advertisements from March and April 1963, respectively. Indeed, whereas the productions in the late 1950s to early 1960s were advertised only via Harry Webb's promotional posters, *Sun* ads for plays at the Cellar began in the spring of 1963. Because the initial run of plays under the auspices of Barry Cramer and Al Neil was promoted via hand-drawn posters rather than newspaper advertisements, and because the ads refer to productions that surviving individuals recall producing years earlier, I suspect that these 1963 productions were restagings. By the mid-1960s, the Cellar was experiencing financial difficulties and increasing competition from venues such as the Black Spot/Flat Five, and the (re)staging of short plays at this time may have been part of a strategy to widen the club's audience. In any case, from 1959 plays formed a regular and integral part of the Cellar's artistic activity. Drawn from diverse but uniformly avant-garde sources, the plays produced at the Cellar enabled non-musicians to involve themselves in artistic work, and encouraged members of the arts community as a whole to embrace the Cellar as a nexus for the artistic counterculture in Vancouver.

During the 1950s and early 1960s, the arts scene in Vancouver was vital and developing quickly in both literature and the visual arts, yet lacked the infrastructure to support and house the efforts of these varied artists. Beyond the Cellar and the scene that was tied to the University of British Columbia, there were few places for developing artists to interact with their peers or to engage in their work. Poet Jamie Reid, who cofounded the influential Canadian literary journal *TISH* in 1961,[34] described the Vancouver art world at the time:

> There was nothing, okay. Believe me. There was nothing. There wasn't ... there would have been the art gallery as a place, but we at that time didn't have any modality, any mode to have access to that. It did come later, but we didn't at that point have access. So, the first art gallery in Vancouver that I remember was the New Design Gallery that opened up on Pender Street, and that didn't open until 1961 at the earliest.[35]

As a result, and with the encouragement of Al Neil, Barry Cramer, John Grinnell, Harry Webb, Don Cumming, and others, the Cellar found itself functioning as a site through which the city's disparate arts groups intersected. While some members of the Cellar co-operative accepted and encouraged these efforts, Al Neil remembered that others were less comfortable, feeling that they took away from the club's focus on jazz: "Some people didn't like it, but I didn't see that they had any reason to, because we did this kind of thing in the middle of the week, or something like that."[36] "The Cellar was the node," suggested Adrienne Brown, daughter of artist Harry Webb, "the meeting point for all these people in these different parts of the arts. They'd all show up [to the Cellar], and they were all friends. It really was a club":

> I was not there myself because I was born in 1957, so I have to qualify it there, this is all based on what my parents told me, and it was a big part of their lives, but I gather from what they related to me about it that there was a tremendous amount of interaction between the visual artists and

> the musicians and the dramatists. Because, I think, because it was a non-profit situation and because it was after-hours it was quite intimate ... Because it wasn't a commercial thing, there wasn't that many people [involved] and I think they all knew each other very well. And [my parents] had such great memories; it was such a positive thing [for them]. I know my father made the posters, and apparently he also acted in some of the plays. There was that sense of crossing over back and forth, and I know that my father's friendship with people like Jim Kilburn was very cherished. They really got on, there was a deep bond ... My father loved music, and he really "got" music. He cared about music, but he didn't play an instrument, and he didn't sing.[37]

Indeed, this interconnectivity between the arts had prompted Al Neil's support of the Cellar as an interdisciplinary space.

Another regular to embrace and add to the interconnectivity of the arts at the Cellar was actor, comedian, and singer Don Francks. Francks had begun his performance career at the age of ten singing on local radio (billed as Don Francks-Sinatra), and quickly expanded his repertoire to include comedy routines. During the 1950s, he found steady employment at the last of Vancouver's vaudeville houses and at downtown supper clubs such as the Cave and Isy's. At these establishments, Francks warmed up the house with a short act that included songs, impersonations, and comedy, and then introduced the main attraction of the evening. With a keen interest in jazz, blues, and other forms of African American popular music, Francks was an early and frequent visitor to the Cellar as an audience member, jam session performer, and later on as master of ceremonies. Al Neil described Francks's act:

> When he started coming to the Cellar, none of us knew anything much about him, and he just showed up. And we were all suitably impressed because he was a worker, right, at that time, in a foundry, doing the heaviest possible work you could do, and he'd clean up and when he came to the Cellar he was all ... I forget if what I'm referring to is called the hipster style back then. A very nice suit, and he'd bring in ... we had

> little square tables at the Cellar, and he'd bring in a red-and-white tablecloth and lay it down, and bring out a bottle of wine. And we couldn't believe it, the first time he [did] it. We didn't have a liquor licence ... any liquor that was in there was under that table, but he put his on the table. And then he asked us, as we got to know him ... if he could do some humour, or I don't know what he called it. And so in intermission ... I said, "Go ahead, Don," and he got up and he managed to find all these totally esoteric and obscene black comics, like ... with names like Lord [Buckley][38] and such ... two or three of them. They were probably released as what were called ... race records.[39] So he got up, and because he was a budding actor, he could memorize like thirty minutes of it, and the accents, pretty close. And he'd get up and ... I don't know if he said, maybe he did, if he introduced them, and said who the work was [from]. He probably did that. And then he'd just start off, and I'd say about two percent or maybe nobody in the audience had heard this stuff, and it was so far beyond. It was beyond Lenny Bruce at the time, for being totally offbeat and erotic and whatever you want. But there was no reason that we couldn't, in that place, let him do it. And then he started singing a bit at the end, and he was very good at scatting like Ella, and of course he went to Toronto and became semi-famous, I guess.[40]

Francks's day job at the foundry paid reasonably well, and in addition to a penchant for sharp dressing, he was able to indulge a passion for automobiles, acquiring and meticulously restoring numerous cars from the 1930s and 1940s. In these cars he made regular trips to Seattle, where he visited record shops in search of rare jazz recordings and other race records, which were hard to find in Vancouver with its smaller black community. The records he found were often badly worn copies that had been removed from jukeboxes, but they enabled him to develop a repertoire that was decidedly unique.[41] At the Cellar he was then able to experiment with a type of satirical, adult comedy that preceded by several years the popularity of Lenny Bruce. Additionally, his interest in the standard song form and vocal improvisation brought the male voice into the monopoly of instrumental jazz at the Cellar, and provided Francks with experience he would later turn into successful recordings in New York at the Village Vanguard, and at the Purple Onion with Lenny Breau.[42]

Blues and Haikus: Poetry at the Cellar

Al Neil's interest in the wider arts scene and his particular fondness for beat literature led to a familiarity with early experiments in combining jazz and poetry, including the 1957 recording *Kenneth Patchen Reads with Allyn Ferguson and the Chamber Jazz Sextet*.[43] Inspired by the album and by what he knew of the San Francisco scene in literature, art, and music, Neil contacted Patchen to see if the poet would be interested in performing at the Cellar. While other Cellar musicians were reportedly less than enthusiastic about the proposal, Neil was aided by artist Harry Webb and designer John Grinnell.[44] Patchen's biography describes the connection:

> Through the combined effort of their old friend, jazzman Johnny Wittwer (now back in Seattle) and another fan and jazz arranger John Grinnell from Vancouver, Canada, a new poetry-jazz tour of Washington and British Columbia was launched that February [of 1959]. Traveling without a jazz group, Patchen was met by John Grinnell in Vancouver on February 12th where he met the Alan Neil Quartet with whom he would be working. He dashed off a note to [his wife] Miriam that night, "Late yesterday afternoon Mike Jeffries, young last year law student and Alan Neil, the piano playing leader of the quartet with which I'll appear, came around to motel and we had supper before proceeding to 'The Cellar' at 8:30 for a rehearsal which lasted until eleven. Worked out a lot of material, and things should pan out pretty well as far as readings-band combination is concerned. Neil is very versatile and quick, full of hero-worship of me; and the alto sax player (18 yrs. old) [Dale Hillary] is almost as talented as Modesto [Briseno]. Drums and bass [Bill Boyle and Lionel Chambers] complete quartet – all young kids. As I say, things should be lively and smooth by time for first appearance.[45]

Though it seems he was at least initially housed at the City Centre Motor Inn, Patchen spent the majority of his Vancouver stay with John Grinnell, with whom he had corresponded frequently regarding the Vancouver dates.[46] Harry Webb's daughter Adrienne Brown remembered the visit well:

> When Kenneth Patchen came up from San Francisco ... my parents, one of their favourite memories was that he came over for tea when he was up here. He stayed with the Grinnells on that visit, apparently, when the Grinnells were living up on South Granville. Kenneth Patchen was my father's favourite poet, and he just loved his stuff, it was so exciting when he came. And also my dad and Al Neil had met when they were working in the airmail section of the post office at Hastings and Granville just after the war ... and they would all socialize and they would come over to my parents' cottage in Ambleside, and this was all going on at the time that his group played behind Kenneth Patchen when they did "As I Opened the Window" and things on that record. So that was a big event in our lives, the making of that record.[47]

Al Neil recalled the experience with less detail some sixty years later, but confirmed his prior knowledge of Patchen, his admiration, and that contracting the poet to perform was a group effort:

> And of course I heard jazz and poetry, through the beats. And from what I heard, there was one really good poet ... I'd heard him reading on one of his early records with a jazz group, and I wasn't impressed by the jazz group but his voice was just like none other for reading poetry. And that was Kenneth Patchen. So we found out where he lived in San Francisco, and we knew that he was doing this stuff right at the very time, and invited him up, and he came. And I had a young eighteen-year-old alto saxophonist [Dale Hillary]. And that went very well. We played ten days together and then did a CBC [show] and that's where the record came from. Recorded for CBC [which] had a *Wednesday Night,* I think they called it, and it went right across, national. So we just

> lucked out, you know. Somebody came down to the Cellar and heard it.[48]

Patchen's trip to Vancouver was part of a Pacific Northwest tour that included dates in Vancouver, on Vancouver Island, and then in the Seattle area, including the University of Washington.[49] Patchen arrived in Vancouver on Thursday, February 12, 1959, and rehearsed with the Al Neil group on Thursday and Friday, possibly performing with them at the Cellar on Friday evening: Al Neil (piano), Dale Hillary (saxophone), Bill Boyle (drums), and Lionel Chambers (bass).[50] On Saturday, February 14, the group travelled to Victoria, where they staged an afternoon concert at Victoria College and performed that evening at the Scene Club.[51]

> On Valentine's Day, he sent [his wife] a special delivery card expressing his love and this report, "Afternoon reading at Victoria College was a standing room smash hit, much to surprise of sponsors, I think. Kids called me back three times – practically tore auditorium down in their enthusiasm. Hope to rest a bit now in hotel room before tonight's sessions: usual night club hours, start around 10:30, probably end about 2."[52]

Following their return to Vancouver and appearances on local television and at UBC, the group was booked by CBC producer Robert Patchell for a local live radio broadcast on Tuesday, February 17. This live broadcast was rebroadcast on the CBC national network from Montreal on October 4, 1959. Released soon after as an LP on the Folkways label titled *Kenneth Patchen Reads with Jazz in Canada,* with the subscript "with the Alan Neil Quartet," the recording is widely regarded as one of Patchen's best (see Figure 18). According to the liner notes for the album, Patchen and the Al Neil group performed at the Cellar late in the evening following the CBC broadcast, to what would have been a fairly select audience of scene insiders. They then performed a series of advertised concerts at the Cellar over the weekend of February 20–22. The *Vancouver Sun* advertisements taken out in support of the Patchen performances were the first by the Cellar since November 28, 1958.[53]

18 *Kenneth Patchen Reads with Jazz in Canada* album cover, 1959 | *Courtesy Folkways Records, Smithsonian Institution*

The original release of *Kenneth Patchen Reads with Jazz in Canada* included a four-page booklet of liner notes written by Al Neil. In addition to brief biographical sketches of the musicians involved in the session and the particulars surrounding its recording, Neil addressed at length the often contentious issue of combining jazz and poetry, suggesting, "God knows most of the attempts have been pretty awful":

> The thing has to be honest: then even when it isn't very good ... nobody will get hurt. But when the attempts are both dishonest – on both sides – and bad, it's not just a cheap scene; it's a vicious, hurtful farce. Which brings me to the fact that most jazz musicians don't dig poetry anyway; and this type of thing [mixing it with jazz] will really close the book on it.[54]

That poetry, in particular when combined with jazz, was something that most Cellar musicians avoided when at all possible was confirmed by bassist Tony Clitheroe:

> It [poetry] would bring in a few different people, no doubt, who otherwise wouldn't have known anything about the place. I got stuck sometimes backing these things up. Sort of the Kerouac thing, and so there'd be some two or three uncomfortable musicians in there trying to figure out, "Well, should we play or not, or should we lay out for a while?" or I don't know ... And there's a guy out front reading poetry.[55]

Neil also noted that though his social circle included visual artists, poets, writers and other prominent members of Vancouver's burgeoning artistic community, he was often the lone Cellar-based musician at such gatherings.

> The Webbs and Grinnell and myself and the other artists would gather on Saturday nights or some nights over in West Vancouver where they lived and party, you know, but that was separate from the musicians. Some of the musicians, they weren't interested in that, most of them weren't. Not only not interested, they thought it was, I don't know ... they thought they were going to, the artists were going to be snobbish. They didn't really know what they were coming to the Cellar for. If they were authentic fans, or ...? That was at the beginning.[56]

Patchen's appeal was different, Neil asserted, and his authenticity of character and artistic presentation in the face of otherwise "falseface" beat posturing was able to reach the musicians in the quartet that played with him at the Cellar.

> Patchen was the one exception. I've heard of many jazzmen who have been digging him all along. Myself, it's been ten years. (On this I should say that it pleased me a lot when Dale Hillary and Bill Boyle went round quoting big hunks of his poetry for weeks after Kenneth left here. They probably dug him more as a man than as a poet, but they did dig him ...).[57]

Patchen aside, attempts to draw other artistic modes into the Cellar space were not always smooth or uneventful, and at times served to highlight the extent to which the performance of jazz in the early 1960s was still very much rooted in the expression and observance of traditional gender roles.[58]

Confronting the Other in the Arts

In the summer of 1961, poet bill bissett staged one of his first public readings at the Cellar on a bill shared with fellow poet Lance Farrell.[59] The reading was a tumultuous one that was not only a significant early event in the career of a notable Canadian literary figure, but provides a clear illustration of the unconscious social conventions that worked to create and defend the Cellar's atmosphere as a masculine space. bissett and Farrell had been booked by drummer and filmmaker Don Cumming to perform during the intermission.[60] The experience proved to be surprisingly traumatic for bissett:

> And, the first poetry reading I ever did was at the Cellar ... And people threw [things at me] ... my first reading there. I used to like reading in different voices ... it was actually an early form of sound poetry, though we didn't actually even have that term then.[61]

bissett's technique at the time was to read in a variety of voices, many of which were pitched in an effeminate, high falsetto. During one of these sequences, a member of the audience threw a glass at the stage, striking bissett on the face and cutting him just below the eye. Poet Jamie Reid was also in the audience:

> bill was reading, and he was reading in one of his feminine voices, and the crowd that was there was the general crowd that used to go there, salesmen who were a little bit interested in jazz and had a bottle of rye under the table and some ginger ale on top of the table to put into it. And bill was reading these poems and they were yelling at him, you know. "Faggot" and stuff like that, you know. And he just kept on going. And finally, someone threw [something] ... at him. Someone had broken a glass or something and threw a piece

> of crockery at him and it hit him right under here [*points at eye*]. And it was just by chance I guess that he was right in the middle of a poem that said, "I'm going to kill you!" So ... he's bleeding from this, and anyway ... he kept going ... And at that point I thought ... bill ... always [used to] be hustling for money for his magazines and I thought he was a bit of a con man at that point. I thought his approach to art was a kind of shuck, but when he did that, I thought, man, this guy's got it man, and ever after that I always had respect for him.[62]

bissett didn't see who threw the glass, and recalled being terrified that it had been one of the musicians – fellow artists he held in high regard. The experience had a profound effect on him, and was recalled years later in his book *Sailor:*

> in vancouvr i was
> skreeching up n down
> i gess a lot uv
> diffrent voices
>
> i dont know   i was reeding my
> poetry   they startid throwing
> glasses at me   breking around
> me avr th floor   sum blood
> i was cut a bit
>
> frend cum up to me she
> sz why dont yu stop bfor
> yu get hurt
>
> i didint   i wa going to reed
> for so long   i red until i
> was redy to stop   ther voices
>
> making a background for me sum
> times riding above thn falling
> away   hyeena frill n gin
>
> n over on the side lines   whun
> a th best bass playrs i evr herd
>
> smiling at me[63]

Immediately following bissett's performance, Lance Farrell took the stage, and Jamie Reid noted that the more orthodox delivery of his poetry did not generate the same response.

> Lance started to read these heterosexual poems with all kinds of swear words and stuff in them in this kind of sweet voice, and these guys sort of liked that. That appealed to their sensibilities, so they didn't throw anything at him. And bill said that after he'd done his set, he sat down and the crowd and the same people that were yelling at him and throwing stuff at him were talking to him as if he was just a normal person.[64]

bissett confirmed that upon the conclusion of his performance he was accepted into the audience and left in peace to listen to the rest of the evening's music. As the reading by Farrell did not generate hostility from the audience, bissett believed the violent reaction to his work had little to do with the performance of poetry as such (despite the indifference or bewilderment of much of the Cellar membership), but rather his bizarre, transgressive recitation.

> That's what I've often thought, but I don't know. Because I did notice that in the higher registers they got very upset. Like men can't do high registers because it would only mean one thing, and they're not like that so they threw things to be separate from it. I dunno. It was a theory I had. Or maybe they just felt like throwing things.[65]

Beyond the physical injury he sustained, bissett found the evening upsetting because the reception his poetry received ran counter to his assumptions about the space and its accommodations. bissett had been hopeful that the Cellar would be a space in which his performance would be accepted and recognized as an exercise in rule bending and improvised expression similar to the risk-taking he observed in the Cellar's musical community.

> That's sort of what I expected, when I read there, at the Cellar, that they would actually appreciate what I was doing

> because I was, like, doing atonal jazz with words. And I was doing nonlinear jazz with words, and I thought they would be able to transition from how they played – nonlinearly ... improvisationally, with lots of surprises – they would be able to transition their appreciation of that to writing ... that you could read that way too. You could write that way too. But I've learned a long time ago that's not necessarily true. People that are multifaceted and adept in one art form may not want some other art form that they've not thought of in that way to be similar ... So that's how, regardless of the response, it [the reading at the Cellar] influenced me.[66]

In the late 1950s and early 1960s, jazz was, at least in Vancouver, still very much a performance of heteromasculinity – an often athletic display of skill and bravado that was often more competitive than it was inclusive, and that generally stuck to the rules and conventions outlined by bebop and other tune-based forms of improvisation.

Though self-consciously bohemian in many ways, musical expression at the Cellar was generally in keeping with mainstream, bebop-oriented forms, and did not often approach the level of experimentation with musical forms that by 1961 could be observed in the (varied) musical approaches of third-stream composers and output by the likes of Eric Dolphy, Ornette Coleman, Sun Ra, Cecil Taylor, George Russell, Jimmy Giuffre, and others who released significant albums in 1960 and/or 1961. Though the early experimentation of Don Cherry and Ornette Coleman was accepted (after some acclimatization) by Cellar denizens, pianist Al Neil's own gradual abandonment of bebop-oriented expression in favour of free improvisation and mixed media was generally considered incompatible with the club's aims.[67] John Dawe commented,

> Well, I don't know what he got into [musically] after that. Al was weird. He started to get too weird for the Cellar. [Dave] Quarin would lay into him. Al would jump up off the piano seat and start playing the wall, and stuff like that. That's when we knew something had changed in Al. He's a great ... he loved to be on a stage. Because he does

> presentations beautifully, that sort of thing. Visual stuff. He's into everything.[68]

Indeed, so great was Neil's dissatisfaction with the limits of mainstream jazz expression that he quit playing almost entirely during the early 1960s, emerging again in 1965 to perform as the Al Neil Trio with Gregg Simpson (drums) and Richard Anstey (bass). The trio played highly experimental improvised music that often included dance and other artistic mediums during performances. Richard Baker observed in *Coda* magazine that Neil's music from this period

> sounded strange even to ears already accustomed to Ornette [Coleman], Cecil Taylor and Sun Ra. Neil derived as much from John Cage, Alfred Jarry, [and] the I Ching ... as from any trends in free jazz or, for that matter, bop ... Developments during the intervening years make it difficult to realize what a departure these performances represented at the time.[69]

At the time of bill bissett's ill-fated reading at the Cellar in 1961, he and Neil were in many ways the "quintessential representatives" of bohemian art in Vancouver, according to Jamie Reid.

> At that point they [bissett and Neil] would not have been accepted by the general population as artists. I don't know what the general population [would] have thought of them, but you know, they'd think they were odd people or they'd be scared of them, at that time. When the Al Neil Trio first took off in 1966 it was really surprising music in Vancouver, I can tell you that. It was really surprising. He got bored with it [bebop], is what happened to him. He didn't want to do it anymore. You have seen his writing? Here comes C7 ... which he doesn't want any more, and they keep saying, "C'mon Al, play the changes."[70]

As Neil recalled, there was both confusion and some hard feelings at the Cellar surrounding his evolving musical aesthetic in the early 1960s: "They weren't too happy about the way I left that kind of music behind and tried to find another way to present music."[71]

> I copped out around 1962. I figured I had had enough and I was starting to hear stuff that couldn't be played in the harmonic structure we were using. I was going crazy because I could hear it and if I tried to play it [Dale] Hillary would turn around and say "play the fuckin' changes," because if I played what I was hearing I would fuck up the rhythm section and the horn players. One night ... I thought, well, I'm going to screw up the rhythm section, so I just played it [the solo he was hearing] on the wall ... the wall was right behind me. [Dave] Quarin, who was the manager at the time, was really upset. At the intermission he was getting heavy with me at the bar.[72]

Al Neil, bill bissett, Lance Farrell, and other key members of Vancouver's bohemian arts scene were pushing the envelope quite hard in those days, with bissett and Farrell in particular perhaps known as much for shocking the sensibilities of the cultural establishment as they were for their poetry and publishing. bissett was particularly polarizing: named by Jack Kerouac in the *Paris Review* as one of the great poets of his time and later denounced on the floor of the Canadian House of Commons for using arts grants to write "pornographic" material.[73] The Cellar's role as a space for women was similarly complicated. On the one hand, the club provided a liberating space within which women could socialize and consume alcohol free from the proscriptions on such behaviour in larger society. On the other hand, the Cellar was very much a male-dominated space within which women were relegated to support roles and denied full acceptance into the musical community.

The Bebop Girls

As discussed in Chapter 2, not until 1954 did the law permit cocktail lounges where one could openly drink in mixed company. Yet even within the relatively liberal atmosphere of the cocktail lounge, women were subjected to unique rules; for instance, they could not be served at the bar unless accompanied by a man.[74] In addition to the rules imposed by the liquor control board, individual establishments could and did place additional constraints on women: the upscale Sylvia Hotel denied unaccompanied women entry to its cocktail lounge (likely in an attempt to prevent any possible accusation that prostitution occurred on the premises).[75] Although the private members' clubs that flourished in Vancouver at this time provided alternative spaces for social drinking, many of these were associated with historically male social and athletic clubs, and a single woman's ability to obtain membership to the majority of these would have been quite limited.

At the Cellar, however, the only restriction to access for anyone was the payment of a cover charge, and though the Cellar initially enforced a membership policy, a membership was easy to obtain and not restricted to male patrons. The cover charge at the Cellar was also quite low relative to other clubs in the city, and, unlike upscale supper clubs such as Isy's and the Cave, the Cellar did not require that any food or drink be purchased.[76] Operating in typical Vancouver style as an unlicensed bottle club for the duration of its existence, the Cellar was one of the few places in Vancouver where an unaccompanied woman could drink and socialize freely in mixed company.

The great concern at the Cellar with creating a reasonably well-ordered environment conducive to jazz – what fans and players would call a "listening room" – also had the effect of creating a safe space for female patrons, because the etiquette surrounding attentive listening prevented most forms of persistent unwanted sexual attention. Lyvia Brooks, who lived in the area, said she felt comfortable at the Cellar:

> It was an interesting neighbourhood altogether, because when we first came there it seemed very safe, compared to LA, and yet it still was a bit of a rough and tumble neighbourhood. And I was quite young at the time. And when I look back on the pictures I guess I was kind of attractive. I didn't think I was [at the time] ... And I never worried [about being harassed], and I tend to be a bit of a worrier about things like that.[77]

Ricci (Quarin) Gotsch, then wife of Cellar manager Dave Quarin, agreed that the Cellar was a generally safe and free environment for single women: "Oh, that's true. Because I was dynamite on that door. And whoever worked there on the door got that instruction."[78] Saxophonist Gavin Walker, who was nearly a nightly fixture at the Cellar as a youth, noted, "I think that's a very good point. Because if [a woman] went to some other club, she'd be hassled all the time, [but] if she liked the music [at the Cellar] she'd be left alone to enjoy the music."[79]

In addition to the women who attended the Cellar as casual members of the audience, a small core of women were fixtures on the scene and performed key roles in the organization and nightly operation of the club. Central to this group was Ricci Quarin, who shouldered a considerable amount of the daily operational work including management of the food sales and kitchen area.

> I did what Dave couldn't do. I went in early and I went and I bought all the meat for making sandwiches and the bread, and whatever supplies we needed. And 7-Up and whatever – the [soda delivery] guys, they came in and I met them there and let them in and they went through their orders and filled us up. What else? I made what I was supposed to make. I got everything ready to be made fast. The pizzas ... we were still selling the pizzas. And then I would go home and get the kids ready for bed after supper, and then come back [to the club to work the door] ... I didn't do any of the banking, unless Dave prepared it, and then I did it.[80]

Though she describes her work as those things that her husband "couldn't do," she is enumerating domestically associated tasks – cleaning, making food, attending to kitchen inventory – that the male membership preferred *not* to do. Tellingly, Ricci Quarin was not involved in the club's finances unless it was to run an errand (dropping off a deposit prepared by her husband) or to collect the door fee. Though her husband received a small salary from the club, Ricci did not, performing essential yet often overlooked labour in addition to her role as homemaker in order to support and create time for her husband's musical activities.

One of Ricci Quarin's most frequent jobs was working the door: collecting the admission charge and confirming membership credentials, along with the sometimes dangerous task of refusing entry to any demonstrably drunk or unruly patrons. This role made her the public face of the club in many ways, and prompted her to form associations with a broad cross-section of Vancouver's musicians and artists. She often admitted many of the city's younger jazz players without charge, thus facilitating educational and networking opportunities for the likes of Don Thompson, Gavin Walker, Blaine Wikjord, and Terry Clarke.

Because her regular duties on the door often kept her out of the club proper, Ricci Quarin relied on several female friends to handle the nightly food and beverage sales.

> I had three girlfriends that worked once in a while. They got ... maybe five dollars a night. [They would] serve from behind the bar. They would make the coffee, and at that time Tevie Smith had just got involved, he had just purchased the pizza thing in Vancouver ... And before that we were selling Ready Hots or something, which was some kind of really terrible sandwiches out of a silly machine. So when they [audience and musicians] got drunk and it got late, they got hungry, so my girlfriends would come in and help out because it was busy.[81]

Though these women earned a token wage for their efforts, evidently the tasks considered to be domestic in nature – the "women's work" of food preparation and cleaning – were not of interest to the club's male executive membership, any number of whom could surely have performed these duties on a volunteer basis. Though John Dawe suggested that at least early in the club's existence general cleaning duties were shared among the charter members, they were quickly delegated to William Schlossmacher, a jack-of-all-trades associated with Ken Hole's restaurant business. With the departure of Hole and Walley Lightbody in early 1958 and the loss of Schlossmacher's services, nightly cleaning of the club was taken on by Ricci Quarin's mother, Elizabeth McEwan. Arriving at the club in the early morning after babysitting the Quarins' children the previous evening, McEwan would perform the double task of cleaning the venue and ushering out whichever musicians had yet not left for home.

> At six o'clock in the morning my mother would come in ... at five if she woke up. And she'd kick everybody out, she'd wake them up and send them on home, so that she could clean the toilets and the floor, and behind the bar and the fridge ... housekeeping. Why? Because we needed somebody to clean the place, and she used to babysit the kids. They were just babies at the time, so I'd go over and put them to bed, and there was no problem.
>
> We paid her. She [didn't] do it for nothing. She had a man living in the basement and he came [along] ... he had nothing else to do. And it was kinda nice. They had a *job* to go to. And my dad had emphysema and he was usually outside smoking a cigarette coughing to death.[82]

Additionally, a small group of women were regular attendees at the Cellar and often performed small club-related tasks. Affectionately dubbed the "bebop girls" by pianist Al Neil, this ubiquitous group included Joyce Kilburn (wife of guitarist Jim Kilburn), Vivian Cook, Carol Hunter, Helen Brown, Lois Scott, Jessie Webb (wife of artist Harry Webb), Rae Sawyer, and vocalist Doreen Williams. These women were insiders – knowledgeable about jazz, close friends with the musicians, willing participants in the daily operation of the club, and fixtures on the scene. Nonetheless, the realities of domestic life and gender expectations often conspired to remove these women from active participation in the scene once they married and had children. Jessie Webb's daughter Adrienne Brown said,

> When I was born in 1957, [my mother] would have ... been home in the basement suite washing the diapers, and she said that "I didn't remember Harry acting. He didn't tell me that he was acting in the plays," you know, that kind of thing, a little bit of a chip on her shoulder because he was off late at night at the Cellar having a good time while she was at home with the baby. Not that she didn't want the baby, but ...[83]

Chris (Hole) Birdseye, then married to Ken Hole, and Lyvia Brooks had similar experiences themselves:

> But I was sort of out of the scene at that point, busy being a wife and eventually a mother, and with two kids it's really hard to keep up with the scene.[84]

> I got married at age eighteen and proceeded to have two children shortly after that, and my life changed drastically. If we went anywhere, we went to the Cave Supper Club ... or they had a club called Isy's. We went there occasionally. But mostly we were home with the kids ... And I was also trying to help my husband out at his new dental office, so we didn't have oodles of money to call on, and babysitters are [expensive] ... and my parents were working a lot, so they couldn't sit with the kids much.[85]

Though Ricci Quarin had her mother's help with child care, which enabled her to take on responsibilities at the Cellar, for the most part motherhood isolated women at the Cellar from the club's activities, and therefore from active participation on the scene. Joyce Kilburn would occasionally bring her infant son Rick to the club, but she too found herself spending the bulk of her time at home. In her case, the friendships Jim Kilburn maintained with musicians such as Barney Kessel, Wes Montgomery, Don Cherry, and Charles Mingus, along with his activities as a guitar teacher, brought at least some aspects of the Cellar environment into the home.

The "Chick" Singer

In the main, the women who frequented the Cellar were not musicians but rather jazz enthusiasts drawn by the music and hipsters attracted to the scene. "There were," Al Neil said, "a number of women who hung out at the Cellar, but that was just because they liked the jazz scene ... they thought it was hip."[86] Of the women collectively referred to as the "bebop girls," only one, vocalist Doreen Williams, had an identity as a jazz performer (see Figure 19). Yet as has so frequently been the case,[87] in order to be taken seriously

19 Doreen Williams with Chuck Knott (bass) and Al Neil (piano), ca. 1960 | *Photo by Don Cumming; courtesy Jim Carney*

as a musician and permitted to take part in the musical activities at the Cellar, Williams had to negotiate what it meant to be female in a jazz context. Al Neil remembered,

> She was our number one ... I don't think the word "groupie" was around, but she seemed to me, once in a while she'd have a girlfriend [with her], but she was a fixture, you know? And so it came about that at that time jazz musicians, especially ones that are just learning the trade, were not so keen on singers, but everybody liked her, and if she was around she'd get a chance to sing a couple of songs. Not every weekend, but she was very discreet about it. She was just one of the boys. I shouldn't have said that.[88]

Neil immediately regretted his choice of words here, conscious that in order to include Williams in the inner circle of musicians he had unthinkingly engaged in a kind of sexual nullification by positioning her as "one of the boys." When it came to jazz, women could be either "good girls" or they could attempt to "play like men."[89] If she opted for the former approach, a woman had to emphasize her looks over her musicality, using sex to sell a musical product often considered (when the music was considered at all) to be inferior to a comparable male performance; the latter approach required that a woman leverage her musical talent to nullify her sexuality and become "just one of the boys."[90]

Tellingly, Williams was aware of this process at the time, even if subconsciously. She "lived for the weekends," when the club's late-night sessions would occur. These occasions were, for her, "the best times" the club had to offer because they allowed her some measure of participation as an insider to the scene. She consciously made the decision not to pursue romantic entanglements with any of the Cellar-based musicians, and instead ingratiated herself into their inner circle by talking shop and sitting in whenever she was able.[91] In addition to the sexual politics in play, Williams also had to surmount the widespread resistance among jazz musicians to working with vocalists, a resistance based on the assumption that a vocalist would not be accomplished enough as a musician to communicate in musically specific language with the instrumentalists, and would therefore limit the creative freedom of the instrumental improvisers.[92] Ricci (Quarin) Gotsch understood this dynamic:

> She never really had anything to do [romantically] with the guys [at the Cellar] ... And they didn't like singers so it was a sad thing, because she couldn't sing there. But they took her out of town and she could get a job there. Everyone wants a girl singer with the guys. And she got to do some of that. But all the women thought that she was after their husbands, but she wasn't. She was there actually for the music. And the association with hip people.[93]

Despite their initial reluctance to include her, Williams did eventually find work with several of the Cellar groups that toured from Vancouver to Seattle and Vancouver Island. At clubs with a more commercial approach to jazz than the Cellar, a female vocalist was an expected part of public performance, and these excursions enabled Williams to make a musical impression. Soon after these initial engagements, she began to sit in at the Cellar's after-hours sessions whenever possible and began to sing more regularly at the club on weekends, often with groups led by Al Neil or Jim Kilburn.[94] By all reports a talented singer, Williams also played a few engagements at the Queen Elizabeth Theatre and at Isy's. Self-doubt as to the extent of her musical abilities and the domestic demands of a marriage in 1960 put an end to Williams's singing career and took her away from the Cellar, to Calgary and then to Las Vegas, before an eventual return to Vancouver in 1965.[95]

The rarity of female performers at the Cellar reflected the scarcity of female jazz musicians in Vancouver as a whole. Unsurprisingly, there were, as far as can be determined, no female jazz instrumentalists in Vancouver of any note during the period in question, and certainly none with the jazz chops required to play at the Cellar.[96] Jazz, as discussed above, was (and in large part still is) seen as a male pursuit, requiring of its practitioners skills and character traits typically considered masculine, such as aggressive playing, ambition, discipline, and self-confidence. A jazz career required lengthy absences from the domestic sphere of home and family while playing instruments often considered to be unfeminine, such as saxophone, trumpet, bass, and drums.[97] "Most women," bassist Paul Ruhland observed, "were playing violin or oboe. Nobody [female] was playing saxophone in those days."[98] Al Neil concurred:

> You know, I don't remember any instrumentalists ... Vancouver did have some good female singers, most notably, of course, Eleanor Collins, but they were a little bit above [the Cellar]. And Pat Suzuki was another great singer that doesn't get talked about too much. She was Japanese, I think, or part Japanese. But they did commercial work and CBC television shows, and they wouldn't [have] been particularly interested in going to the Cellar.[99]

Though popular Vancouver star Eleanor Collins did play both the Scene Club in Victoria and Vancouver's Flat Five club in the mid-1960s, Al Neil's point is well made. Vancouver's notable female vocalists were far too successful to consider performing at the small

20 Poster for the Jean Hoffman Trio at the Cellar, 1960 | *Designed by Harry Webb; courtesy Adrienne Brown*

co-operative club, and generally performed music that, heavily influenced by American popular singers of the time, was jazz-inflected without actually being jazz.[100]

In addition to Doreen Williams, the only locally based vocalists who performed at the Cellar with any regularity were comedian, actor, and vocalist Don Francks; "crooner" Barry Dale;[101] in later years, Lynne McNeil (a UBC music student who would go on to perform with Dal Richards and Hagood Hardy); and Donna Wright, who began performing at the Cellar after ownership of the venue transferred to her husband in the mid-1960s.

Aside from the scarcity of locally available talent, the Cellar's focus on bebop and instrumental jazz (there were no vocalists among the founding members) meant that the venue featured guest vocalists infrequently. In what was something of a unique presentation, pianist and vocalist Jean Hoffman from Portland, Oregon, appeared at the club for a week in November 1960 (see Figure 20). Her performance in Vancouver was reviewed by the UBC correspondent for *Coda*.

> The following week we heard the Jean Hoffman Trio. This comparatively unknown group had just completed an

21 Poster for Ernestine Anderson at the Cellar, 1961 | *Designer unknown; courtesy Don Thompson*

> engagement at the Blackhawk in San Francisco and, as is often the case with these lunch-time concerts, the trio appeared by arrangement with the Cellar, a local nightspot which books some of the finest talent into Vancouver. Accompanied by Bill Underwood on drums and Bill Knuckles (?) [sic] on bass we were treated to an hour of fine jazz. With complete lack of announcing or showmanship Jean Hoffman and accompanist held their audience captive relying more on ... her excellent technique to give us something which is ... rather rare on the jazz scene today – real musical entertainment.[102]

Though her 1957 debut recording for Fantasy Records had been well received by the critics, Hoffman did not record again and remained little known outside the west coast.[103]

In the summer of 1961, Ernestine Anderson appeared at the Cellar from June 27 to July 9, perhaps the highest-profile vocalist to do so. The club's reputation was growing, largely due to efforts of its members and beneficial links to the CBC. It had become an important venue for jazz expression that would continue to draw remarkable instrumental talent to Vancouver during the early 1960s.

5

In the Swing of Things

Growth, Maturation, and Mingus

> *They just showed up one night and walked through the door again, out of the pouring rain and dumped their stuff on the bandstand and kinda said, "Here we are." Actually, a lot of word had spread down to California about the Cellar, and people just kind of showed up in town here.*
>
> – *John Dawe*

The initial idea for the Cellar was simple – to create a place where local jazz musicians could hang out, rehearse, play, and improve themselves in front of a knowledgeable and generally sympathetic audience. Though the club needed to generate a steady cash flow in order to keep the doors open and the lights on, it was never intended to be a commercially successful venture. In its early years the club relied only on word of mouth and advertisements in local student newspapers to attract an audience. However, after early experiments with bringing in American jazz artists proved to be both economically viable and artistically gratifying, the Cellar's executive slowly expanded the club's public profile in order to support more of these events.

As previously mentioned, the first mainstream newspaper ad taken by the Cellar ran in July 1958, but such a promotional effort was not repeated until November of that year. The Cellar then placed no further ads until February 1959, when ads were taken out in support of the Kenneth Patchen poetry reading. Sporadic ads followed – in March for the Jim Kilburn Trio, and in September for the Chris Gage Trio.[1] The Cellar's erratic placement of ads in the *Vancouver Sun* continued until the spring of 1960, when ads began to appear more regularly in the weekend edition, whether advertising a specific act or simply the club in general.

Growth

Following early successes with Art Pepper, Paul Bley, Lou Levy, Ornette Coleman, Don Cherry, the Montgomery Brothers, and others, the Cellar continued to bring in American artists whenever possible. In November 1958, tenor saxophonist Harold Land played a three-night engagement, bringing with him from Los Angeles pianist Elmo Hope, drummer Lennie McBrowne, and a very young Scott LaFaro on bass. Club manager Dave Quarin had by this time installed rudimentary recording equipment under the Cellar's stage, which he used to record rehearsals and performances at the Cellar. The microphones were well concealed, and unbeknownst to most visiting American artists, their performances were often captured as well. Though the vast majority of these tapes have never been heard publicly, portions of this engagement were eventually (and somewhat accidentally) released in Europe on the Fresh Sound label. Running nearly eighty minutes, the album presents one evening's worth of music complete with stage announcements by Barry Cramer, and though slightly marred by issues with recording quality, *The Harold Land Quartet: Jazz at the Cellar, 1958* remains the only recorded evidence of this remarkable quartet.[2]

The group that Land brought with him to Vancouver was not his usual working group, though Land did work with Elmo Hope with some frequency.[3] The talented and eccentric Hope had struggled with heroin addiction throughout much of his life, and had moved to Los Angeles in 1957 following the loss of his New York City cabaret card due to a drug conviction.[4] In Vancouver, Hope's issues with addiction continued, as Gavin Walker and Tony Clitheroe observed:

> Oh, Harold Land was here at the Cellar twice. The first band was one of the best bands I've ever heard and there's a tape of it. Elmo [Hope] and Scott [LaFaro] ... I sat with Dale Hillary the opening night there, because my parents let me out because I wanted to hear this, and remember sitting with Hillary and [Jim] Johnson and we were right down

> front and Harold kicked off "Just One of Those Things" at a Max Roach tempo, but no piano. You see Elmo, Elmo was late. He'd been out trying to find his shit, you know. And he came in in the middle of the tune, and kind of wended his way between the tables, and went up and just ... and this thing is going by at a mile a minute, and Elmo just splatted down some chords exactly in the right place. And I remember looking at Hillary and listening to Harold and just ... it was like, wow.[5]
>
> But, yeah, there were some interesting things going on there. Harold Land is so cool. He's so cool. There were a couple of times during the gigs when Elmo disappeared underneath the piano and was rolling around yelling, right? And Harold Land didn't even look. Just carried on playing. "Oh, that must be Elmo down there."[6]

Hope had little trouble scoring drugs in Vancouver. Dealers were a regular presence on the scene, including two who made a habit of shadowing out-of-town players and became known by Cellar insiders as the "two horsemen."[7] Vocalist Doreen Williams recalled that one evening of the Harold Land engagement culminated with her and Scott LaFaro walking Elmo Hope between them, trying to keep him moving and on his feet to avoid suffering the effects of an overdose.[8] So regular was Hope's habit that he ended the engagement in debt to the Cellar, which had loaned him money over the course of his stay. Bassist Tony Clitheroe spent time with him:

> Oh, man. So Elmo, as you know, had a terrible habit. So when the other guys left, Elmo had to stay behind to work off his debts. And I wound up working with him ... I can't remember who was playing drums, but I played with him for probably a week or something. It was fun, because he's a fun guy to play with, you know.[9]

The Harold Land engagement also provides a useful juxtaposition between the co-operative, artist-focused nature of the Cellar and the often exploitive relationships that existed between musicians and agents of the music business in the larger jazz industry. Tony Clitheroe remembered,

> They had a manager called Tilley Mitchell. And Tilley Mitchell had a Pontiac. This would be about a late-fifties Pontiac, anyway. And this thing was as long as a ship, you know. Mostly trunk. I think it was a two-door, but it had a trunk like ... it went on forever. And she brought the guys up. And one night the guys had been playing, the gig had been on for two or three nights already, and we were sitting at a table during an intermission and Harold was sitting there with us and we were having some coffee or drinks or whatever, and somebody – it wasn't me, it was whoever else was sitting at the table – made some sort of joking remark to Harold about the advances that he was getting on the gig, right? Payment. Advance payment. And Harold looks at the guy and says, "What do you mean?" And the guy says, "Well, we're giving you these advances ...," and Harold Land says, "Who are you giving them to?" And whoever it was says, "Tilley, Tilley's getting them." "Oh really?" says Harold, and he gets up from the table and goes and has an intense conversation with Tilley. Apparently Tilley hadn't said anything to him about taking the advances.[10]

According to several interviewees, following this confrontation, the band's manager abruptly left town, leaving the group stranded. While Hope stayed behind to work off his personal debts, Harold Land apparently phoned New York to ask the Baroness Nica de Koenigswarter for help getting the group back to Los Angeles.[11] The Cellar was not, generally speaking, a significant financial opportunity for the American artists who played there, and it was in large part the collegial, artist-run nature of the club that attracted them. At the Cellar there was no fear of not getting paid, no fear of musical censorship, no fear of racial prejudice, and the guarantee of (in the majority of cases) an enthusiastic and supportive reception.

Following the Harold Land appearance, Don Cherry returned to Vancouver, this time on a personal visit with his wife, and stayed with drummer Chuck Logan for more than a month. Though

22 John Dawe (trumpet) and Harold Krauss (piano), ca. 1959 | *Photo by Bill Boyle; courtesy Jim Carney*

Cherry did not headline any shows, he sat in regularly at the Cellar with local groups, and on one occasion filled in for trumpeter John Dawe on an engagement backing Herb Jeffries, a vocalist known for his work with Earl Hines in the 1930s and with the Duke Ellington Orchestra, with whom he recorded in the early 1940s.[12] Cherry was also a featured guest with Jim Kilburn and John Dawe at a Vancouver New Jazz Society concert at the Georgia Auditorium on April 26, 1959, a performance that may well have been the last concert at the venerable hall before it closed and was torn down. Cherry's extended visit to Vancouver speaks volumes about the atmosphere cultivated by the Cellar, and the personal relationships that developed there between local musicians and their American counterparts. Though Cherry seems to have spent most of his stay with Chuck Logan, he also spent considerable time with guitarist Kilburn, an avid fly-fisherman, who recalls taking Cherry with him on a fishing trip to the nearby Vedder River. Cherry, Kilburn recalled, "sat on the bank and attempted to lure the fish with some fine trumpet solos."[13]

Between 1958 and 1959, the Cellar also hosted trombonist Carl Fontana (who worked with bassist Tony Clitheroe, drummer Bill Boyle, and pianist Tom Thorsburn), pianist Pete Jolly, and trumpeter Joe Gordon, though the precise dates of these performances remain unclear. Art Pepper returned for an engagement that ran for ten days between July 24 and August 2, 1959; and *Vancouver Sun* advertisements confirm that trumpeter Conte Candoli played the Cellar the weekend of March 9–10, 1960. In late April, guitarist Howard Roberts appeared for three days,[14] followed in June by Harold Land, who returned to the Cellar for a three-day engagement bringing Shorty Rogers (trumpet/flugelhorn) with him. The advance advertisements for this engagement mention jam sessions at the Cellar on Sunday evenings at 9 p.m., which were presumably open to members of the public.[15] In July 1960, the Cellar welcomed tenor player Bill Perkins, who worked with a local group including trumpet player Ed Roop, pianist Tom Thorsburn, drummer Chuck Logan, and bassist Tony Clitheroe. Photographs of informal sessions at the Cellar during Perkins's stay show tenor player and "downtowner" Fraser MacPherson sitting in, and also provide the only known photos of bassist Earl Freeman and tenor saxophonist Bill Holmes (Figure 23), African American musicians who apparently moved to Vancouver specifically to play at the Cellar (discussed below).[16]

Drugs

Many of the American artists who performed at the Cellar were well known for having substance abuse issues, and while Elmo Hope and Art Pepper had perhaps the highest profiles as addicts, numerous other artists were similarly afflicted. Those who wished to obtain hard drugs in Vancouver were generally able to do so, but for most of the Cellar's regulars, including poet Jamie Reid, alcohol remained the intoxicant of choice:[17]

> We used to drink a lot in those days. Marijuana didn't come to Vancouver until 1962, at least to our group. We were all sort of on the alert for it all the time, but there was nobody bringing it in our direction. And at that time it was just a

23 Bill Perkins plays with local musicians during informal sessions at the Cellar, July 1960. [*top*] Fraser MacPherson (seated), Bill Holmes (saxophone), Earl Freeman (bass), Bill Perkins (saxophone), Chuck Logan (drums), and Tom Thorsburn (piano); [*bottom*] Ed Roop (trumpet), Tony Clitheroe (bass), Bill Perkins (saxophone), Chuck Logan (drums), and Tom Thorsburn (piano) | *Photographers unknown; courtesy John Dawe*

> trickle. LSD arrived earlier than 1965, but in 1965 it became a bit more general and it was a bit more available.[18]

Though most of those attending the Cellar stuck to alcohol and what marijuana may have been available, harder drugs such as heroin were available to those who were interested, including visiting American artists. This activity was not unknown to the local police, and the drug squad made its presence felt from time to time.

> They just nosed around and did what they were supposed to and they didn't bother anybody and then they took off. It was just highly suspicious that they would come in just when [Art] Pepper happened to be there. They didn't bother anybody. It just kind of interrupted the music for about ten or fifteen minutes, but that was it.[19]

Hard drug use was of course not limited to American musicians, and several members of the Cellar became addicted to heroin during the early 1960s. Al Neil wrote about his experiences at length in the novel *Changes,* and saxophonist P.J. Perry was similarly open regarding his own struggles with drug and alcohol addictions, which began during the late 1950s and were very much associated with the jazz and counterculture arts scene of the period.[20] As poet bill bissett and another Cellar regular described it:

> I knew everyone was shooting up. I mean a lot of people, and I was dabbling a bit. Because it seemed very cool. And I've always liked needles because I've been in the hospital all my life. So they didn't freak me out. But I could never shoot someone else up. It frightened me, what it would do to them. But I didn't care what happened to me.[21]

> I heard later on in 1961 and 1962 when all of us started messing around with bad kind of dope that [the cops had] been watching that place twenty-four hours a day, and nobody knew about it. Not the regular cops. The narcotics squad had their eye on it. But the reason apparently was not so much us, it was ... we found out long after the place had been closed that the place had been used by heroin dealers as a place to come in and drop off large bundles of heroin. They would go into the washroom and tape it underneath the sink or take the toilet lid off and tape it under there, and then somebody else who was supposed to pick it up

> would come in later and know exactly where to go and pick it up. This had been going on for, god knows, years. And we didn't know a thing about that. That was news to us. I heard about that later.[22]

It should be noted that while some of those associated with the Cellar succumbed to heroin addictions, many others avoided hard drugs and their associated lifestyle.

Black Music, Black Musicians?

As already mentioned, Vancouver's black community was quite small during the period, and very few musicians involved in the Vancouver jazz scene were black. The significant exception was trombonist, bandleader, and club owner Ernie King, an entrepreneur originally from Edmonton, whose Harlem Nocturne Cabaret in Vancouver's East End was in many ways the heart of the black music scene in Vancouver.[23] Known primarily as a home for rhythm and blues, the Harlem Nocturne also hosted jazz, blues, music of Afro-Cuban and Afro-Caribbean origins, striptease artists, and occasional big-name acts from the United States, including the Mills Brothers, Ike Turner, the Montgomery Brothers, and T-Bone Walker.[24] Ernie King is quoted at length in Becki Ross's work on the Vancouver burlesque scene, *Burlesque West: Showgirls, Sex, and Sin in Postwar Vancouver,* particularly with regard to enforcement issues surrounding liquor licensing that he felt were racially motivated: "No one was harassed more than me. No one ... Because I was the only man that owned a black nightclub! I couldn't get a liquor licence. I could only sell food and soft drinks."[25]

While King may well have faced closer scrutiny due to his unique position as a black nightclub owner, an inability to obtain a liquor licence was an issue shared by clubs across the city, the vast majority of which either operated outside the law as "bottle clubs" (including the Penthouse, the Commodore, the Panorama Roof until 1955, and the Cellar), or marginally within the law as private members' clubs (including the Pacific Athletic Club, Arctic Club, and Quadra Club). Indeed, the popular upscale Cave Supper Club, one of the few nightclubs to obtain a liquor licence in the mid-1950s, suffered significant financial losses as a result of the restrictions the licence placed upon its operation, and bottle clubs remained a staple of Vancouver nightlife well into the 1960s (as discussed in Chapter 2).

Before opening the Harlem Nocturne, Ernie King worked extensively as a bandleader and trombonist throughout western Canada in the 1940s, with a small mixed-race jump blues band and with the larger, all-black Harlem Kings orchestra. Upon the disbandment of the Harlem Kings in 1948, King settled in Vancouver, where he managed a trucking company in addition to the Harlem Nocturne, which he opened in 1957.[26] When interviewed by Ross, King attributed his inability to find steady full-time employment as a musician in Vancouver during the 1950s to systemic racism.

> I was qualified enough to play in the Cave, but they didn't want a guy like me. The owners wanted an all-white band, not a coloured band with me sitting in there. I would have never got a job as a houseman, in the house band at the Cave – there were never any black musicians, unless it was a black band from the States. They knew our black musicians had as much talent or more than anybody else ... So I said I'd prefer to be with a couple of coloured guys, and maybe a couple of white guys, in the East End clubs.[27]

While it is more or less impossible at this juncture to determine if the downtown clubs such as Isy's and the Cave did indeed have a policy (official or otherwise) against mixed-race bands, we have already seen that employment in these clubs and in the Vancouver studios was both highly competitive and highly insular. Tensions surrounding employment in these venues was palpable even between white musicians, and the downtown scene was referred to as a "musical clique" even by those, such as bassist Paul Ruhland, who benefited from the situation. During the 1950s and 1960s, competition for trombone vacancies in the downtown clubs and studios would have included Dave Robbins, Dave Pepper, Ray Sikora, Bill Trussell, Jack Fulton, Ted Lazenby, John Capon, Ian McDougall, and Dave McMurdo, all of whom were more than competent players, readers, composers, and arrangers (in particular Dave Robbins and Ray Sikora), able to provide a varied set of employable skills to the bands and venues in which they worked.

African American pianist Mike Taylor, whose trio acted as the house band at the Harlem Nocturne in 1959–1961 and who regularly sat in after hours at the Cellar, suggested that the situation may have been a bit more nuanced than King perceived it. Taylor said that although King "played well," in order to play in the downtown clubs

> he'd have had to step up to the plate and practise more. He was more a businessman than a musician [running the Harlem Nocturne and his trucking business] ... Coming from the States, I had a bit of a racial thing in my own head [until I] found out how things were different in Canada. Though [it wasn't perfect] ... in the music genre, I didn't find [much racism]. It was about how you played. If you played good, you had an open door.[28]

Nonetheless, bassist Don Thompson, who was employed regularly by the CBC and in downtown clubs, as well as at the Cellar and Five Spot, observed:

> There was a funny scene with white guys and black guys in Vancouver. It wasn't a very friendly mix. A lot of the time ... there were different parts of town and everything, and I really picked that up, because I hardly ever played with the black guys. I actually asked Mike [Taylor] and Chuck [Logan] one time if I could get together with the two of them and play. And just play some tunes, because they were so damn good. Mike was ridiculous. And Chuck was really a beautiful drummer. But there wasn't a crossover ... it's getting better. It's still not great, but it is getting better. And it really wasn't very good then. Because they were in a different part of town, and their gigs were not in the same places as my gigs.[29]

Whether the lack of interaction between white musicians and the few black musicians in Vancouver was a result of an established clique, lack of work, mutually exclusive musical interests, or systemic racism, many white musicians recalled that during the period of the Cellar's operation comparatively few black musicians in Vancouver were playing in a jazz idiom, and even fewer of them performed at the Cellar (and later the Black Spot/Flat Five).

> There were very few blacks living in Vancouver. There was one black trombone player called Ernie King, who sort of played rock and roll gigs. I played in his band ... many of us did play with him, he'd sort of tailor the band to whatever the client wanted, and sometimes it would be a fairly large group and other times a small group. But Ernie King was the only black musician that I can recall. And then Chuck Logan of course came along, but he wasn't a native Vancouverite I don't think.[30]

> There wasn't a heck of a lot [of black musicians at the Cellar, or in Vancouver]. It wasn't like Halifax. We didn't have a huge black population. And what few people that were around town that I knew ... black guys in music, there were very few, and mostly they were into R&B more than jazz.[31]

> Well, there was a club here called the Harlem Nocturne, and that was pretty well [the black club] ... There weren't that many black players here. There was a piano player that I worked with in the 1970s a lot, piano player and organ player, Mike Taylor, he was around. He was originally from LA, and then he moved up here. And he was one of the few black players that were around. Chuck Logan was one of them, and of course he was a regular [at the Cellar]. And, there was a really good tenor player named Lionel Mitchell, who was a very fine big-sounding, no-bullshit tenor player that a lot of people liked. And he was an infrequent kind of sitter-in [at the Cellar]. And then there was the owner of the Harlem Nocturne, Ernie King, who was a trombonist. But, you know, he had his own club ... Mike [Taylor] would come

> down and sit in [at the Cellar], or come down after hours after they'd finished their gig, but the Harlem Nocturne went on pretty late too, so ...[32]
>
> There weren't that many [black players] ... maybe ten or twelve guys, that's it.[33]

The first black jazz musician to be closely associated with the scene at the Cellar was drummer Chuck Logan, who relocated from California in 1955 following his marriage to a Canadian. Born in San Diego, Logan had been given music lessons as a child but had been most active as a dancer, working with the famed Bill "Bojangles" Robinson in the late 1930s. An injury sustained in the Pacific during World War Two eliminated dancing as an option for Logan, who then turned seriously to the drums. Upon moving to Los Angeles, he gained experience working behind the likes of Big Mama Thornton, Johnny Otis, Pee Wee Crayton, and T-Bone Walker, as well as Dexter Gordon, Conte Candoli, Wardell Grey, Hampton Hawes, and others. Logan moved to Vancouver in 1955, met Jim Kilburn and Ken Hole in early 1956, and quickly became a regular fixture at the Cellar, playing sessions, in organized groups, and backing visiting American artists. Indeed, his connections to the jazz scene in Los Angeles made many of the Cellar's early attempts to bring in American musicians possible.[34] Logan shared how he had experienced the racial dynamic in Vancouver:

> I found that it was the French, the East Indian and the Native [who] were worse off than I was. But there was still the unsurety of the black, because of Fort Lewis down in Washington, and the Seabee base in Bremerton. They used to come up here and basically, there was nothing but white girls, and the blacks really didn't know how to handle that situation. You know ... which would create some problems in due time ... My colour came into it on occasion, but not much.[35]

In addition to Chuck Logan, two other African Americans became, at least for a time, an integral part of the Cellar scene – tenor saxophonist Bill Holmes and bassist Earl Freeman, who relocated from the United States together specifically to play at the Cellar. As Tony Clitheroe remembered their arrival,

> John Dawe and I and two or three others guys were sitting around the Cellar one night, drinking and chewing the fat or what-have-you, and we heard the door open at the top of the stairs, and we heard footsteps coming down, and we sort of looked to see who would come through the door at the bottom, and it was two black guys. One guy is carrying a bass, the other guy is carrying a tenor saxophone. So they looked at us, and we looked them, and they asked, "Is this the Cellar?" and we said, "Yeah, come on in, have a drink." So they came and sat down and we poured them a few drinks and asked, "Where are you guys from?" "Miami." They'd heard about the Cellar all the way from Miami, right? So anyway, I thought, I'm off the hook. There was a bass player here and he was probably going to stick around. And they both stayed around for a while, but I think the climate got to them. After about a year and a half or something they disappeared.[36]

While Tony Clitheroe believed Freeman and Holmes had arrived from Miami, John Dawe recalled that they had come from Los Angeles,[37] and had moved north in order to play and practise at a club that had a reputation for offering few artistic limitations, a sense of community, and less pronounced racism than they experienced south of the border.

> And there were a couple of other black guys that played the Cellar, they were from [the States]. They moved up here, why I don't know. It was a bass player named Earl Freeman and a tenor player, really good tenor player, named Bill Holmes. They just showed up one night and walked through the door again, out of the pouring rain and dumped their stuff on the bandstand and kinda said, "Here we are." Actually, a lot of word had spread down to California about the Cellar, and people just kind of showed up in town here.

> Uh, maybe they were fed up with [racial] problems in the States, and kind of got the idea to try up here, but those two guys, Bill and Earl, were in town for [a while].[38]

Earl Freeman in particular was a popular addition because bass players were still in short supply, a situation exacerbated by an increasing demand for Tony Clitheroe's services outside the Cellar. Freeman and Holmes stayed in Vancouver for a few years before relocating – Holmes to Toronto and Freeman to Europe, where in the late 1960s he recorded with Archie Shepp, Alan Silva's Celestrial Communication Orchestra, Kenneth Terroade, and Clifford Thornton, and played at the Amougies Actuel Festival in the fall of 1969.[39] Following sojourns in Holland and the UK, in the mid-1970s Freeman returned to the United States, where he continued to record and perform until his death in the mid-1980s.[40]

The only other black musician with a regular profile at the Cellar was pianist Mike Taylor, another American who had moved north from California.[41] Taylor was predominantly active on the East End scene, where he led the house band at the Harlem Nocturne and played the Smiling Buddha Cabaret with some regularity. Taylor would also sit in at the Cellar's late-night sessions and headlined there with his own groups from time to time. Don Thompson thought Taylor's career was affected by racism:

> Mike was a fantastic jazz player, he really was. [But] because of the race thing, I suspect, I hope I'm wrong, but I don't think so ... he never wound up on any of the [downtown] gigs I played, in the studios or the clubs or anything. I was never on a gig with him, and I played really a lot. And I was hardly ever a leader, either.[42]

Decades later, saxophonist Jim Johnson would end his professional playing career working in a band led by Ernie King that included Mike Taylor.

> I knew [Ernie King] when I was at the Cellar. I used to go down there and jam at the Harlem Nocturne, but that was

> the last I saw of Ernie for twenty years or so, until 1983, when he called me and said, "Do you want to play?" and I said yeah. So we played from 1983 to 2001. Club dates, that's all it was. Here, there, and everywhere. UBC and hotels. So I finished playing [professionally] with Ernie King.[43]

God Bless the CBC

One of the keys to attracting American artists to play at the Cellar was the extent to which visiting players were treated with dignity and respect at the artist-run space, and word of the collegial atmosphere at the Cellar spread quickly through the jazz community on the west coast. In addition, the Cellar did what it could to ensure that the trip north paid well enough to be worthwhile. In what would become a decades-long trend, the CBC played a vital role in ensuring the economic viability of these out-of-town bookings.[44] "We made it as lucrative as we possibly could" for American musicians visiting Vancouver, John Dawe said.

> You know, some of the guys in LA, some of the white guys down there at least, were working studio gigs and other pretty good-paying gigs. So they weren't going to take off for three days and come up here and work for fifty bucks a night. Because that's what we paid them at the Cellar, fifty bucks a night. So Dave [Quarin] would line them up some CBC studio work if possible, and Jim Carney was another guy who helped us a lot, because he was going to UBC, and he was a trumpet player, and he became a CBC producer. So he let us know – at that time the CBC had certain ... local TV shows, and the format for those shows was very loose; they could change what they had in mind if suddenly we had someone that they could put on for thirty minutes or an hour. They'd just switch it and put that on instead of what they normally had. They had some loose local shows where they could just put someone in on short notice. So someone like Art Pepper or Conte Candoli or someone like that could make themselves another three hundred and fifty or four

> hundred bucks doing that, plus have the hundred and fifty bucks from doing the weekend at the Cellar, so it was worth their while to come up. We had to throw them a plum. Some came up without doing a show, you know, and I don't know how they worked the finances for that.[45]

In the first few years of the Cellar's operation, the Cellar contacted the CBC and local radio stations to see what interest could be garnered for co-presentations. Thus Art Pepper was presented on the *Cool Pepper Show* in 1956, Lou Levy performed opposite the Fred Massey Quartet on a half-hour broadcast in 1957, and several other early Cellar presentations were similarly facilitated. Later, trumpeter Jim Carney's employment at the CBC gave the Cellar more direct access to the network's programming flexibility and financial resources.

> I was at that time starting to work at CBC television. I was a so-called production assistant or floor director in 1958–1959, and then in 1960 I became a producer. I mean, a television producer at the age of twenty-five shows you how nascent the industry was. And I had this fondness, this avid interest in jazz, so I ended up producing a series of jazz shows, it was a random ... I say series, but it wasn't a weekly thing, it was whenever we had ... the deal with the Cellar was this: if Dave Quarin, the de facto manager of the Cellar, he would have an interest in, say, booking Charlie Mingus for a week, and then I would produce a television show. Get the go-ahead to produce a television show. And pay the Mingus group, I forget what it was, $750, and Dave Quarin would pay them $750, and the $1,500 was enough to bring them up here for a week. And under that formula I produced shows, Charlie Mingus was the first one, and I forget exactly ... there were about nine shows all in all, and some of them were just local musicians, but Barney Kessel, I remember doing a show with him ... Ernestine Anderson ... my memory is definitely fading.[46]

Between January and July of 1961, Carney produced a series of jazz programs for the CBC that featured local artists Eleanor

Collins, the Ray Sikora Jazz Orchestra, and a live performance from the Cellar featuring the Al Neil Quartet (see Figures 24 and 25),[47] as well as performances by Barney Kessel, Ernestine Anderson, the Mastersounds, and Charles Mingus. The only one of these programs to survive in the CBC archives – "The Mind of Mingus" – intercut studio performance footage of the Mingus group with an interview recorded earlier at the Cellar.[48]

> I did this Mingus show that was shot in the studio. Studio 41 at CBC television, in what you call a limbo studio, which was pool lighting ... there was Charles Mingus and Dannie Richmond and Lonnie Hillyer and Charles McPherson just in

24 Live CBC broadcast from inside the Cellar, March 21, 1961 (produced by Jim Carney). Shown performing are Jerry Fuller (drums), Tony Clitheroe (bass), and Dale Hillary (sax). Al Neil is obscured. | *Photo by Franz Linder (261–14); courtesy CBC Still Photo Collection*

25 The audience attending the live CBC broadcast at the Cellar on March 21, 1961. [*L-R*] Terry Hill, Barry Cramer, Helen Brown (seated at bar), unknown woman (seated foreground), Jim Johnson, Gavin Walker, unknown person (striped jacket), unknown person (seated), and Glenn McDonald | *Photo by Franz Linder (261–14); courtesy CBC Still Photo Collection*

> pools of light. But we also did an interview ... A local anchor dinnertime conversation talk show host called Bob Quintrell interviewed Charles Mingus, and it was my idea to do that. And we got this quite startling interview with Charles Mingus at the Cellar. There was nobody else there, just us and the film crew.[49]

In an unrelated experiment also facilitated by the CBC, Carney engaged in an ultimately futile attempt to make a solo recording of Wes Montgomery, a late-night session that took place at the Cellar sometime after 1961 and was scuttled due to the technical requirements brought on by the sudden popularity of stereo recordings.

> And Wes Montgomery came to town once and played at the Cellar ... before he was the stellar attraction that he became. I remember trying to produce a record with Wes. I found this music producer in New York ... and said, "I've got this guy Wes Montgomery, and he's a really great guitar player, and I could record it," because I had access to CBC television equipment, "but I was looking for a US distributor, and how do I go about that?" And he said, "Well, that's a good idea, I'll help out as much as I can, but make sure that it's in stereo." And I said, "What?" And he said, "Make sure it's in stereo." And I said, "Stereo? What's that?" So he explained to me, and the CBC sound technicians were pretty savvy, of course. We had no stereo recording capability at CBC, but with film, in those days, you recorded the sound separately on a 16-millimetre sprocketed tape, and that's one of the reasons for the clapboard, so that you can sync up the tape and the film image. And I thought, well maybe if we got two of these Magnasync 16-millimetre sound recorders and synced them up, and kept our fingers crossed, we could do the double track then ... we could use two mics and mix it, and all this sort of stuff. And we tried that. And poor old Wes Montgomery sat there until three in the morning, not that that was late for him, but we never could get it synced, because the machines were drifting. That was long before they came up with Nagra, and eventually the wireless connection, which the NFB [National Film Board], who I worked with, later developed.[50]

In addition to the financial help provided through cross-booking artists with the CBC whenever possible, the Cellar relaxed the rules surrounding memberships during performances by out-of-town players. Rather than turn away a paying customer, anyone able to pay the cover charge who was not visibly drunk or belligerent was admitted, membership or no. Ricci Quarin let in "whoever could pay. We would be foolish [not to do it that way]. At that point we had to get the money and save the money. Still, people were not working for money," she said, referring to the staff and local musicians at the club.[51] This open-door policy for performances featuring out-of-town artists also made it possible for advance tickets to be sold at venues such as the 711 clothing shop operated by Barry Cramer's family, Just Jazz Records, and the H. Kaye Bookshop, businesses that would also display posters for upcoming Cellar performances. These posters, often designed by Harry Webb, appear to have been the only advertising materials produced by the club to supplement their sporadic advertisements in the *Vancouver Sun* and the UBC campus papers. While no conscious effort was made to increase the club's profile beyond these small local efforts, in 1959 *Coda* magazine began to include news from Vancouver in its "News and Notes" section, and these brief columns at times included information about activities at the Cellar.

Coda *Magazine*

Coda was established in May 1958 by John Norris as a magazine dedicated to traditional, or Dixieland, forms of jazz.[52] Headquartered in Toronto, *Coda* was initially available only by subscription and at Toronto's Maison D'Or, which operated as something of an unofficial clubhouse for Toronto's Traditional Jazz Society. *Coda* relied upon just a few columnists in addition to editor John Norris, and made an interesting plea to its readership to supply information on the traditional jazz scenes of their own cities and regions.[53] First expressed in the magazine's inaugural editorial, the message would be repeated over the years: "First and foremost there will be news and views on the Toronto jazz scene. Then, any news on Traditional Jazz will be published that we receive from other parts of Canada, the U.S., England and, for that matter, anywhere else in the world."[54] Reliance on its readership explains why jazz news from England, Australia, the United States, and even South America was printed in *Coda* before any news from western or eastern Canada made the magazine's pages.

The first mention of a Canadian city other than Toronto, Montreal, or Ottawa came in March 1959, when the magazine's review of the Timex All-Canadian Jazz Show expressed the hope that future programs might include Lance Harrison's Dixielanders, since "Vancouver B.C. is in Canada too."[55] Vancouver appears in the "News and Notes" section for the very first time in the same issue, with mentions of Bob Smith's *Hot Air* program on the CBC and the existence of the Vancouver New Jazz Society.[56] Vancouver appears again briefly in the "News and Notes" section of the next issue in April, with another mention of Lance Harrison's Dixieland group and the activities of the Vancouver New Jazz Society. These early Vancouver blurbs have no byline, and it is not known who submitted them. Mentions of Canadian cities beyond Toronto, Montreal, Ottawa, and London then cease until an anonymous submission from Edmonton in July 1959 mentions that the Yardbird Suite had opened in 1957, and that the city was also home to a traditional jazz society.[57]

In November 1959, *Coda* includes its first mention of the Cellar, which is limited to a single line: "The Cellar club has featured the odd attraction with Art Pepper there a short while ago."[58] Vancouver is not mentioned again until January 1960, when the expanded Vancouver section of "News and Notes" for the first time carries the name of its author, John Moller, at the time secretary for the Vancouver New Jazz Society.[59] More than a page long, this section is posited as "the first in a series of reports from Canada's west coast," needed because "for too long jazz news from Vancouver has been rather sparse in *Coda*." Moller reviews the past year's presentations by the Vancouver New Jazz Society on Sunday afternoons at the recently built Queen Elizabeth Theatre, and as part of this recap, refers to a jazz society presentation that featured "the Tony Clitheroe Quartet, the Jerry Fuller Quintet, and the Dave Quarin Quartet. This was a night for modern sounds as all three combos play regularly at 'The Cellar,' the city's jazz night spot. Doreen Williams was the vocalist of the evening."[60]

John Moller continued to contribute Vancouver news to *Coda* through the mid-1960s, spending most of his space on activities outside the Cellar, but making mention of key appearances such as that of Kenneth Patchen with Al Neil in February 1959.[61] In May 1960, John Moller's column was joined by that of Pete Wyborn, who contributed a second segment of Vancouver news titled "Jazz Is Where You Find It." Though the column was meant to tilt the emphasis back toward a traditional and Dixieland focus, Wyborn's opening paragraph neatly paraphrases many Cellar musicians' attitude toward the Vancouver music scene:

> I am writing this additional column on jazz in Vancouver as I feel that John Moller, being a professional man, does not have enough time to cover the whole unusual situation here. Vancouver is a city with the mind of a small town, due mainly to the fact that it outgrew itself in too short a time. As a result, professional jobs, musicianwise, are limited in number consisting of a few larger clubs, CBC studio work and the Vancouver New Jazz Society. This has created a situation which I will classify as [a] "closed shop," for lack of a better phrase. The same musicians hold the jobs which means that literally dozens of fine jazzmen are reduced to the odd cut-rate one nighters at weddings and banquets etc. This is not meant to be an attack on those musicians ... but merely a criticism of a situation that is holding back the growth of jazz here. The same old faces and sounds time after time, good as they may be, are not inspiring the audiences as only new ideas and additional new blood can.[62]

The June 1960 issue contains no column by John Moller, but Wyborn's news report includes Howard Roberts's engagement at the Cellar. Wyborn seems to have been enough of an insider to note, "An unusual sight for a 'modern' club was the presence of several leading traditionalists in the non-union jazz field among the audience. Also a surprise was the drumwork of Howard's wife, Jill, sitting in on several sets."[63]

Though no mention of Vancouver was included in the July issue, in August 1960, Wyborn discussed the Cellar's ongoing presentations of American jazz artists, a policy he deemed to be musically successful, and which he surmised was economically prudent due to the size of the crowds he witnessed, particularly at a Harold Land engagement. In September 1960, he mentioned the performance of *The Tender Edge,* though does not provide a review, and announced that Barney Kessel was due to perform at the Cellar in coming weeks.[64]

The October 1960 issue of *Coda* provided significantly expanded coverage of the Vancouver jazz scene, including not only Wyborn's "Jazz Is Where You Find It" news section, but a separate section on the activities of the UBC Jazz Society, as well as a brief review of the Vancouver scene by *Coda* editor and founder John Norris, who had visited the city on his way to the Monterey Jazz Festival in California in September. Wyborn's report includes a glowing review of the September Barney Kessel engagement at the Cellar, and a brief one-line mention that the Montgomery Brothers had also appeared at the Cellar during the same month. Of Kessel, Wyborn had this to say:

> The electric guitar has probably become the most abused instrument ever over the past five years. However, when taken away from the greasy-haired caterwauling rock and rollers and placed in the hands of a great musician like Barney Kessel it again becomes a thing of beauty to listen to. The Kessel Quartet direct from Los Angeles played a six day stand in August to standing room only crowds at the Cellar. I caught the Thursday night show, which unfortunately was my only free evening, otherwise I might have been tempted to do a six day stand at the Cellar as a member of the audience. There is no doubt about it that Barney Kessel is great! He not only plays jazz but creates relaxing mood music out of it which quite literally holds the listener in its spell.[65]

For this engagement, Kessel was backed by his working group of Marvin Jenkins (piano, flute), Gary Peacock (bass) and Ron Lundberg (drums), and it is worth noting that the experience was recalled quite differently by some members of the Cellar involved with the concert's staging. John Dawe recalled that the music was less well received by some of the Cellar musicians.

> Unfortunately this group was a bit of a disappointment to us beboppers, musically speaking. Barney, at this time was "cashing-in" on the then popular "soul-jazz" craze ... It brought in the "mink-coat" crowd, who definitely did not like our uncomfortable metal chairs and wooden tables ... Barney canceled out the last 2 days of his booking.[66]

The Cellar had run an advance ad in the *Vancouver Sun* on August 6, and followed this initial advertisement with ads on Friday, August 12, Saturday, August 13, and an unusual Monday ad on August 15. The Cellar continued to run ads once the engagement began, buying space on Tuesday, August 16, Thursday, August 18, and Friday, August 19.[67] No ads were placed for the final two days of the engagement (August 20–21), which may support Dawe's assertion that Kessel cancelled his last two appearances.[68]

That the Cellar took the unusual step of running advertisements in midweek editions of the newspaper perhaps suggests the hope that Kessel would appeal to a broader audience than some of the other artists it had presented. Indeed, the advertisements made repeated mention of Kessel as a "Poll Winner," and of his having been voted "the greatest guitarist" by *Downbeat, Playboy, Metronome*, and *Melody Maker* magazines (see Figure 26). The jazz cognoscenti who constituted the Cellar's regular audience would probably not have needed such enticements, but these ads may have targeted more casual jazz fans who may well have had a passing familiarity with Kessel due to his high profile in the contemporary jazz press, and the series of Contemporary Records releases that referenced the "poll-winning" status of Kessel, drummer Shelly Manne, and bassist Ray Brown.[69]

Coda's inaugural news bulletin from UBC made brief mention of the fact that visiting American artists appearing at the Cellar often presented clinics and performances at UBC, a co-presentation arrangement which was another way that the Cellar executive sought to make an appearance in Vancouver economically viable for visiting artists.[70] The brief introduction to the UBC Jazz Society estimated its membership at some three hundred members, a significant audience pool from which the Cellar could draw on any given evening.

In his October 1960 feature story on Vancouver, *Coda* editor John Norris correctly identified that many of the most skilled musicians – those playing the downtown clubs – were in situations that prevented them from demonstrating what were no doubt admirable jazz chops.

> In a quick round of the Vancouver spots we heard a number of jazzmen but in most instances they weren't able to play

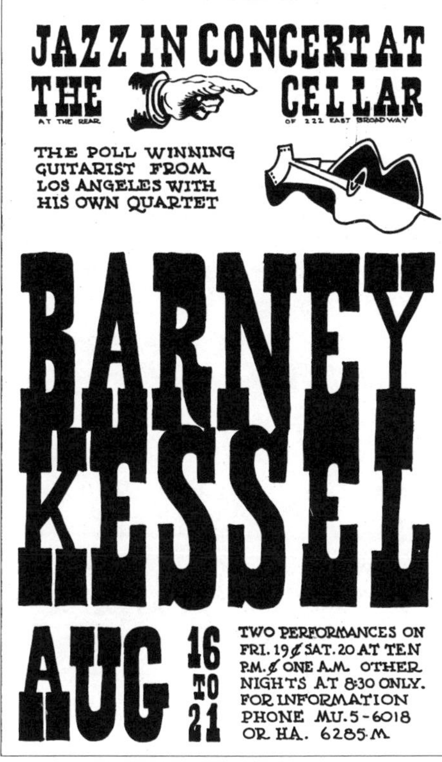

26 Poster for Barney Kessel at the Cellar, 1960 | *Designed by Harry Webb; courtesy Adrienne Brown*

> jazz ... The type of clientele [prohibited] an out and out jazz policy ... at the Cave ... Once again the jazz numbers remain at the bottom of the book.

Perhaps unsurprisingly, Norris's favourite group during his brief visit was that of clarinetist and soprano saxophonist Lloyd Arntzen, whose traditional jazz band was performing material associated with Jelly Roll Morton the night that Norris stopped by for a "delightful evening." His review of the Al Neil group at the Cellar was not nearly so kind.

> At the Cellar was the Al Neil Quintet. This is a pleasantly set out club but to attract a steady audience they must offer music of a higher quality than that offered by this group. They were ragged and uninspired. There was no fire or finesse. This may, to a certain extent, have been caused by

> the overloud and unsteady drumming of Bill Boyle. A drummer's job is not to play over the rest of the band.[71]

Norris didn't mention the date or time of his visit to the Cellar, so it is unclear whether he attended a paid evening performance featuring the Al Neil Quintet, or if he happened by one of the club's late-night sessions. Regardless, his assessment of Boyle is quite a departure from the usual regard in which the drummer was held, and is perhaps more indicative of a listener more attuned to traditional and Dixieland forms of jazz drumming than it is an accurate reflection of Boyle's skill (see Figure 27). Bassist Don Thompson, who played with Boyle on numerous occasions, recalled that

> Bill was ... very much like Jimmy Cobb, because he didn't have a ton of chops, but he had a groove that just wouldn't quit. And everything he played worked. He couldn't actually ... he couldn't do a roll. He didn't know how to do a roll, but he could really play. [He had] time that was just amazing, and it was very easy playing with him, because he didn't play busy either. He left lots of space, and it was really nice playing with Bill ... He was crazy about Philly Joe [Jones], but he still came out like Jimmy Cobb. Because he didn't have the chops. If he'd had the chops he probably would have played like Philly Joe.[72]

Boyle was self-taught as a drummer, but his lack of technical skill did not prevent him from becoming one of the most in-demand players on the Vancouver jazz scene, a scene that included such notable young drummers as Jerry Fuller, Stan Perry, and Terry Clarke. Clarke said:

> I guess I should have got the message, but the reason that everybody wanted to play with him instead of us hot-shot young drummers was that he wasn't busy at all. He just played straight down the middle, and to this day, a lot of people, that's really what they want you to do. You know, the same rules apply ... everybody just wants to hear "one." And he played simply and a lot of air, and in situations where

27 Bill Boyle | *Photographer unknown; courtesy John Dawe*

> there might not have been a piano player or guitar player, they liked the space. He just played the time. He had a nice sound.[73]

As one of the more experienced players on the scene, Boyle was the focus of attention for many of the city's up-and-coming young drummers, most of whom were studying with the now somewhat legendary teacher Jim Blackley.[74] John LeMarquand, for instance, observed Boyle's style:

> Bill Boyle was one of those drummers that if you look at him playing, he looks so awkward. But if you shut your eyes and listen to his playing, it's really good ... Billy was an excellent drummer, but he didn't have a lot of technique. But he got a lot of work, and he sounded ... it sounded really good. He

> wasn't particularly loud. Of course at that age I was very critical of all drummers, and technique and all the rest of it, and I had to put all of that aside and just shut my eyes and listen to what he was doing, and then he was very, very good. I mean, he was right into the music. I mean, he played with everyone. He was a downtown heavy. I think of him more as a Jimmy Cobb–type drummer. You know, that's how I heard him play. Swing the bridge kind of thing, and cut time. Nothing like what they do today. Yeah. Very tasteful. Very good ... I couldn't say anything negative, other than that he was a little awkward to watch.[75]

In the December 1960 issue of *Coda,* both Pete Wyborn and Vancouver New Jazz Society secretary John Moller bemoaned the state of jazz in Vancouver, with Wyborn reporting that the "bottom seems to have dropped out of the jazz market in Vancouver" and that crowds at the Cellar were becoming poor, though he did not mention which groups he heard. John Moller reported that a series of financial misfortunes had placed the Vancouver New Jazz Society in a perilous position, while the high-priced American "acts" that were performing in Vancouver with increasing frequency had made competition for audiences increasingly fierce.[76]

Following the engagements of Barney Kessel (August 16–21, 1960) and the Montgomery Brothers (August 30–September 4), the Cellar appears to have kept mainly to local musicians for the remainder of 1960, with the Bob Winn Quartet (September 16) from Seattle and the Jean Hoffman Trio (November 22–27) the only non-Vancouver group the club advertised in the *Vancouver Sun* through 1960. The next year, however, the Cellar played host to perhaps its most famous American visitor – bassist, composer, and bandleader Charles Mingus.

Mingus

In January 1961, the Charles Mingus Quartet arrived in Vancouver to perform at the Cellar, and also appeared at UBC under the auspices of the UBC Jazz Society and on CBC television in a program produced by Cellar member Jim Carney. Advance promotional materials for the engagement list performances from December 15 through December 24, but in actuality Mingus's stay at the Cellar began on Friday, January 6, and extended through January 21 (see Figure 28).[77] The quartet comprised Mingus (bass), Dannie Richmond (drums), Charles McPherson (saxophone), and Lonnie Hillyer (trumpet), and appeared in Vancouver directly after a series of performances at San Francisco's Jazz Workshop. Billed by the Cellar as "the most provocative musician in jazz," Mingus's two-week stay at the Cellar represents what is perhaps the most widely attended and most frequently recalled presentation in the club's history, as well as being the centrepiece of a great deal of Cellar lore.[78]

Plagued by stomach troubles, Mingus was forced to sub out the second set during one of the group's first performances, and pressed Tony Clitheroe into service playing bass with the rest of the band, which, due to the paying crowd, remained behind in Mingus's absence and completed the night's performance.

> Well, it was one of those situations where I was working downtown, and I'd left my bass downtown, you know, because I figured I wasn't going to need it. But I couldn't wait to get up to the Cellar and listen to the group ... it was a great group. And I got up there as soon as I could and there was nothing going on. And ... I got down to the bottom of the stairs and walked in, and whoever was taking the tickets in the box saw me and said, "We're glad you showed up, we weren't sure you were coming." And I said, "What do you mean, who cares if I come or not?" And they said, "You're playing." And I said, "What? Where's Mingus?" And Mingus, apparently – I didn't know this before, but Mingus had an ulcer, a really bad ulcer, and he wanted to go back to the hotel. So I walked through the door, and here's Mingus pacing up and down with a carton of cream in one hand and a package of arrowroot biscuits in the other, you know, looking fierce. And somebody took me over and introduced me to him, you know, and he says, "You're the bass player?" and I said, "Well, I ..." And he grabs me by the shoulders and kind of spins me around and aims me at his bass up on the stand, and he says, "There it is." And then he says to me, "Don't hurt it."[79]

28 Advance posters for Charles Mingus concerts at the Cellar, 1960. Dates and personnel differ from actual 1961 dates. | *Designed by Harry Webb; courtesy Adrienne Brown*

Unsurprisingly, Mingus's stay in Vancouver was not without its share of drama, including drummer Dannie Richmond running into some legal trouble sufficient to whittle the group down to a trio for a few evenings.[80] No incident, however, lodged in the collective memory of Cellar audiences more than the night on which Mingus became involved in an altercation with a member (or members) of the BC Lions football team. Fifty years later, the exact details of that evening, including the date, remain somewhat muddled.[81] Common consensus suggests that it was near the end of the Mingus engagement, possibly on the closing weekend (Friday, January 20, or Saturday, January 21). Poet Jamie Reid, who was at the Cellar that evening, recalled it this way:

> Mingus played two sets that night. When I came in, at the beginning of the second set, there were rumours abounding that Mingus had already had some kind of altercation with somebody in the crowd. That he had thanked the audience for their attention, in particular the "latent homosexual who was pounding on the cigarette machine." So Mingus was in sort of a high mood, right from the very outset.[82]
>
> ... But anyway the second set began and Mingus starts to play and he's got the entire band there with him, and there's a pretty good crowd there for the Cellar. It was pretty near full. And Mingus is on the stage here [*gestures*] ... and over to the side, on his left, is a kind of small platform on which there is some sofa-type chairs, as I remember it ... It was the only space in the place like that. All the rest was sort of regular chairs. [In] the crowd there, the one person I recognized was Steve Cotter, who I went to high school with, who was a football player there, and a bit of a thug, in my recollection. He played for the BC Lions at this time. He played guard with them. And so they continued to talk throughout the entire set. And at one point Mingus asked them, and when he spoke he never quite spoke in a polite tone of voice, but you know his request was polite, in the sense that he did request that they be quiet so that others could hear, you know, "like

this lady here who's sitting all nice and quiet," and he points to a woman named Birgit.

Then at the end of the first half of the second set, he went to the bathroom and he came out with a bathroom plunger, and he stepped up on the platform and had words with them. I couldn't hear what he said. You know, they went this way and they went that way, and finally there seemed to be some kind of agreement, and so Mingus was satisfied that they weren't going to make any more noise and as he stepped off the platform Cotter made some kind of sneering noise at him and Mingus just turned around and hit him with the bathroom plunger. And so Cotter got up and took a swing at him, and Mingus just caught it in his hand – like that – and just sort of flung him, you know, behind him, so he spun through three tables, and then he gets back up and Mingus is going towards him and in jumps Warren Tallman, who I hadn't even seen, from this other direction, and he says, "Charlie! Charlie! Think about your career!" And so Mingus just kind of diverts. He just turns, slightly, on his heel, and goes off like a bear, you know, who's just going to forget about it, and Cotter's friends just pushed him up the stairs. And then the whole thing went on from there.[83]

Though the final resolution of the incident, including UBC poetry professor Warren Tallman's intervention, was not recalled by most contributors, it was corroborated by poet bill bissett, who was at the Cellar that evening, though not sitting with either Reid or Tallman.

And one night Charlie Mingus came [to the Cellar], and he was huge everywhere, and at home we were all listening to Mingus and Coltrane [records], and somebody said something during his playing ... And then, Mingus got really mad at them. He reacted as a human being rather than a performer, if there is a fine-line difference there, and [the audience member] got really angry back, and then Warren Tallman was there, and he jumped on the stage ... and hugged Mingus and said, "It's your career. Don't react. Don't get into

> this. Let it go, keep playing." And it was one of those gasping situations ... it was very amazing, and I never forgot it.[84]

Interestingly, the most widely circulated report of the incident contains the least detail, holds the least in common with other recollections of the incident, and is quite probably the least accurate version of events that I obtained.[85] Jamie Reid, for example, said, "The story that I've read in the posting that Gregg has made about the history of the Cellar is entirely different from my memory of it," referring to the online report by John Dawe, published on the website run by artist Gregg Simpson. This version of events is as follows:

> One nite [sic] Charlie became highly agitated with a table full of noisy football players ... He shot off the stand, grabbed one of them by the back of the neck and ran this mother up the stairs so fast he didn't know what hit him! ... They settled the rest of the dispute outside ... I think Charlie won.[86]

John Dawe himself was not at the Cellar that night, and composed this brief outline after speaking to several people who claimed to have been there. Though many of the details are at odds with the recollections of those who attended the performance, it captures the spirit of the incident and illustrates both how firmly the evening has become lodged in the mythology surrounding the Cellar, and just how many disparate versions of the event exist.

A teenaged Terry Clarke was also at the Cellar that night:

> The last night I went there [to hear Mingus], I think it was a Saturday night, and the place was packed, and I was sitting [*points out how close he was to the stage*], and Dannie and Charles and Lonnie, and I'm sitting there like this [*mimes rapt attention*], and Mingus is playing a bass solo, and all of a sudden you're aware of a lot of noise coming from over in that [*points away*] corner of the room. And there were three BC Lions football players talking, and Mingus is just playing away, and he keeps on playing and says, "If you motherfuckers don't stop talking I'm going to come over there and

> beat the shit out of you." That was verbatim what he said. He kept on playing the solo, they kept on talking. He then put his bass down, and he walked right past me to the bathroom and got a toilet plunger and went over, and started. And the tables were in the air, and shit was flying, and ... it was like, just fisticuffs, and the whole club cleared. Everybody freaked out. Lonnie Hillyer walked past me and said, "I don't want any part of this, I'm a peaceable man." Those were his words. This is, like, etched in my brain, and it so freaked me out – I'd never seen anything like this in my life, and, uh, and that's how serious [Mingus] was about his music.
>
> I mean, the whole thing was (a) this is serious music, yes we should understand [that], (b) this man is crazy, (c) he's justified, and (d) the whole thing is insane, and I hope my mom and dad never find out about this. But I watched the whole thing go down.[87]

Mingus's Cellar performances had a profound musical impact on those who heard them and, as a student, this was Clarke's main takeaway from the evening:

> I'd heard about the Charles Mingus band, but I knew nothing about it, and I said I'm going to go and hear this band. And I took the bus. Down Broadway, whatever, by myself, in my little suit and tie, and got there really early. And I remember sitting by myself, and it was Mingus, Dannie Richmond, Lonnie Hillyer, and Charles McPherson. It was the quartet. And I had no idea what I was about to hear. I had not heard them, I just knew this was somebody I ought to check out. And that first, that evening, completely changed my life. I was so terrified, and blown away. My head just blew off. And I remember sitting there for the hour break that they took, just thinking ... my whole life flashed before me and what music was all about, and why did I understand it. What blew me away is that what Jim Blackley and I had been talking about, as far as rhythm sections and rhythms and three-beat rhythms and vamps and riffs and things ... Mingus and

> Dannie were doing it. And Dannie was a self-taught drummer, or Mingus had taught Dannie how to play, he had been a saxophone player ... I knew nothing. I was a virgin. And I was just so blown away. And I said, "This is exactly what we had been talking about. Now, I get it." The light bulb had gone on. "I get it," you know.
>
> And so he was there for two weeks ... Jim Blackley was down there, Jim had Dannie Richmond over to his house and he played a tape of *me,* and he said, "You gotta hear this young student I've got, he's fifteen."[88]

Bassist Don Thompson also vividly recalled his first encounter with Mingus:

> So you open the door to go in, and it's really, really dark, because Mingus is onstage and they're ready to begin. And it's really dark. You can't see anything. But there's a light behind the door I guess, and Mingus ... the door opens and he turns around and he glares right at me, and he says, "Good evening, you're just in time to shut up." So that was my first meeting with Mingus. It was really funny.[89]

Those Cellar members who were fortunate to spend time with Charles Mingus outside of his performances related that their interactions with him were both meaningful and surprising. Jim Carney, for example, hosted him for several nights:

> What impressed [me] ... he had this reputation of being this very angry man, this very bitter, angry man, and his music tended to reflect a lot of that. But I found him very gentle, and in fact he stayed in my apartment for several days, down in the west end, and he loved Scotch, but he couldn't drink it straight, he had to drink it with milk, because he had an ulcer. And ... he said things like, "The most any artist can do is leave a little truth, a little beauty." This wasn't exactly the thinking of a mad, an angry, bitter [man]. He was quite poetic.[90]

Indeed, on the CBC show "The Mind of Mingus," which Carney produced, Mingus expressed a similar sentiment:

> The message to pass on ... it's a duty of all people that do love and have found the beauty in life to sort of talk to each other, and if, well ... there's bound to be one among them who's not in love with life enough to save life, or the earth, and by just talking to each other the whole thing will grow. By passing on the truth ... by passing the truth on to people. ... I can't play beauty to someone if I'm not feeling beautiful. But if they give me hate in return, I have much of that to give also. And probably more ... that's why I have the ulcer.[91]

This half-hour program is in many ways a startling and complex presentation that introduces the viewer to Mingus's music through live performance footage shot in the CBC studio and through a remarkably candid interview shot earlier at the Cellar. "The Mind of Mingus" received a glowing review from John Clayton in *Coda* just ahead of its national rebroadcast in March:

> Mingus answered the questions in a full and articulate manner, a pleasant change from the welter of platitudes and mumbled incoherencies strung together with "you knows" one so often encounters when musicians are being interviewed. His personality, as projected from the glass screen, appeared warm and human. He knows what the relationship of the musician to music should be – "feel it, understand it, have an opinion on it." ... All in all this was one of the best jazz programs I've seen – because of Mingus himself, his convictions and expression of same in a relaxed, and, at times, humorous manner, and because of the excellent program direction allowing Mingus to put over the fact that his type of jazz is closely connected to and dependent upon life.[92]

In addition to his nightly performances at the Cellar and the CBC filming, Mingus also performed a short daytime concert at UBC presented by the UBC Jazz Society, which was reviewed in *Coda:*

> After a very late start (not his fault) and playing one number Mingus noted a dozen or so people standing at the rear who

> had not been able to get seats, more were outside the auditorium. He enquired as to whether they had paid, he thought they should. Gavin Walker, in charge of proceedings for the Jazz Society, shrugged off the suggestion that he should take the hat round. So Mingus put down his bass, found a hat and made the collection personally and thoroughly. As he shambled up the aisle the crowd melted away, but one fellow stood his ground, alone and isolated when all had fled and told Mingus he had paid, at which the hat and Mingus passed him ... Now, up to a point, this all seemed quite hilarious, but he dragged it on to such an extent that one began to have an uneasy feeling about it ... there was a certain tension.[93]

Though this UBC presentation was a concert rather than a workshop, the young players involved with the Cellar found other opportunities to learn what they could. Bass player Terry Hill recalled that Mingus would sometimes remain at the club after hours, which enabled some interaction between the American star and some of the more junior Cellar members.

> I was there one evening, I don't know what time it was in the morning. About four of us sitting around, I don't even remember who was sitting at the table, [though] of course I remember Mingus, and what he was letting us know was how you played. How you become whatever you are. And I can't take his voice off, because it was very gruff. He'd rather punch you out than talk to you, I think. He was a pretty rough guy, but what an incredible player. And anyway, he said, in his voice, "What you do, man, is you practise and you practise and you practise, and you get down all the licks of all the great players, and then one day you play yourself, and if it's no good, you kill yourself." [*Laughs*] And at that point I thought about trying to kill myself.[94]

Mingus's extended engagement in Vancouver provided a unique and valuable opportunity for Cellar members, who were able to interact with the visiting artists not simply as enthusiastic members of the audience, but also through informal sessions, rehearsals, and simply "hanging out" – receiving valuable musical experience and forming personal relationships.[95] In addition, Mingus's stay at the Cellar demonstrates the process of mythologization central to the life of a scene; raised consistently as a point of reference by interviewees, it served as a tool for recognition, as a social entry point, and as a point of mutual experience that still, several decades later, separates those who were part of the scene from those who were not.

6

Altered Chords

New Blood and the End of an Era

It was kind of a template for what I think the kids should be doing now.

– Terry Clarke

Throughout 1961 the Cellar continued to program a mix of local artists and visiting American stars despite a rapidly changing musical marketplace that presented increased competition for the attention of Vancouver's jazz audience. In February 1961, Phineas Newborn Jr. played a widely advertised six-night engagement at the Harlem Nocturne, providing high-profile competition at a time when Cellar newspaper ads were now often run only in the Friday newspaper.[1] The club was also advertising a new program of Sunday evening sessions, which were low-key affairs consisting of either a rehearsal band (often Ray Sikora's) or jam sessions.[2] These casual sessions represented the lowest financial outlay for the Cellar executive as the musicians were generally not paid,[3] so whatever cover charge was collected could be directed entirely to the operational costs of the club. This reduction in paid advertising and turn to ad hoc, economical sessions suggests that the Cellar was starting to feel a financial pinch and significant decline in audience as early as 1961, though it remained a vital part of the Vancouver scene. As bassist Tony Clitheroe told me,

> At one point we adopted a policy of opening on Sunday nights, which we hadn't done for quite a long time. Unless we had somebody there ... a high-profile import. I keep using that term, but that's the one I think of. So if we had somebody come in, we'd certainly be open on Sunday night, probably slightly earlier, maybe nine to one or ten to two or something like that, as Monday would be the next day. But we decided to start opening the place on Sundays no matter what, with the proviso that it was a rehearsal band ... the local band would work for nothing. So that went on for quite a while, and it went right up, I believe, until the closing of the Cellar.[4]

In the spring of 1961, both the Montgomery Brothers and Barney Kessel returned for short stays – Barney Kessel from March 17 through March 26, and the Montgomery Brothers from March 31 through April 16 (see Figure 29)[5] – followed by Dick Forrest in May, and Ernestine Anderson from late June into July. Though *Coda* magazine reported in its December 1961 issue that the Cellar was planning to move to a downtown location that would permit more foot traffic, I found no other evidence that such a move was seriously contemplated.[6] The bulk of the Cellar's advertised engagements during this period were local artists, most of whom were drawn from the ranks of what had been an influx of younger players to the scene.

Drummer Stan Perry arrived from Halifax, Nova Scotia, where he had been involved in a similar co-operative performance space in the late 1950s (777 Barrington Street, see Chapter 7). Shortly after his arrival in Vancouver, Perry began studying with Jim Blackley and participating in the Cellar scene.

> I went to Dal[housie University in Halifax] for one year and flunked everything. I got a job in British Columbia working at a mine, and decided to go back to school, so I went out to Vancouver and I went out to UBC and graduated from UBC, barely. Just arts, English, basically. And I did okay at first, but I got more and more involved with music, and that's when I

29 Poster for the Montgomery Brothers at the Cellar, 1961 | *Designed by Harry Webb; courtesy Adrienne Brown*

> got involved with the Cellar club out there. And I wound up playing down there all the time.[7]

Vancouver native Terry Clarke, also a drummer, was only twelve years old when the Cellar opened in 1956, and first went there as a teenager.

> My first time was 1960 or 1961 ... I was about fifteen years old ... So I'd started taking drum lessons with Jim [Blackley], who used to live up on Commercial Drive ... I remember going down [to the Cellar] with my jacket and tie. And I'm pretty sure my mom was a little freaked out that I'd be going over there ... Just to go there was exciting. I didn't really care [who the bands were]. It was the learning ... And anybody that played the Cellar had to be good. That was the idea, that

> they wouldn't let you in there if [you couldn't play] ... the bar was really set pretty high, in my mind. And Jesus, I can remember just sitting and listening there over and over and over ... I just sucked in everything. And I learned just as much from Jerry [Fuller] and Stan [Perry] as I did from Jimmy Lovelace ... but in a different way.[8]

Jerry Fuller, who began drum instruction at an early age in his hometown of Calgary, had also continued his studies under Jim Blackley in Vancouver, where his father worked as a saxophonist in the downtown supper clubs.[9] Following a year at the Westlake College of Music in California (1958–59), Fuller returned to Vancouver where he became a vital and regular part of the Cellar scene, playing frequently with the likes of Don Thompson, P.J. Perry, and Dale Hillary, as well as with long-time Cellar members such as John Dawe and Tony Clitheroe.

Saxophonists Dale Hillary and P.J. Perry arrived on the Vancouver scene at more or less the same time. Hillary, born in Edmonton in 1940, was something of a startling protégé and was chosen, along with (Edmonton-based) drummer Terry Hawkeye, as one of twenty-four young musicians to attend the prestigious Lenox School of Jazz in Massachusetts in the summer of 1957.[10] Instructors at the school during Hillary's stay included John Lewis, William Russo, Ray Brown, Jimmy Giuffre, Herb Ellis, Max Roach, Dizzy Gillespie, and Oscar Peterson, who acted as Hillary's small ensemble director.[11] Two years later, in 1959, Hillary was not yet nineteen years old when he appeared with Kenneth Patchen and Al Neil on the Folkways recording *Kenneth Patchen Plays with Jazz in Canada,* garnering a special mention in *Downbeat*'s three-star review of the album. Hillary went on to spend the 1960s as something of a musical nomad, drifting between Vancouver's Cellar, the Yardbird Suite in Edmonton, and Toronto's MINC and First Floor clubs, in addition to working with drummer Philly Joe Jones on a tour that apparently included a sojourn in Cuba.[12]

One year younger than Hillary, Calgary-born P.J. Perry grew up in a musical family. His father, Paul Perry Sr., led the dance band in the popular Alberta resort town Sylvan Lake from the late 1940s through the mid-1960s. P.J. found early work in his father's orchestras, and he and Hillary played together in the band at Sylvan Lake before meeting again in Vancouver. P.J. discovered the Cellar while still a teenager, because his family spent the fall and winter months in Vancouver. Trumpeter John Dawe remembered P.J.'s first visit to the Cellar:

> He came down one night, I don't know how old he was, maybe seventeen or eighteen or something, and he said, "Hey man, can I sit in?" First he sent me to the liquor store to get him a bottle. And he got up and played. He sounded like he was going to play real great, but he didn't know the tunes. Didn't know the chord changes. He had been playing with his dad's band as a kid so he actually played the saxophone really well, but his jazz wasn't together at all. And I think that very night Don Thompson, who was brand new in town and still learning, leaned over and said to him, "Hey kid, go home and learn some tunes, and come back in six months." He did. I think he came back in less than six months, and the next time ... wow! Watch out! Because P.J. had gotten a hold of it, and he was down in the Cellar after that all the time.[13]

Multi-instrumentalist (bass, vibraphone, piano) Don Thompson also arrived on the Vancouver scene in 1960 at the age of twenty from rural Powell River, some two hundred kilometres north, though he had visited the Cellar a couple of times as a teenager.

> I'd actually been to Vancouver before that, just to visit. A friend of mine was a drummer ... and [he] went down to Vancouver [and] came back talking about the Cellar. And talking about this fantastic drummer, who was Chuck Logan, [and] said this guy is as good as anybody, he was just amazing. Talking about Chuck and all the guys he'd heard. This was before I'd ever been to Vancouver. But it made me want to go and check out the club and everything. But I couldn't really play. I really couldn't play for a long time.
>
> I think the first time I actually played in a session was with Dave Quarin. I remember ... I didn't know how to play,

> but I got up anyhow, and we played a blues or something, and then we were going to do another tune and we couldn't think of anything to play so Dave said, "Well, let's just play 'Just Friends,'" and I said, "Well I don't know that," and Dave said, "Well I've got the chords here." So he gave me the paper and I got through it somehow ... I can remember all the guys: John [Dawe] was playing, and Tony [Clitheroe] was playing bass. And they were so good. And here I am, not really knowing how to play, just sort of hanging on, and not really even hanging on, just kind of getting through it.[14]

Thompson found employment quickly, working at the Black Spot, the Inquisition Coffee House, the Espresso, and the Cellar with a variety of groups. Thompson's popularity on the Cellar scene was aided by the fact that Tony Clitheroe frequently worked other engagements, and Earl Freeman had left the city. During the hours he wasn't performing, Thompson could be found either sitting in on piano at the Espresso Coffee House in exchange for a meal, or shadowing Vancouver's pre-eminent bassist, Paul Ruhland.

> Paul was my first bass hero. I mean, I loved Tony, but Tony was different. I'd listen to Tony play and I just really, really liked it. But I listened to Paul, and it was like getting a bass lesson. Because Paul knew stuff about the bass that none of us knew. I'll never forget ... I used to follow him around. I'd go down to the CBC because you could walk into the CBC anytime, there was no security in those days, so I'd just go down to the CBC and see what was happening ... where the radio studios were, and there was a rehearsal studio actually, on the same street as the Espresso. Just down a couple of doors. And I went in there one day, and Dave Robbins was rehearsing his band for the *Jazz Workshop* radio show they used to do, and Paul was playing bass. So I just went in, because I knew Paul, and sat down right beside him while they were rehearsing.
>
> And first of all, he was like Tony ... he had a sound that was unbelievable, and a really good French bass. And I was just sitting there listening to him, and the first thing they

> played was a thing of George Russell's, and it was all twelve-tone music, and so I'm listening to Paul play, and the bass line is just so bizarre I couldn't believe it. And I was looking at the part, and when they stopped for a minute I said, "What is that?" And he said, "Oh, it's a twelve-tone row," and he explained to me what it was, and how the notes don't repeat and all that stuff. And then the next thing they did was a thing he'd written, and it was a blues or something. I can't remember what it was called ... And the whole first chorus that he played was in the thumb position and four-note chords. All these big four-note chords, just like classical guitar. Perfectly in tune. And I'm sitting there listening to him play this thing, thinking, Jesus! I just couldn't believe it, that anyone could actually do that. And even right now, that's not that easy. Most of the guys around couldn't do it now. But he just had the bass together. He'd just go [*strums*], and there would be this perfect chord. And there was a whole chorus like that. And I thought to myself at the time, "I hope I never have to play that."
>
> And then of course Paul packed up and left for LA and Dave Robbins called me to take his place in the band, and that was the very first thing I had to play. But when I looked at the part, it was just chord symbols. He had just been improvising the part just for fun. But that's how good Paul was. He was amazing. And so ... I used to go to the Cave and sit up in the balcony and watch his hands. And with no microphone or anything you could hear him. He was the first guy you heard when you walked in the door. He had a sound that was unbelievable. Paul was really something. As a composer ... in his own class as a composer. I mean, he was light years ahead of anybody around, to the point where the guys used to ... they just didn't understand him at all. They really didn't. They had no idea at all what he was doing.[15]

When Ruhland left for California in 1963, Thompson took over from him in many instances, and was soon featured with his own group on a weekly half-hour CBC broadcast. These short programs featured the Don Thompson group (usually with Terry Clarke) in showcase performances or backing up invited guests ranging from Vancouver vocalist Eleanor Collins to Americans such as Stan Getz.[16]

A New Scene: The Black Spot

When the Cellar opened its doors in 1956, it was the only available space in Vancouver for young musicians interested in jazz to meet and play. Almost instantly popular, the Cellar not only drew from the age demographic of the players who had started it, but quickly attracted younger players still in high school at the time. Though musical skill was something of an equalizer within the scene, the age gap between the Cellar founders and those who discovered the club in later years could nonetheless be startling. Bassist Terry Hill was on the young side of this gap:

> The thing was, these guys, they were such good players, but there was a difference in the ages of about eight to ten years, and when I'm playing with Al Neil I'm thinking he's the same as me, but he's ninety and I'm seventy-five. There was a difference, and when you're twenty-two, that's a big difference.[17]

Even saxophonist Gavin Walker, who as a teenager became a fixture at the Cellar, recalled that his introduction to the scene involved acknowledgement of a generational gap. Walker was in high school when his family relocated to Vancouver, and one of the first people he happened to meet in his new city was saxophonist Jim Johnson, who at the time was still working days at Western Music.

> The first thing I looked for was a music store. And I walked into Western Music ... and had a few dollars in my pocket and I saw a record that I hadn't seen before and I remember it was a J.R. Monterose record ... And I took it to the counter and the [clerk] said, "Wow! For a young guy you're really digging the real stuff." And he said, "I'm going to go on a break. Do you want to join me for a coffee and a sandwich around the corner?" So I said yeah, and we went around the corner to a place called Mother's Café, it was on Dunsmuir Street,

> and we sat there and he told me all about the Cellar, and it was like I'd struck gold. Because I had no idea that Vancouver had something like that at all. When we were in Mother's Café, John Dawe came in. So he was the second person I met in Vancouver. And so, Johnson introduced me, and said, "This is a young cat who's really interested in jazz," and he says, "We're having a rehearsal on Tuesday night ... why don't you come down to the club and check it out, and we're going to have a rehearsal with our group." And so the group consisted of Jim Johnson on tenor and alto, John Dawe on trumpet, Al Neil on piano – it was actually his group – Tony Clitheroe on bass, and Bill Boyle on drums. So those were the Cellar beboppers. That was my intro. So I sat and listened to them rehearse.[18]

Much as the sessions at the Penthouse in the 1950s were essentially closed to the young players who ultimately formed the Cellar, in the early 1960s the Cellar itself was a scene that was closed, at least initially, to many young players. With active participation in the Cellar tied to a certain level of musicianship, most younger players in Vancouver were relegated to the audience. As a result, they, like the Cellar founders before them, lacked the performance opportunities necessary to develop as jazz musicians, a situation which led to the formation of the Black Spot as a co-operative jazz space in the summer of 1960 (see Figure 30).

Located at 4345 Dunbar Street near King Edward Drive, the Black Spot began in 1958 not as a jazz club, but as one of the first coffee houses in Vancouver. The space was known variously as Mother's and the Living End before being renamed the Black Spot, possibly in some sort of hip opposition to the iconic Vancouver restaurant chain White Spot, or perhaps simply in reference to its largely black interior design.[19] The venue bore no signage other than a large black circle painted above the door, and quickly became popular with students with an affinity for beat culture (see Figure 31). The venue operated as a commercial, albeit quite casual, endeavour, and relied upon its clientele to amuse themselves by playing chess, staging poetry readings, or using the house piano. In poet Jamie Reid's assessment,

30 Promotional material for the Black Spot, ca. 1961 | *Designer unknown; courtesy John LeMarquand*

31 Exterior of the Black Spot, ca. 1961 | *Photo by John LeMarquand; courtesy John LeMarquand*

> The Black Spot crowd was a younger crowd. University students and young people aspiring to be beatniks, in the main. It was a beatnik club, that's what it was. Everybody in black turtleneck sweaters and pretending to write poetry and getting up and reading poetry and drinking awful coffee and so on. And the musicians from the university used to go there and play.[20]

By late 1959, the scene at the Black Spot had tilted toward a regular jazz policy because of its adoption by young players from UBC and nearby Lord Byng High School, which had a noteworthy music program. It was also starting to draw the ire of local residents, who were unimpressed by the activities at the space and circulated a petition in the summer of 1959 to shut down the Black Spot.

> Attempts of a group of young people to turn Dunbar into "beat street" have drawn the ire of neighbourhood residents. They're passing around a petition to have the "Black Spot" closed ... P.S.: the only thing "beat" about the kids I saw around the place was the fact that they were all tired out from working so hard to make the place go as a coffee shop.[21]

The attempt to shutter the club was unsuccessful, but by early 1960 the Black Spot's owners found themselves in economic difficulty and were looking for additional partners. At this point John LeMarquand, along with his friends Ron Dobson, Morris Jenkins, and Tom Killam, stepped in to help keep the space open. LeMarquand was an aspiring drummer studying under Jim Blackley, though the other partners were not musicians.

> The original owners had sold to two people that I knew, a couple of years older [than I was], and they were looking for some co-signers, because the lease was coming up and they were afraid that they might not be able to make it, and the more people they had on the lease the more the financial burden would be spread. So that's how I got involved, you know, as one of the co-signers. So in 1960, I was an owner ... I was an aspiring drummer ... but neither of the other three

> were musicians at all. And the club sort of had a beat poetry thing ... nothing very structured, and then the trio from Victoria came, and they were pretty hard-core jazz. Sax, bass, and drums.[22]

From its inception in 1958, the Black Spot had required inexpensive memberships, and cardholders paid a reduced admission in the evenings when music was offered.[23] Though the club was open from Tuesday through Sunday, formal performances were usually only on Friday and Saturday nights, with the other evenings left free for informal jam sessions and rehearsals.[24]

As John LeMarquand alludes above, the arrival from Victoria of saxophonist Claire Lawrence, bassist Bob Keziere, and drummer George Heller helped to reset the focus of the Black Spot, and it quickly transitioned from beatnik coffee house to jazz-based music club, taking out ads in the *Vancouver Sun* alongside the Cellar in the summer of 1960.[25] While these advertisements positioned the Black Spot in competition with the Cellar for Vancouver's limited jazz audience, for those in the know the Black Spot functioned less as direct musical competition, and more as an alternative, more youth-oriented space (see Figure 32). Poet Jamie Reid compared the two venues:

> The musicianship was not professional musicianship. In the Cellar it was generally professional, or at least to my understanding it was professional. They didn't break up in the middle of the set ... and they [the Black Spot guys] would play a couple of things and then casually get off the stand. There wasn't any set thing, and they were more or less jamming more than anything else, I expect. They didn't have any headliners at any time, it was whoever got up and played for them, and if there wasn't anybody playing for them then there wasn't any music, and they would play it on the jukebox.[26]

The Black Spot served as clubhouse and creative incubator for those Vancouver jazz musicians who were just young and inexperienced enough to be left out of direct participation in musical activities at the Cellar, such as Terry Clarke.

32 Inside the Black Spot, ca. 1961. [*top, L-R*] Bob Keziere (bass), Bill Fawcett (guitar), George Heller (drums), Claire Lawrence (saxophone), John Capon (trombone), and Ron Proby (trumpet) perform. Ken Clarke is seated in the audience with his back to the piano, and Terry Clarke is next to him. [*bottom*] Al Wiertz (drums) and Ron Proby (trumpet) perform. | *Photos by John LeMarquand; courtesy John LeMarquand*

> I had a paper route. I was really young. I just enjoyed going there and they let me come in and the beauty of that is that I was studying with Jim [Blackley], and everybody was all caught up in the scene, so the beauty of it is that we could go to our lesson and think about music and then go and play. Dave McMurdo had a big band, you'd go there and play Sundays. But I didn't contribute financially to it, I just was always [there]. My mother would come up and drag me out of there, if she had to ... Because we'd be there until seven in the morning.[27]

Though the younger players who frequented the Black Spot were regular attendees at the Cellar, few managed to perform there with any regularity, and the two scenes operated as distinct, though at times overlapping, social scenes. In John LeMarquand's opinion,

> There was quite a separation between the two. Though we would go to the Cellar, particularly if they had some notable person playing there, they never came to our club. We were a lot younger, probably three or four years younger. But I was nineteen, you know, and the guys were of that age group, and these [Cellar] guys were twenty-five, twenty-six, and they ... a lot of them [were] professional musicians working downtown Vancouver. So we were just sort of the kids. And it was pretty much that way while the Black Spot was in existence. It wasn't until the Flat Five came around that we became more accepted and actually outlasted the Cellar ... I mean that was still, from our point of view, the mecca in town at the time – 1960, 1961. Because they were bringing in some notable people. Charlie Mingus comes to mind. And he caused quite a stir there and impressed everyone. And Art Pepper was there. They were just like on a whole different level, so we more or less ... Glenn McDonald, who was a saxophone player that did play at the Cellar, was the only one that consistently played at the Black Spot.[28]

The Vancouver correspondent for *Coda* magazine concurred with this general assessment in the June 1962 issue:

> The Black Spot continues to function every night except Monday, though it is somewhat haphazard. A phone call in advance is recommended, but this is the place to see the new blood of the Vancouver jazz scene in action. At the weekends, for a more sophisticated approach to jazz, the Cellar is the place to go.[29]

In late 1961 or early 1962, with the Black Spot facing further financial difficulties and in danger of closing, a group of musicians who regularly performed at the club approached John LeMarquand and his co-owners about the possibility of collective ownership as a means to keep the club open. Under the name of the Contemporary Jazz Society, a group of some fifteen musicians and fans, John LeMarquand still among them, pooled their resources and took control of the Black Spot.

> What was happening, I think, is that the handwriting was on the wall that there was talk of the Black Spot closing when the lease came up, and so people were enjoying playing there so much, I guess just through sheer talk they figured they ought to do something about this. So they actually pooled some money and approached me and the other three guys and made us an offer, and we said sure. It was a lease thing that prompted it. And so it carried on from there ... So that was the formation of the Contemporary Jazz Society. It was just a name we thought up, it had no relation to anything, and it was never officially registered as a society. It was just a collection of people, and actually the original people that put money into it, to buy out the original owners of the Black Spot.[30]

Terry Clarke recalled that the scene at the Black Spot was prompted by circumstances nearly identical to those behind the Wailhouse and the Cellar – the need for young musicians to have a place to meet, share ideas, practise, and play in an environment that was welcoming of experimentation and failure.

> We all knew, the Cellar *is* the club. And as a backlash to the Cellar, we ... Claire Lawrence and Al Wiertz and a whole

> bunch of people, we opened up the Black Spot, which was a club up on Dunbar. And I lived up on Dunbar and Twenty-Seventh. So that was our club, which was like a co-op club. If you could play at the Cellar you'd arrived. You know? So ... we had the Black Spot going because we weren't good enough in our minds to play at the Cellar. We weren't good enough musicians. "But one day, I'll be able to play down there." And I didn't play there very much. When I did, I was really nervous.
>
> It was a brilliant idea. Because the Cellar ... the main guys played down there ... and it wasn't that we couldn't get in, because there was no liquor, so we could get in there as kids, I guess ... But the Black Spot was our club where we could get our shit together. And it was a co-op, which I thought was a great idea. A bunch of guys just chipped in twenty-five dollars a month, paid the rent, one of the guys lived above it, and we had access to the club and there was a piano and drum set and ... we would go to the Cellar and hear Charles Mingus, and then run up to the Black Spot, open the club up, and play until six in the morning. And then go to high school.[31]

By June 1962, even the collective efforts of the Contemporary Jazz Society were not adequate to maintain the operation of the Black Spot, and the club closed its doors, a situation that *Coda* regarded as regrettable but unsurprising.

> This month sees the demise of the Black Spot, which claimed to be the oldest coffee shop in Vancouver, being inaugurated in October of 1958. For some time it had been operating on a very shaky financial footing and the attraction of cash customers was not encouraged by the haphazard method of operating – open six nights a week as it was, often little was offered in the way of entertainment. When music was played it was usually well worth the moderate admission fee, but the uncertainty was not conducive to steady business ... The really amazing thing about the Spot was that it ever functioned at all considering the number and variety of characters who all had a hand in its operation ... In addition to the

> directors many others were instrumental in keeping the place functioning – not only musicians who played for the fun and experience, but also the voluntary kitchen help, book-keepers and general lend-a-handers.[32]

Before the club's closure, the Contemporary Jazz Society was approached by restaurateur Anthony Thorn, who was opening a coffee shop on Marine Drive near Locarno Beach in English Bay, and wanted to offer live music there. The society quickly agreed to relocate to the rear of his establishment in a venue that would become known as the Java Jazz. However, it was short lived, as *Coda* reported:

> The end of October saw a less happy occasion that is the predicted demise of the Java Jazz Club came about. But this was not the end of this ambitious group of young musicians. Packing their tents and more or less silently stealing away, this group of ex-Black Spot arabs [sic] is now encamped at another oasis – 3623 West Broadway, due to open officially Dec. 1st. One of our promising young drummers, Jim Chivers, will manage it and spaghetti, pizza, cold drinks and coffee will be served upon request. It will be run on the more practical basis of weekends only – Friday, Saturday, and Sunday from 10 p.m. to at least 1 a.m.[33]

The Java Jazz was open only from the summer to October of 1962, but John LeMarquand recalled that the society easily moved on:

> Actually, [the Java Jazz] was a very good deal for us. What happened was we got the money for the door, and he got the food sales. And, well, people didn't buy a lot of food, and so he couldn't carry on. And around that time he was coming to us and asking if we could change the relationship, and boy we were hard core, and said no. But someone had found this building on Broadway, which was pretty much made up ... honestly I don't know what it was originally. Never a club. Pretty much everything was there [though], we didn't do a whole lot to it. We built a stage, and put in some lights for

> the tables ... and we went down and had a look and I guess we got a hold of the landlord and made a deal and the next thing you know, we're moving.[34]

The Flat Five

Originally and briefly known as the Flatted Fifth, the Flat Five at 3623 West Broadway (see Figure 6) marked the last experiment in club ownership by the Contemporary Jazz Society, as well as the most significant development in Vancouver's jazz scene since the inception of the Cellar in 1956. The Flat Five marked a new level of professionalism for the Contemporary Jazz Society, both from its own musicians, who had developed considerably over the last few years, and in the level of imported talent presented at the venue. This mixing of local artists (many of whom were members of the managing co-operative) with well-known stars was yet another way the Contemporary Jazz Society modelled their venture on the Cellar. John LeMarquand recalled:

> At the Black Spot time, the Cellar wasn't competition; by the Flat Five they were a little bit of competition. Our skill level went up, we had better players, Don Thompson had moved down from Powell River of all places, and was playing in the downtown music scene, and Terry Clarke, and they played together a lot, and of course joined the John Handy band. But the quality of music just took a leap upwards in the Flat Five era.[35]

The transition from Java Jazz to Flat Five was overseen primarily by drummer Jim Chivers, who acted as manager of the Flat Five, along with John LeMarquand as the club's secretary and treasurer. In 1962, LeMarquand was working for the CBC as a member of the stage crew, and was able to facilitate the remodelling of the Broadway location to suit the needs of a jazz club.

> I was able to use my contacts and hired the carpenters to build the stage, and the painter foreman actually had a job on the side where he made decorative lights, so we got lights

> from him for the club. And CBC was throwing out some risers, so we snagged those, for some seating at the back of the club using those risers. So my contacts with CBC came in handy.[36]

The jazz society's ambitions for the Flat Five also required that they confront a great deal of red tape that had largely been avoided by the more casual Black Spot and Java Jazz. As at the Cellar, a deal was worked out with the local chapter of the American Federation of Musicians to accommodate casual sessions and performances by co-op members as well as formal presentations of high-profile artists. LeMarquand recalled that the Flat Five dealt with the American Society of Composers, Authors, and Publishers (ASCAP), since replaced in Canada by the Society of Composers, Authors and Music Publishers of Canada (SOCAN):

> So we actually did hire musicians, right from the start, and then we got nailed by SOCAN or whatever they were, ASCAP before that. Fortunately they were, I dunno, we didn't have to pay very much money, fifty dollars or something like that. Though fifty dollars in those days was probably four or five hundred dollars today.[37]

The club was originally intended to open in December 1962, but initial advertisements announcing the Flat Five as Vancouver's "newest contemporary music club" along with weekend performances by singer Lynne McNeil and the Don Thompson Trio did not appear until January 4, 1963.[38] Though the Flat Five took out regular ads alongside the Cellar and other established nightclubs in the *Vancouver Sun*, the club also established itself as a regular presence in the UBC student newspaper the *Ubyssey,* which wrote: "Flatted Fifth? We've all been wondering what it is. It's a jazz club – a real jazz club – not just a wine-bottle checkered table cloth, atmospheric condition. It's a jazz sound – a fine high swinging jazz sound – with high fine swinging jazz musicians."[39] The campus paper carried nearly weekly announcements of concerts by such newcomers to the Vancouver scene as multi-instrumentalist Don Thompson, bassist Robert Witmer, pianist John Gittins, vocalist Lynne McNeil, drummers Al Wiertz and Blaine Wikjord, saxophonist Claire Lawrence, vibraphonist/pianist Ralph Dyck, and others, and offered a student admission rate of seventy-five cents on Sundays.[40]

In a move further reminiscent of the Cellar's practices, John LeMarquand's CBC contacts led to the taping of a half-hour broadcast live from the Flat Five in September 1963. Featuring Eleanor Collins and the Don Thompson Trio, the engagement was a resounding success that introduced the club to a wider audience than attended many of its less mainstream jazz presentations.

> We even got a television show done, by CBC, and I often wonder whatever happened to that. It was just a half-hour, I can't remember who was playing. The biggest draw we had was Eleanor Collins, and we were sold out the two nights she sang, and we even opened the fire doors and people were outside, listening. The club was absolutely packed.[41]

In addition to live music, the Flat Five presented visual art shows in the club's spacious lobby, which ultimately led to the opening of the Peter's Ear Gallery in 1965. In another move probably borrowed from the Cellar, the Flat Five also hosted short theatrical productions, staging *Around the World in 80 Seconds* in March 1963,[42] and a high-profile charity event featuring the Gastown Players in February 1964. Al Neil, unsatisfied with what he perceived to be musical limitations at the Cellar as he began to back away from mainstream jazz performance, began playing at the Flat Five with some regularity in 1963 and 1964, apparently finding greater creative freedom there. Between the involvement of Al Neil and the establishment of the Peter's Ear Gallery, the club acted as an important site of intersection for Vancouver's burgeoning experimental arts scene, much as the Cellar had for earlier countercultural developments. In many ways the later activities of organizations such as Intermedia and the Sound Gallery and the work of such artists as Al Neil, Gregg Simpson, Michael de Courcy, and others can be traced to the Black Spot and Flat Five (as well as to the Cellar, to a lesser degree). With only minor changes in management within the co-operative group, the Flat Five continued as a co-operative venture until the summer of 1964, when it was sold to new owners who operated it briefly as a regular, commercial club.

The Plot Thickens: Other Venues

In the early 1960s, other venues emerged in Vancouver that, along with the Black Spot/Flat Five, placed increasing pressure upon the Cellar. While not co-operative spaces in the vein of these clubs, these venues presented similar types of jazz, often with better-known artists than the co-ops could afford to hire. Paradoxically, greater jazz activity across a multiplicity of competing venues fractured the city's small jazz scene, weakening the social bonds and cohesion necessary for scenes to function as community spaces and sites of identification and participation rather than simply as places for musical consumption. It's hard to be "on the scene" with any consistency if that scene occurs in multiple places, often simultaneously.

The most high profile of these new venues was the Inquisition Coffee House at 726 Seymour Street in the downtown core, run by local impresario Howie Bateman.[43] The Inquisition opened in the spring of 1961, offering a mix of local and imported artists in the worlds of both folk and jazz. The Inquisition operated as a coffee house without a liquor licence, and quickly became a focal point of the Vancouver music scene, eventually hosting such performers as the Montgomery Brothers, Ernestine Anderson, and Cannonball Adderley.[44] Some of these artists had previously played at the Cellar, yet despite the positive relationships fostered there, opted for engagements at the Inquisition because it offered higher performance fees than the not-for-profit Cellar could guarantee.

In April 1963, however, the Inquisition presented the Miles Davis Sextet to a disappointingly small audience, an economic failure that was bookended by the costly appearances of Cal Tjader in February 1963 and Stan Getz in October 1963.[45] The limited turnout for these presentations was a crippling financial blow and led to the club's closure in December 1963, as reported by *Coda*:[46]

> Some people didn't get their stockings filled this Christmas ... bad business forced [Bateman's] Inquisition coffee house

> to close anyway. In its short two year life it brought a handful of jazz stars and a host of folk to Vancouver. As Cannonball said when he played there, "This coffee is sure great for keeping you awake, but ..."[47]

Bateman's difficulty making a profit with such high-profile acts may well speak to the failures of a business model predicated on the limited revenue potential of a coffee house, but is also likely indicative of the size of the audience for jazz in Vancouver at the time – an audience that was becoming increasingly dispersed across available venues for jazz. Anecdotal evidence suggests that the ticket prices for concerts at the Inquisition were often discouraging to the younger, less affluent regulars who formed the core of the Vancouver jazz scene – those musicians and students who relied upon the Cellar and Black Spot/Flat Five as interactive scenic spaces rather than as intermittent listening venues. In many cases, regulars at the Cellar or Black Spot/Flat Five did not attend the concerts at the Inquisition, hoping instead that the artists involved would find their way down to the Cellar for an after-hours session.[48] After the Inquisition closed, the venue passed to Ken Hole, who reopened it briefly as The End.[49]

The other significant addition to the Vancouver jazz scene in the early 1960s was the Espresso Coffee House on West Georgia at Howe Street, near the Hotel Georgia (see Figure 33).[50] Ken Hole, who after his departure from the Cellar in 1958 had opened the Scene Club in Victoria with Walley Lightbody, had returned to Vancouver in the spring of 1960. Hole remained active in the restaurant business through a series of overlapping ventures, and inherited ownership of the Espresso from a business contact. Though the exact date of the Espresso's opening remains hard to pin down, it appears that Ken Hole took control of the operation sometime in 1960, and quickly brought in pianist Neild Longton as the venue's manager.[51] In addition to his managerial duties, Longton performed on the house piano when required, often during the earlier portion of the evening.

The Espresso never formally hired musical entertainment, relying instead upon musicians dropping in to organize informal sessions

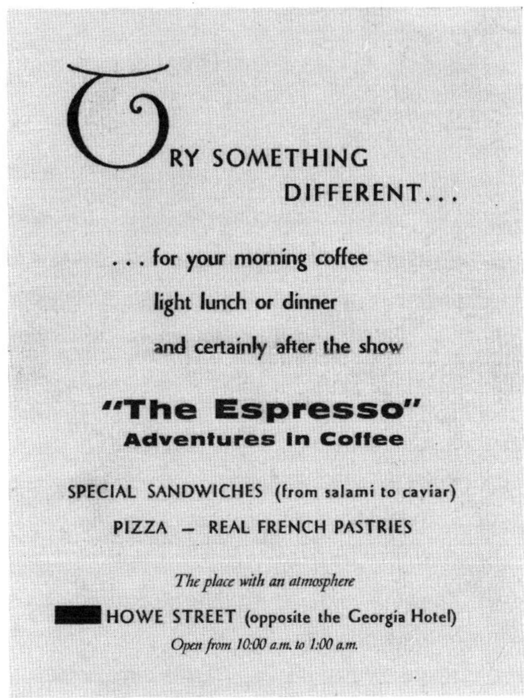

33 Advertisement for the Espresso Coffee House | *Designer unknown; courtesy Chris Birdseye*

using the house piano, bass, and drums. The Espresso benefited from being close to Isy's, the Cave, and the CBC studios, and Ken Hole recalled that it rarely lacked for musicians willing to play late into the evening:

> The boys started coming in, Don Thompson and th[em], and we started having jam sessions. And I'd go down there after work, and I'd sit in there and have a couple of drinks and play a couple of tunes. And next thing you know it caught on.[52]

One regular visitor to the Espresso was teenaged Don Thompson, who would often fill Longton's role as piano player in exchange for a meal, and was a frequent member of the ad hoc evening groups that formed.

> It was a very loose thing. It was a drop-in. It wasn't a "hire them for the weekend, come and see them," kind of thing. It was anybody who came ... Neild Longton was there all of the time running the place, and he was the piano player, a very good one. So that's where Don [Thompson] started sitting in with him, and Don would use Ken's bass I think.[53]

> Oh, I spent hundreds of hours in that place. With Neild Longton. I'd just go in and play the piano and they'd give me food for nothing. They wouldn't charge me for food, and then I'd just play the piano for an hour or so. That was a fantastic place. I remember countless times, because there would be sessions every night, and sometimes the sessions wouldn't start until one o'clock in the morning. Buddy Rich's band was in town once for a couple of weeks, and we played every night, but we didn't start until about 1:30 a.m. And we'd go home, and the sun would be coming up, you know. And that's when we'd finish. Because they wouldn't shut down until everybody left. It didn't matter. It was just like that, and all the guys in Buddy's band came down. Pat LaBarbera, Don Menza and all these guys and they'd ... that's when I met Pat LaBarbera.[54]

The emergence of the Espresso as a popular centre for downtown musicians to meet and play in informal sessions following their paid gigs reduced the once unique late-night atmosphere at the Cellar to simply one of an increasing number of musical options. Though players such as Tony Clitheroe continued to return uptown to the Cellar for sessions and socializing, changes in Vancouver's musical culture meant that it no longer held a unique after-hours allure for jazz fans or musicians. For young players such as Don Thompson, there were simply more playing opportunities to take advantage of.

The Cellar, 1962–63

In response to the changing musical marketplace in Vancouver and the increased competition for both audiences and performers from

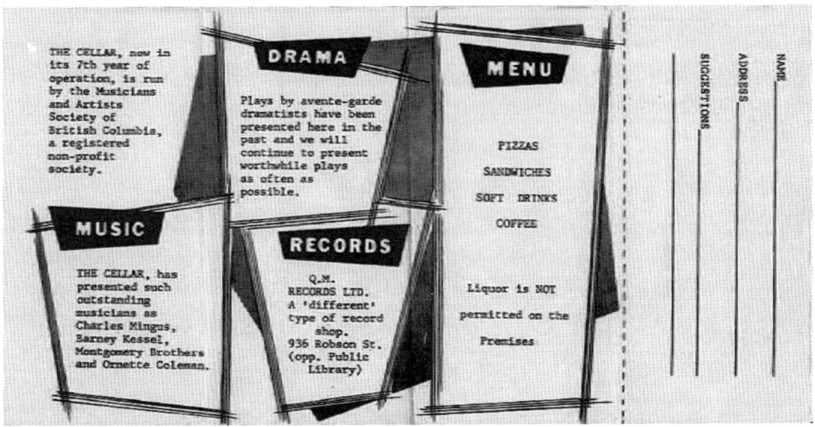

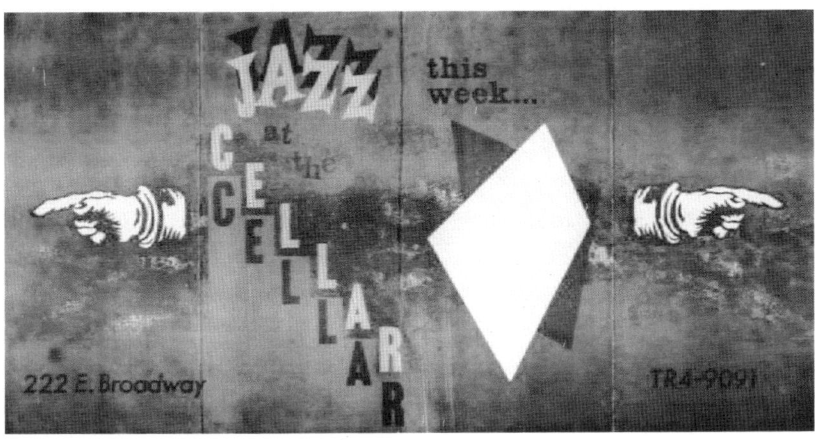

34 Brochure for the Cellar, ca. 1962 | *Designer unknown; courtesy Chris Birdseye*

the Black Spot, the Inquisition, and the Espresso, the Cellar's activity in 1962 was rather low profile and stuck largely to the presentation of local artists (see Figure 34). Early in the year, the Cellar narrowly missed out on what would have been a significant booking – tenor saxophonist Dexter Gordon. Gordon was booked to play the club March 8–11 (see Figure 35), and the club had gone so far as to produce promotional material in support of the dates along with advertising in the *Vancouver Sun* beginning on March 3.[55] However, the gig was cancelled at the last minute; Gordon attempted to cross the border with his saxophone but without the appropriate work

35 Poster for Dexter Gordon at the Cellar, 1962 | *Designed by Harry Webb; courtesy Don Thompson*

permits, and was denied entry.[56] It appears that Gordon attempted to enter Canada on March 8, the day of his first advertised booking at the Cellar. The *Vancouver Sun* advertisement on that day featured Gordon, but on March 9, the Cellar instead advertised Conte Candoli, who happened to be in Vancouver and was booked as a hasty replacement.[57]

Following the three-night stand by Candoli, the Cellar stuck largely to local groups for the remainder of 1962. The only significant exceptions were engagements by vibraphonist Warren Chiasson, alto saxophonist Lee Konitz, and drummer Jimmy Lovelace. Warren Chiasson had grown up in Nova Scotia, where he honed his musical skills with the Royal Artillery Band stationed in Halifax, and at Halifax's own co-operative jazz club, 777 Barrington Street (see Chapter 7). Nearing the end of his military service in 1959, Chiasson found employment with George Shearing and relocated to New York City. In 1962, no longer with the Shearing band, Chiasson joined the orchestra of a touring theatrical production that took an engagement in Dawson City, Yukon. Through his association with fellow Nova Scotian Stan Perry, Chiasson was hired to play the Cellar June 15–28, 1962, as he passed through Vancouver on his way to Dawson City.

In an attempt to make the Cellar premises more inviting to audiences, the club closed for remodelling in the month of August, reopening over the Labour Day weekend to once again feature Warren Chiasson, who was back in Vancouver on his way home to New York. Chiasson also headlined from September 14 to 16, and was quickly followed by alto saxophonist Lee Konitz, who was living in California at the time. Konitz performed from September 22 to 30 in a trio with bassist Tony Clitheroe and drummer Stan Perry.

> Since I was a newcomer to the bass, I was listening to a lot of Percy Heath and Paul Chambers. If it wasn't for those two guys, I wouldn't have known what to do. So when Lee Konitz came up, I thought this was going to be kind of strange. Because I'd heard Lee Konitz and Warne Marsh years earlier when I was still in the UK, and they were doing a lot of stuff that was ... I thought, "What is all that!" So, I didn't really know what to think about it when the gig started, but it got to be a hell of a lot of fun as the week went on. At least it was for me, it might not have been for Lee. It was for me.[58]

Following Konitz's engagement, the Cellar returned to presenting local musicians, relying heavily on saxophonist Dale Hillary, who headlined the club three weekends out of four in October alone. As the original musicians who founded the Cellar matured, they became less available to play at the Cellar for questionable financial returns. Musicians who had started families were compelled to take their day jobs more seriously, and some, like Al Neil, had begun to move on to other interests. Others, such as Tony Clitheroe, Dave Quarin, and Stan Perry, were quite active on the downtown scene, which greatly reduced their availability at the Cellar:

> You see, I started working in the downtown clubs around 1959, and of course they were six-night-a-week gigs. So there were fairly lengthy periods when I wouldn't be hanging out at the Cellar as I was beforehand. But every now and then something special would happen and I'd book off the gig at the club and go and do the Cellar ... you know, if somebody asked me to or something like that. I think a period of ... years elapsed ... when I was mostly at Isy's. Then we got fired, after the predictable conflict with Isy. And of course by that time the Cellar was just about done, and I was doing less formal things ... a lot of casuals, and at one point I was working the house band, as a matter of fact with Quarin, at this place in Chinatown. I can't remember the name of it. It might have been the Mandarin Gardens.[59]

> We got these places [the co-ops] so that we could go out and play. We could play whatever we damn well pleased, you know. And we didn't have to be beholden to anyone else. But of course, as we get older, all our attitudes change and now we'll play anything. I played Tommy Hunter's show for a year, you know, in a country and western band. Toured with it and did a television show and everything else. Because it was money. Your values don't change ... but your, what's the word I'm thinking of, your priorities change a little bit.[60]

The last available evidence of Cellar programming in 1962 shows that the Jimmy Lovelace Trio performed November 23–25.[61] Following Lovelace, the Cellar's December advertisements did not indicate any particular performer. These generic ads also began to advertise free admission for "ladies" before 1 a.m., a marketing strategy perhaps aimed at making the Cellar more competitive with the Black Spot/Flat Five, Espresso, and Inquisition. In 1963, the Cellar's newspaper advertisements began to announce that no memberships were required for admission, marking the end of one of the Cellar's most distinctive features – its nature as a private members' club.[62] Strangely, the September issue of *Coda* reported precisely the opposite state of affairs, stating that

> the Cellar appears to be going downhill – it has changed its policy now to function as a private musician's club operating by subscription. For the sake of Dave Quarin and the others that have supported and guided what used to be the Mecca of the Vancouver scene it is hoped that a long needed transfusion of new blood will occur.[63]

As *Coda* generally reported events a month or more after they occurred, it is possible that before eliminating the membership policy the Cellar tried to increase revenues by becoming more strict about the membership requirement.[64] Negative reception to a tightening of the original membership rules could perhaps then have led to the decision to remove the membership requirement entirely.

Presentation of short plays resumed at the Cellar in 1963; it's unclear whether these productions had been ongoing since the first such experiments in 1958, though that seems unlikely. In March 1963, the Cellar presented both *The Red Sock* (March 1–2) and *Freddy* (March 8–9 and 15–16), both staged at 12:15 a.m. between the second and final musical sets.[65] The Cellar executive may well have been hoping that the theatrical audience would choose to come early, and perhaps stay late. In April 1963 the Cellar staged Edward Albee's *The Zoo Story* (April 5–6 and 12–13), and then presented what appears to be the club's final theatrical production on June 25–26, a restaging of *The Red Sock*.[66] As discussed earlier, the recently opened Flat Five club also began to experiment with theatre in March 1963. As the two clubs were sharing numerous musical performers by this time, the same individual(s) may have been responsible for the renewed theatrical activity at both venues.

The Cellar faced significant competition for its audience in early 1963, as the Inquisition presented Cal Tjader in February, and both the Miles Davis Sextet and the Modern Jazz Quartet in April.[67] Isy's Supper Club presented Billy Eckstine, and the Cave began to advertise the Chris Gage Trio in addition to its regular featured entertainment.[68] At the Cellar, meanwhile, the only recurring performer from the club's earlier years was guitarist Jim Kilburn, who headlined repeatedly, often alongside vocalists Barry Dale, Doreen

Williams, and Lynne McNeil. The appearance of vocalists with such frequency marks a further departure from the Cellar's previous programming model, and signals perhaps both an attempt to appeal to a wider audience and that there was a more limited pool of musicians from which to draw. Other local artists to perform at the Cellar in 1963 included saxophonist Claire Lawrence (a key member of the Black Spot and Flat Five clubs), saxophonist Glenn McDonald, the Mike Taylor Trio, and, on Sunday evenings, the big bands of Ray Sikora and Bobby Hales. The only American artists advertised at the Cellar in 1963 were Barney Kessel, who returned May 17–25; Jimmy Lovelace, who returned June 7–9; and Freddie Schreiber, who performed on cello with his quartet August 16–17.[69] Trumpeter John Dawe recalled the competition:

> A lot of other places were springing up and siphoning off the [audience for jazz]. Vancouver was a pretty small-potatoes kind of town, and there were only so many jazz patrons to go around. Even in the earlier days, we had a lot of months in there where patrons and patronage fell off to hardly anything. A lot of time we had to play for nothing down there, just to crack the nut for the rent.[70]

The End of an Era

The details surrounding the closure of the Cellar are murky, but sometime in late 1963 the club's management passed from Dave Quarin and the Cellar executive to entrepreneur Bill Wright. Whether the club was sold or simply changed management is unclear. No meeting of the executive or board of directors was called, according to John Dawe and Tony Clitheroe, which suggests that a major breakdown in club operations had occurred by this time. The first definitive evidence of Bill Wright's takeover of the club comes in September 1963, with an advertisement in the *Vancouver Sun* for a performance by Donna Wright, Bill's wife, alongside the Don Thompson Trio.[71] *Coda,* however, reported that the club had changed hands as early as August, and that the Freddie Schreiber performance that month had been under Wright's auspices.

> The Cellar club is not closing after all ... Bill Wright is the new backer and manager of the Cellar, and has shown himself interested in maintaining the modern music policy. A group with Freddy [sic] Schreiber (from San Francisco) on Cello played last month. Since then local jazz groups have been employed and also Wright's jazz singing wife.[72]

The last ad for the Cellar to appear in the *Vancouver Sun* ran on November 15, 1963, and announced "the exotic sounds" of the Clinton Solomon Quartet. Solomon was Trinidadian, and his group played a mix of steel pan and bongos along with a style of song and dance that would not previously have met the Cellar's standards for jazz performance.[73] Despite the lack of advertising, the Cellar apparently remained open for some months longer. Tony Clitheroe recalled playing in what was likely the Cellar's final Sunday performance of Ray Sikora's orchestra:

> I think it's entirely possible that the last date that I'm aware of was on December 8, 1963. And Ray had his band in there, and I used to play with Ray's band, and I have it down as December 8th, which was a Sunday, and I have nothing else [for the Cellar] afterwards.[74]

The December 1963 issue of *Coda* mentions that the guitar/vibraphone duo of Jim Kilburn and Ralph Dyck performed at the Cellar in November 1963, and that pianist Bud Glover, formerly of Victoria's Scene Club, had been hired on as something of a house rhythm section along with drummer Al Wiertz and bassist Ted Gawks.[75] No advertisements can confirm that this arrangement was finalized.

Finally, in March 1964, *Coda* correspondent Adrian Tanner reported that the Cellar had closed its doors in February:

> It may be a symptom of something, I don't know what, but the Cellar died quietly last month. I hate to report this, for more than the obvious reason that the Cellar was one of the best centres for jazz around here in its day. There is also the

> uncomfortable knowledge that Vancouver jazz clubs have a tendency to die, but refuse to lie down. By the time you read this it may be open again, but I doubt it.
>
> In its heyday around 1957–1958 the Cellar was the avant-garde music centre of Vancouver. Week after week the crowds would pack in to hear local cats battle it out in cutting contests, or hear the truly fantastic sounds of some of the then-unknown names that were being brought in from San Francisco and Los Angeles. One group had Harold Land, Scott LaFaro, Elmo Hope and Lennie McBrowne. Art Pepper played there three times. In 1957 Don Cherry brought in a group. Later he convinced manager Dave Quarin to let him come up with a group led by an absolute unknown – Ornette Coleman. Billy Higgins and Don Payne were also in the group. Many other greats played there – either as booked stars, or as sit-ins – Lee Konitz, Paul Gonsalves, Herb Jeffries, Shorty Rogers, The Montgomeries, Joe Gordon, Barney Kessel, and more. In 1961 Charles Mingus was there, and after one particularly powerful solo, leaped into the audience and started to threaten a B.C. Lions football player with a bathroom plunger. I guess it's OK for the Cellar to close now. There aren't those sort of things happening anymore.[76]

Minor inaccuracies aside, this short eulogy neatly encapsulates the place and importance of the Cellar both within the musical life of Vancouver and in one of the most intense periods in the development of jazz, Canadian or otherwise. For a good many years, the Cellar had not simply been an important part of Vancouver's jazz scene, it had, in many ways, been the jazz scene itself. By the time it closed, however, its role had largely been assumed by the Flat Five, which through 1962 and 1963 had become the more significant club. In John LeMarquand's view,

> Oh, god, you know [the Cellar] ... it seemed to me it suffered a death, and then all of a sudden it started chugging along. It kept going, but it wasn't the hard-core, this-is-where-everyone-goes-when-they-finish-their-gigs kind of place that it used to be. And our club had taken that position. We had

> lots of musicians who were passing through come to the club, and playing or just hanging out, which was always pleasing. I don't really know when the Cellar closed. It just sort of lingered and lingered, you know? They weren't advertising that many people, and somehow they were scrambling to get people to play there and, I guess one day the doors didn't open, but I couldn't tell you when.[77]

The reasons behind the decline of the Cellar were varied, and included the rise of alternative music venues and complementary scenes such as those surrounding the Black Spot/Flat Five, the increasing popularity of rock and roll, and the gradual drifting away of its core members, many of whom had been closely associated with the club since its precursor, the Wailhouse, in 1955. In John Dawe's opinion,

> It wore itself out. When we started out, we were real rank amateurs, that was sure. And seven years later, we, some of us, were starting to play awfully damn good. And a lot of guys who wanted to play jazz also wanted to start getting out and doing studio work and nightclub work ... they wanted the money. They had decided to become professionals, and some of us did not go that way. And so, there was not a lot of guys available to play gigs any more on the weekends. Getting the picture? I mean, when Dale [Hillary] and I went in [to the Cellar] in October [1962], we couldn't find a rhythm section! It was impossible. Everybody was working other gigs. Better-paying gigs elsewhere at downtown clubs. So everybody had ... the musical skills had escalated like crazy, and some of the people around the Cellar were getting offered really good gigs in other bands around town. Commercial bands. Commercial gigs. And everybody wanted to make a living, so ... you know, it's pretty simple. The place no longer had a group of musicians there to keep supporting the club. They just played down there, maybe after another gig and play later on. [And] we'd all grown up a bit, in some ways. Everybody was starting to mature a bit and get other ideas.

> P.J. [Perry] was off all the time, he was in and out and back in Toronto, and doing some other gigs. And Ray Sikora was down in LA a lot, and Dick Forrest and those other guys were doing other gigs. I know in 1961 I wasn't available to do a whole lot of gigs, and neither was a whole bunch of us. We landed a steady gig in a big band. And a steady gig was unusual for a fourteen-, fifteen-piece band, and we were working every night until one o'clock. So we weren't available either to go down there and play. We'd go down after the gig was over, maybe. But, you know, professionalism reared its ugly head.[78]

John Dawe recalled being particularly burnt out on the realities of the music business after having worked the summer of 1962 playing in a dance band at the resort town of Sylvan Lake, Alberta:

> When we got back from that summer gig around Labour Day, I had no incentive to play anymore at all, and I hung my horn up and I didn't hang around at the Cellar. I played a gig there in October [1962] with Dale Hillary, and that was the last I ever played there ... One of the main factors, [was that] the main group of players down there started to lose interest in it. The main body of players started to lose interest in the place. After Labour Day [1962], a whole bunch of us just wanted to get the hell out of music.[79]
>
> Dave [Quarin] was trying his best to keep that place open ... but quite a few of us had been on the same gig all summer, June, July, and August, and when we got back into town, most of us were so fed up with the music business or anything to do with it, that when we got back into town in September of 1962, a lot of us didn't even go near the club. We were just fed up, and we went out and started to look for day gigs. It was all over, the fun was over. You know, we'd been working a commercial dance gig all summer and there were hardly any jazz musicians left in town to even play at the place during the time that we were all out of town, and when we came back the place had really disintegrated.

> Looked like it had fallen apart, and none of us seemed to care. We'd lost interest ... By the time I'd been in music for so many years, I found that most of the music that really good players around town were doing didn't interest me in the least. I mean, I didn't want to work at the Cave, or Isy's, and back up a chorus line, or back up a comedian. Or, you know, some really bad acts. Which is what a lot of really good musicians are relegated to doing ... they're making good money at it. But to me, I'd sooner work a day gig then do that.[80]

Dawe dropped out of music shortly thereafter, training as a chef and finding employment in the food services department at Vancouver General Hospital. Not wanting to deal with the intensive practice required to maintain his chops on trumpet, he switched to valve trombone and played around "for a few years here and there, nothing serious."[81]

With some musicians drifting away from the Cellar entirely and others pressed for time due to other commitments, it became hard to find musicians to play at the Cellar, a situation made clear both by Jim Kilburn's repeated appearances through 1962 and 1963, as well as the Cellar's regular use of younger players more closely associated with the Black Spot and Flat Five clubs. At the same time, musicians such as Al Neil, Glenn McDonald, Don Thompson, and P.J. Perry took work at the Flat Five, essentially performing in competition with the offerings at the Cellar. High-profile acts at the Inquisition Coffee House such as Miles Davis, Cannonball Adderley, the Montgomery Brothers, and the Modern Jazz Quartet placed additional pressure on the available audience for jazz on any given weekend in Vancouver, though the economic pressures of such bookings ultimately led to the Inquisition's closure in December 1963.

Others believed the end of the Cellar had more to do with changing musical taste:

> There were a lot of problems, and Elvis Presley had reared his head, and all the people that we'd regarded as our staunch fans at the Cellar all of a sudden departed like rats

off a sinking ship and became rock and roll fans.[82]

It worked for a while, I guess. Then, while I was still working at Western Music and selling records, Elvis Presley came along, and then the Beatles, and I knew right then and there that things were changing, and that ... I didn't know that it would go down so badly as it has, but yeah ... [rock was more popular] and [there was] a new generation of younger people coming up and they were pretty well hypnotized by Elvis Presley ... and then the Beatles and all that stuff ... and then it all turned into a generational thing, more than anything, I think. The same thing happened with us and we did the same thing to the Dixieland players. We had the same kind of thing going on where we started playing swing and, well, bebop later, but we started putting down the figs ... the mouldy figs, and stuff like that. Although ... we learned not to put it down, and even be willing to play it, commercially and wherever. But yeah, when I was in [the] Western Music store I could see that things weren't going very well for the sale of jazz. Jazz records were like special orders at the music store. And classical music was still pretty good, though. They're [classical fans] loyal and true.[83]

No people. Rock and roll. What's his name ... Elvis. The Beatles. There was no money and there was no up-and-coming jazz musicians, really. They were all going with the crowd [toward rock] so ...[84]

I was probably one of the first, in the early 1960s, when I saw things slowing down, to realize that we were coming to an end. I think it was about the era of Coltrane's *A Love Supreme,* or something. A similar era, in any case, to the Rolling Stones and the Beatles coming in, just that history ... you could say that right across the country the jazz, except for some isolated pockets, was finished.[85]

While not the death of jazz in Vancouver, the mid-1960s saw a major reduction in the number of venues that presented jazz on a regular basis and an end to co-operative ventures such as the Cellar

Musicians and Artists Society and the Contemporary Jazz Society that had operated the Black Spot/Flat Five. Though the Flat Five did manage to outlive the Cellar, the Contemporary Jazz Society voted to sell the club in the summer of 1964. The Flat Five then passed to Dave and Karen Parkin, who continued to operate it as a jazz club though with a more conventional business model. In the summer of 1965, the club was sold once again, to Graham and Gloria Humphries, who renamed it the Blue Horn. The venue closed its doors for good at the end of 1965, having succumbed (at least in part) to the widespread cultural shifts of the 1960s that tilted countercultural activity away from jazz and jazz-based expression toward other forms of popular culture.[86]

part three

Other Canadian Scenes

7

Co-ops from Coast to Coast

Edmonton, Calgary, Halifax

> *On Sunday night there was nothing in town. No movies, no places to go, nothing to do. So on Sunday nights we had jam sessions.*
>
> *– Don Palmer*

The conditions that prompted young musicians in Vancouver to organize themselves into what would become the Cellar and the Black Spot/Flat Five were not unique to the Canadian west coast. Inspired by the Cellar, players in Edmonton banded together to form the Yardbird Suite; while some five hundred kilometres to the south, Calgary made room for the Foggy Manor. The latter enjoyed regular support from the musicians who had established the Yardbird and was occasionally visited by Vancouver-based groups, and the development of this grass-roots circuit foreshadowed later developments in domestic jazz touring. Remarkably, on the other side of the country, young players with no connection to what was going on in the western jazz scene responded to a similar dearth of playing opportunities by establishing their own co-operative club at 777 Barrington Street in Halifax, Nova Scotia.

Edmonton: The Yardbird Suite

In March 1957, the Yardbird Suite opened in Edmonton, Alberta. The brainchild of local drummer Terry Hawkeye,[1] the club was

36 Terry Hawkeye | *Photographer unknown; courtesy Edmonton Jazz Society and the Yardbird Suite*

expressly modelled after the Cellar in Vancouver, which Hawkeye had visited some months earlier (see Figure 36). Excited by what he had seen developing there, Hawkeye recruited several other young Edmonton musicians who were interested in jazz, and began to hunt for a suitable location.[2] Pianist Tommy Banks recalled their efforts:

> Well, the driving force person was Terry Hawkeye. All of those people were in the Ron Repka Big Band, except for Neil Gunn. And they were all aspiring musicians. And the idea, the impetus behind the whole idea was Terry Hawkeye, who said, "Let's do this!" and they all jumped in, but it was his ambition to do this, to make the Yardbird Suite. And to call it the Yardbird Suite, and he designed the first logo for the Yardbird Suite. He was an artist, among other things. Not the present logo, but it was on the wall of the original location where there were a lot of distinguished signatures of people that had played there. [Hawkeye] was a blinkers-on, one-single-minded-purpose jazz musician. But he knew that he wanted to make this happen, and just recruited people into doing whatever the hell they had to do. And he also got out the hammer and nails. These guys physically built the place.[3]

37 Inside the Yardbird Suite, ca. 1958. Ray Magus (saxophone), Ken Chaney (piano), and unknown musicians | *Photographer unknown; courtesy Edmonton Jazz Society and the Yardbird Suite*

Aided by saxophonists Ray and Zen Magus, bassists Gary Nelson and Ron Repka, pianist Ken Chaney, and jazz enthusiast Neil Gunn, Hawkeye rented space in the basement of 10444 82 (Whyte) Avenue NW (see Figures 37 and 38). Much like the Cellar, the location was largely free from concerns regarding excess noise. Tommy Banks recalled that the upper floors of the building were occupied by a clothing store, and the club's basement space was shared with the Jacobs Sheen & Morris School of Music:

> Those guys went out and found a little space with a back-alley entrance which they rented and they went out and scrounged chesterfields. They actually built the tables in the club. They went and bought a bunch of plywood and those metal screw-on legs and put them together to make the tables. They built a little stage to put the piano on ... they did it all by themselves.[4]

38 Entrance to the Yardbird Suite, ca. 1957–58 | *Photographer unknown; courtesy Edmonton Jazz Society and the Yardbird Suite*

In the late 1950s, a wide variety of nightclubs and other entertainment venues in Edmonton's bustling city centre hired bands of differing sizes. Though they rarely offered jazz, these establishments nonetheless provided steady employment for many of the city's jazz musicians, most of whom would congregate at the Yardbird Suite after hours.

> Well, Edmonton was going through one of its various booms. Edmonton has had lots of booms and busts, and it was going through one of those, and there were a lot of clubs here, and a lot of music, and they were hiring musicians. They were all very busy ... And [the Yardbird] let all the musicians in Edmonton, of which there were a lot, at that time, know that this was happening, and everybody finished their commercial gigs that they were working to make a living, and converged on the Yardbird Suite on that opening night.[5]

The founding musicians split the rent for the space, though the concept proved so popular that with a modest door charge the after-hours venue quickly became self-sufficient. Like the Cellar, the Yardbird operated as a private members' club that provided membership cards and required a small fee to join, though for quite some time its clientele remained closely linked to the musicians that played there. Unlike the Cellar, the Yardbird did not possess a business licence and did not initially seek to establish itself as a public entertainment venue. The club was open only on Saturday nights and didn't offer a regular program of concert presentations; initially it operated solely as an after-hours location for informal sessions, which musicians like Tommy Banks attended.

> Nobody got paid scale for playing at the Yardbird Suite initially, because it was an after-hours ... it's important to remember what the reason [for the club was]. The reason the place was put together by seven guys, was to have a place to play the music that we wanted to play, that they wanted to play, after they had finished playing the music that they had to play. Until midnight we played the music that we had to play to make a living, you know, commercial music. To play jazz, we needed a place with a piano and that was it. And that could sustain its rent, so that was the whole reason, was having a place to play. So there was nobody ... nobody was ever paid to play at the Saturday night sessions, ever.[6]

Programming did soon expand to include Sunday, which featured more formal presentations by members, and the remainder of the week members were able to use the space to practise and rehearse. During its informal beginnings, the Yardbird employed no advertising, relying instead on direct mailings to its membership and word of mouth among musicians to spread news about what was happening at the space. As the Yardbird matured and began staging more formal concerts, these events were included in the *Edmonton Journal*'s entertainment listings, but the club did not pay for advertisements.

The club was operated by the membership on a volunteer basis, and, as at the Cellar, memberships were broken into two categories – executive members who bore some financial risk and were eligible to use the space throughout the week, and social members who formed the bulk of the audience. Tommy Banks was in the former group:

> It was stupid, but they were called the executive, which meant that you had the privilege of cleaning the toilets when it was your turn, and sweeping out the floors, and getting your girlfriend to run the bar, as it was called, though it served Coke and coffee. Or the door. Those jobs were meted out on a rotation basis. My partner [drummer] Phil Shragge and I became part of what was called, absurdly, the executive, I think maybe less than a year after it opened.[7]

To help defer costs, the Yardbird Suite offered a limited menu of soft drinks and coffee in its original 82 Avenue location, though when the club temporarily relocated to 106 Street in 1959 and took over the premises of what had been the Club Anton, the menu was expanded considerably. In possession of a full kitchen, the Yardbird began to offer sandwiches, burgers, and salads – simple food able to be quickly prepared by a kitchen staff composed of musicians and whatever friends could be persuaded to help out. Word of the Yardbird Suite reached *Coda* magazine, which included a brief mention of the club in the "News and Notes" section in July, 1959:

> "The Yardbird Suite" is a jazz club formed over two years ago by Edmonton musicians desirous of a chance to play jazz. Since January of 1957 the club has been open every Saturday and Sunday evening at their premises located at 10443 82nd Street [sic]. The Saturday sessions, which are of an informal nature, start at midnight and have been known to go on well after dawn has broken. The Sunday show takes the form of a concert. Currently playing there are Tom Banks (pno), Dale Hillary (alto), Phil Shragge (dms). The sessions are further highlighted by the excellent singing of Mark Cohen. Terry Hawkeye and Ken Chaney, now in Toronto, and George Urson (dms), now in Vancouver, were amongst the founding members.[8]

Between 1957 and 1965, the Yardbird was forced to move three times; from its original location on 82 Avenue to 106 Street,[9] back briefly to 82 Avenue, and then to 9801 Jasper Avenue, where it replaced the Steak Loft.[10] Still entirely volunteer-driven, the Yardbird began to open as many as five nights a week to feature local performers and regional Canadian jazz artists such as P.J. Perry, Jerry Fuller, and the nomadic Dale Hillary. In 1961, a band billed as the Vancouver Jazz Quintet, and comprised of several Cellar members, played an engagement at Calgary's Foggy Manor club (discussed below), and it is quite likely that they played the Yardbird Suite in Edmonton as well.[11] Following a brief closure, the Yardbird reopened in 1967 in a converted garage at 10122 81 Avenue NW near the corner of 102 Street, and in this location the club began to expand its offerings to include poetry and theatrical presentations, and occasionally showcase American guest artists.[12]

> The club began to expand the presentation of things, including very serious concerts and they of course were paid, and everyone was paid quite well for playing there. But never at the Saturday-night sessions ... The union here understood what the place was, and said that it was none of their business. They weren't interested in it ... until the Yardbird started presenting concerts. That was a different story, and when they did that ... first of all the initial sessions were only on Saturday. And then Friday and Saturday nights, and then they started a Sunday concert series. And then they started doing concerts of chamber music, and classical guitar music, and plays, and poetry readings and all of this stuff, as well as jazz, on other days of the week. Wherever there was a formal presentation of something, those people were all paid.[13]

This incarnation of the Yardbird Suite hosted such notables as Zoot Sims and Phil Woods before closing its doors in 1967. Although this marked the end of the club as a co-operative venture operated by like-minded jazz musicians, the Yardbird Suite was revived in spirit in 1973 by the newly reformed Edmonton Jazz Society, which presented concerts at a variety of locations, before it found a permanent home in 1984 at the Malone Warehouse (11 Tommy Banks Way). Celebrating its sixtieth anniversary in 2017, the Yardbird Suite remains a vital cultural institution, and is the only volunteer-run, not-for-profit jazz club in Canada. The club is a vital part of the Edmonton jazz scene and, through its support of domestic touring activity, has positioned itself as an important site of linkage for the national scene.

Calgary: The Foggy Manor Club

Though comparatively little historical detail is available on Calgary's Foggy Manor Club, it appears that sometime in the fall of 1957 a Calgary jazz co-operative was organized,[14] likely inspired by similar activities in Vancouver (1956) and Edmonton (1957). In 1959, *Coda* included a brief mention of the Calgary club in a notice about the upcoming Banff Jazz Festival: "Calgary Musicians have got together and formed a club similar to the Minc and the Yardbird Suite. Called the Foggy Manor Jazz Society they meet at 210A 8th Ave. S.E., Calgary, but we have no further details at time of going to press."[15] Apparently named for the clouds of cigarette smoke that would accumulate in the unventilated room, the Foggy Manor occupied the basement of a building that may originally have housed the Utopia Club, a meeting place for black railway workers in Calgary.[16] Operated by a not-for-profit jazz society that went by the same name, the Foggy Manor operated much like the Black Spot, Cellar, and Yardbird Suite, as a private members' club open only to those in possession of a membership card, along with a limited number of guests. Unlike the Cellar and the Yardbird, the Foggy Manor admitted musicians free of charge, perhaps as a way to encourage as many players as possible to attend the late-night sessions given the somewhat limited musician pool.[17]

Drawing on a mix of older, established players from the city's dance and local military bands, as well as younger, less competent players motivated by an interest in bebop, the Foggy Manor Club was nearly an overnight sensation when it opened in 1957.[18] Bassist Ray Mah recalled, "We were playing once a week in a militia band at Mewata Armouries ... after the practice, every week four or five of us would talk for hours about this new jazz and finding a place to play it."[19]

The Foggy Manor's core group appears to have consisted of pianist Pete Martlinger, bassist Ray Mah, trumpeter Follie Foss, drummer Shelly Gjertsen, and jazz enthusiast Morris "Moe" Levinson. Martlinger, Mah, and Gjertsen seem to have acted as the house band much of the time, though little else is known about these players. Though the club relied almost exclusively on this small core of local Calgary musicians, Dale Hillary, Terry Hawkeye, and Tommy Banks made frequent, though irregular, appearances from Edmonton, with ex-Calgarian Banks leading and writing arrangements for the Knights of the Manor, the club's resident big band.[20] In 1958, the Foggy Manor relocated from its original basement space to another, slightly larger one further along the same street. In November 1960, E. "Red" Ockwell, who edited the Foggy Manor Club's newsletter, wrote to *Coda* that in Calgary,

> The jazz scene is centred around the Foggy Manor Jazz Society – an after-hours spot. Foggy has a varied history – which is probably duplicate of most jazz clubs on the American continent. Most of them have solved their problems – Foggy has yet to find a format which is satisfactory to musicians and public alike. Starting out in a hole as a musicians after-hours club – was a small success practically overnight. Musicians who hadn't seen each other for years suddenly found themselves shoulder to shoulder – playing – talking – or sharing a jug. Concerts were organized – arrangers and little and big bands sprung up like jackrabbits for concerts – but after 3 years, the enthusiasm has gone. Maybe everyone has heard everybody else – maybe there's no sparkplug to lead the way – whatever it is that's needed, it had better come along soon.[21]

The club did manage to continue operating, and in 1961 welcomed the Vancouver Jazz Quintet, featuring several players from the Cellar:

> This past weekend, Foggy Manor Jazz Society spotlighted the Vancouver Jazz Quintet. This group is about the most exciting I have heard here in a very long time, with the

> possible exception of Elmer Gill's own group that was here about 2 summers ago. The VJQ is comprised of five people who are young in age, but a lot older in their attitude and approach to music. The group plays all the modern hard jazz sounds, but, though they copy the themes, there is individuality in all the choruses ... Trumpet, baritone, piano, bass, and drums all seem to feel each other and work together to the same end ... and they all appear to have a ball while playing. This is particularly obvious between the bass player and the drummer.[22]

However, that year *Coda* also reported a change in management as well as plans to expand the club's programming to include folk singers, indications that the club was having a hard time financially. Though few details are available, the club appears to have closed for good in late 1962 only to be reopened by John Uren as the Depression Coffee House in September 1963.[23]

Halifax: Jazz Unlimited

While the Black Spot/Flat Five in Vancouver, Yardbird Suite in Edmonton, and Foggy Manor in Calgary were all influenced by the pioneering efforts of the Cellar Musicians and Artists Society in establishing their co-operative jazz spaces, in Halifax a group of young musicians embarked in isolation on a similar project in 1957. The postwar years had seen the formation of numerous military bands in Canada, three of which – the Black Watch, Stadacona, and Royal Canadian Artillery – were stationed in Halifax and became a breeding ground for young musical talent in the area. These young players received steady pay, exceptional musical training, time to practise, and access to like-minded peers. Saxophonist Don Palmer was among them:

> They'd only actually started having army bands about ten years earlier. Post–World War Two. So what they did was they went to Europe and hired all these experienced musicians, many of whom were in their forties. They told them to come to Canada, get paid, get a pension, become a citizen ...

> all this stuff ... these guys were good musicians. In a fifty-five-piece band there were twenty-eight Dutchmen, and there were only eight Canadians in the band. And they had to get some more Canadians ... Warren Chiasson was one of them. So they gave me an interview with Ken Elloway, the conductor of the Royal Canadian Artillery band, and he said that they would take me. It was sort of like getting a gig with Duke Ellington or something, in comparison to the level that I was at. It was crazy. The next thing I know I'm in the band. And there was a guy named John Schalkwijk, an older Dutch guy who was playing third clarinet, and his job was to teach me. I was not allowed to play a note in rehearsal for two weeks. I had to sit there and watch the music and watch John play it. I was not allowed to make one noise for two weeks, and then I was allowed to work on little parts, and I'd play these four bars and then lay out, and then these four bars ...[24]

While many of the older musicians considered the military bands their career choice, several of the younger players inducted in the 1950s harboured ambitions of playing jazz. These included Warren Chiasson (vibes), George Carroll (drums), Dick Crowe (piano), Bob Mercer (guitar), Ron "Moose" Maas (saxophone), Cy True (saxophone), Don Palmer (saxophone), Frank Ridgeway (trumpet), and Keith Jollimore (saxophone), who were employed in Halifax's various military bands. In addition, young players outside the military such as Ernie Fong (piano), Stan Perry (drums), David Caldwell (saxophone), Charles Frederick Pearson "Skip" Beckwith (bass), Don Vickery (drums), Glenn Sarty (piano), and vocalist Pat LaCroix were actively seeking an outlet for their developing interest in jazz.

Halifax was a relatively small urban centre with a limited selection of musical venues, and younger players often found themselves unable to find work in the city's few dance bands and jazz orchestras, where positions had long been held by more established local players.[25] Seeking places to play, this group of young jazz musicians initially performed at fraternity house parties at nearby Dalhousie University, or made the hour and a half drive out of town to the Shore Club in Hubbards to host jam sessions. The risks and time involved in such a lengthy drive at night on winter roads prompted the group to try renting space at a local hotel, but the predictable issues with noise soon rendered that idea unfeasible. Sometime in 1957, a core group of these young players met at the Nova Scotian Hotel adjacent to Halifax's CN railway station for what would turn out to be the inaugural meeting of the Halifax Jazz Society.[26] Joined by supporters Don Warner (leader of the area's most famous dance band), and Ron Roberts (local radio disc jockey), the group decided to search for a space in which to operate a club centred on their musical activities.

They soon located space in the basement of 777 Barrington Street, once the parish hall for nearby St. Patrick's Church. Located near Cornwallis Street in the city's north end, the space was conveniently situated between the Halifax Armoury and the Stadacona naval base. During World War Two, the building had housed a dancehall known as the Silver Slipper, a venue so famous for the servicemen's fights that occurred there that it was known colloquially as the "bucket of blood."[27] Though the basement jazz room would enjoy a more genteel tenure, this older nickname was still often used. Known officially as Jazz Unlimited, the venue was popularly referred to by its address, which is how it is perhaps best known, though local newspaper reports referred to the space variously as 777 Barrington Street, Jazz Unlimited, and the Jazz Room. Membership cards for the space bore the name the Jazz Room, though none of the participants interviewed ever used this name (see Figure 39).

The club operated on a co-operative basis, much like the Cellar and the Yardbird Suite, with the musicians themselves chipping in to construct the bandstand, tables, chairs, sound system, and other necessary fixtures. Pianist, photographer, and artist Ernie Fong was one of the members chiefly responsible for these renovations, and also provided the Jazz Unlimited stage poster (see Figure 40). Drummer Stan Perry credited his efforts in getting the club together:

> Ernie Fong did the heavy lifting. He was a jack of all trades, and he played a bit of trumpet and a bit of piano and a bit of drums, and this, that, and the other thing. But we were all looking for a place to play, and Ernie had the connections ...

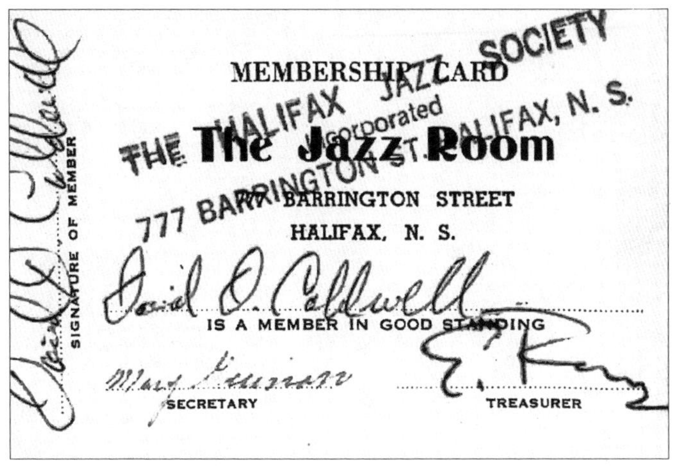
MEMBERSHIP CARD

THE HALIFAX JAZZ SOCIETY

Incorporated

777 BARRINGTON ST. HALIFAX, N. S.

The Jazz Room

777 BARRINGTON STREET

HALIFAX, N. S.

SIGNATURE OF MEMBER

IS A MEMBER IN GOOD STANDING

SECRETARY

TREASURER

39 Membership card for the Halifax Jazz Society, aka the Jazz Room, aka 777 Barrington Street | *Courtesy Dave Caldwell*

> I shouldn't say connections but, I guess, the business sense to ... he rented the place, and he got it for us. As I recall. Remember, it's a long time ago, so sometimes my memory is a bit sketchy. But he basically was the mover for us. The rest of us did a little bit of painting and moving furniture and stuff like that.[28]

Jazz enthusiast Buddy Burke was brought on as the club's de facto manager, and soon moved into an apartment upstairs. Burke was responsible for ensuring that the rent was paid, the venue was cleaned, and the musicians could gain access to the space when needed. Though the venue was open to the public only on Sunday nights, it was available to the membership during the rest of the week for informal rehearsals and sessions.

The club opened on Sundays rather than Saturdays because the Lord's Day Act in Nova Scotia greatly limited the types of businesses permitted to remain open on Sunday. As a not-for-profit private members' club that skirted the provisions of the law, 777 Barrington Street was essentially the only option for those seeking Sunday-evening entertainment. Saxophonist Don Palmer described the offerings:

40 Interior of 777 Barrington Street, aka Jazz Unlimited, ca. 1957. Note the Jazz Unlimited poster behind the bass player, as well as the homemade cardboard music stands. [*L-R*] Ernie Fong (piano), Jean (last name unknown, on saxophone), Roy Eastman (bass), Don Palmer (flute), Don Vickery (drums), Cy True (alto saxophone), and Bob Mercer (guitar). | *Photographer unknown; courtesy Don Vickery*

> On Sunday night there was nothing in town. No movies, no places to go, nothing to do. So on Sunday nights we had jam sessions. They were somewhat organized. You know, we'd present a trio, quintet, big band, and guys would work on things to play and we'd charge seventy-five cents to get in. And that's how we paid the rent.[29]

The club became popular as word of its existence spread, and those musicians not playing on a given Sunday evening would be tasked with taking the cover charge and selling potato chips and bottled soda, much of which was used as mixer for the alcohol smuggled in by patrons. These revenue streams enabled the club to remain in operation, and the venue provided an opportunity for the musicians to play for an audience. As the crowds got larger, the club could sometimes pay the bands as well as cover operating expenses from the proceeds brought in at the door. Vibraphonist and bandleader Warren Chiasson recalled how the scene came together:

> There were a lot of jam sessions, and advertising people were pitching in to make up posters for the club, and word was really getting around. We took some money at the door, and found some way to pay [for things]. I guess Buddy Burke took care of that. I remember long phalanxes of tenor players lining up to take a chorus. That was kind of fun.
>
> Halifax was really happening, and people were really into the music. Because we had our records, and our records were giving us a lot of information. There were three bands, there was the Navy band, the Black Watch band, and the Royal Canadian Artillery band, which I was a part of. Now the Navy band had done trips right around and into the States, and stopped at a lot of ports in the LA area at the time when a lot of west coast jazz was being played. Shelly Manne, Bud Shank, Chet Baker, Art Pepper ... and the drummer, George Carroll, had sat in with a lot of these people. So he had the ego that provided him with a germinating influence on the rhythm section. So all these nice forces were happening. You know, I'd done my studying a lot, and I was bringing something new to it. The rhythm section ... Roy Eastman was playing terrific bass, and everybody was pitching in. It was a great time.[30]

Though the vast majority of the groups that played 777 Barrington Street consisted of local musicians, visiting jazz artists who played Halifax's larger venues would at times make their way down to the jazz club for informal sessions. Perhaps most famously, in 1958 Lionel Hampton made a guest appearance at 777 Barrington Street along with pianist Oscar Dennard, playing into the early-morning hours with guitarist Bob Mercer, bassist Roy Eastman, and drummer George Carroll.[31] Charles "Buddy" Burke also recalled this visit:

> It was a good time ... and we had lots of guys coming in ... Lionel Hampton. The [Hampton] band played all night and we put them on the bus in the morning. Lots of all-night sessions, and you never knew if someone was going to show up, or what ... It was a good ride. And it was all free. It wasn't money, money, money, it was just a free ride. Everyone was pleased just to have a place to jam.[32]

In addition to the odd visiting American star who dropped in after playing the Halifax Forum, aspiring jazz artists from around the Maritimes would make the trek to 777 Barrington Street both to listen and to play. As one of the more popular spots in Halifax, the club drew young artists from outside the jazz scene as well, including aspiring singer-songwriter Denny Doherty, who was a regular fixture at the club before forming the Colonials with Pat LaCroix. After landing a recording contract with Columbia records, the acoustic folk group changed their name to the Halifax Three, and enjoyed brief success before their dissolution led Doherty to a connection with Cass Elliot, and ultimately to the formation of the Mamas and the Papas in 1965.

Owing largely to the experience and confidence gained through their association with 777 Barrington Street, 1958–60 saw a minor exodus of the club's core players as they sought to expand their jazz ambitions beyond the limited opportunities in Halifax. In 1958, multi-instrumentalist Warren Chiasson (piano, vibraphone, trombone) lucked into an audition for George Shearing while on leave in New York City, landing the position of vibraphonist in Shearing's quintet. Chiasson originally had an appointment to audition some compositions for Shearing's publisher, but when he asked if he could play them on a vibraphone that was in the room rather than on the piano, the publisher quickly exited the room and returned with Shearing, whose vibraphonist had just left the band. Chiasson auditioned on the spot, playing through several Shearing charts, and was hired. Though still in the army, Chiasson was able to secure an early release on compassionate grounds. It probably helped his cause that a friend of the Royal Canadian Artillery band director was simultaneously seeking admission to the band on trombone, the position occupied by Chiasson.[33] In July 1959, Chiasson joined the Shearing band at the Newport Jazz Festival, the first engagement in an association that would last some three years.[34]

In the spring of 1958, David Caldwell began studying at the Berklee School of Music, and was joined there that fall by bassist Skip Beckwith; they may have been the first Canadian players to attend the prestigious program, still in its infancy. While Beckwith had the financial resources to complete his studies in two years (four consecutive semesters), Caldwell had to return to Halifax at the end of 1959 to earn more money, returning to Berklee in September 1961 and graduating in spring 1962. Beckwith, who returned to Halifax during semester breaks, brought a small ensemble of Berklee students including Gary McFarland (vibraphone), Tommy Check (drums), and Jack Stevens (saxophone) to play 777 Barrington Street at the end of 1960. The following spring, Beckwith returned with Berklee's "A" big band led by Al Ware, which performed at 777 Barrington Street in addition to a number of performances for the local CBC, the fees from which helped to fund their trip.[35]

Buoyed by Warren Chiasson's success, in the fall of 1959 saxophonist Don Palmer left Halifax for New York City, where between 1959 and 1964 he studied jazz and improvisation with Lee Konitz and Lennie Tristano. The skills Palmer had developed playing with the Royal Canadian Artillery band helped him enormously in New York, where his ability to sight-read earned him a reputation as a reliable and capable replacement player. Perhaps best known for his work with Latin bands, Palmer played with the Machito Orchestra in 1967–69, the Tito Puente Orchestra in 1969–72, and regularly subbed for alto players Jerry Dodgion and Eddie Xiques in the Thad Jones/Mel Lewis Orchestra from 1973 to 1975.[36]

Inspired by the earlier success of David Caldwell and Skip Beckwith, bassist Athan Katsos also studied at Berklee (1961–63) before moving to Toronto in 1966 to pursue a successful career as a producer and director with the CBC. Following an unsatisfactory tenure at Dalhousie University, drummer Stan Perry struck out in 1959 for British Columbia, where he would become a contributing member of Vancouver's Cellar co-operative. Drummer Don Vickery also left Halifax in 1959, arriving in Toronto where he would attend Oscar Peterson's Advanced School of Contemporary Music.[37]

Despite the departure of several key members of the co-operative to pursue musical opportunities elsewhere, the 777 Barrington Street club continued on for several years. In 1961, however, it was forced to relocate several blocks south to 599 Barrington Street, and in late 1962 the club closed. What is perhaps remarkable about 777 Barrington Street is that it managed to perform a very similar role to that of the Cellar in Vancouver and the Yardbird Suite in Edmonton, clubs that benefited from the knowledge of one another's existence and the casual mixing of players from one scene to the other. Halifax, isolated on Canada's east coast and quite far from any major urban centre, lacked such resources. Indeed, despite the striking similarity in their organization and operational time frame, the western clubs and their eastern counterpart remained ignorant of each other. As Vancouver-based bassist and composer Paul Ruhland put it, "You had to be there," because jazz wasn't broadcast nationally.[38] Other Vancouver musicians concurred:

> I don't think we heard of the one in Halifax. Now I'm speaking for myself, obviously. I don't think I'd heard anything of a club in Halifax, although years later I did hear about a district of Halifax called Africa-town? [Africville] But the Yardbird Suite ... I think we knew about that, yeah.[39]

> We heard about the Yardbird Suite, mostly from Dale Hillary, who was a very good saxophone player who came from Edmonton, but I think the Yardbird opened up about a year after the Cellar. But we certainly heard about it. Probably opened sometime in 1957 ... [but we had never heard of 777].[40]

While Stan Perry no doubt commented on the similarity of the Cellar to the club he had left in Halifax, without national radio broadcasting or a domestic recording industry interested in disseminating Canadian jazz, musicians across Canada remained largely ignorant of each other outside of the few groups (such as the bands of Dave Robbins and Phil Nimmons) able to secure national broadcasts from Vancouver, Montreal, or Toronto. For those working in smaller centres or in more marginal forms of music, there were few ways to make lasting musical connections outside of one's geographical region.

Montreal and Toronto

Montreal and Toronto presented entirely different musical realities from smaller centres such as Halifax, Edmonton, Calgary, and even Vancouver. While jazz musicians in these cities were not necessarily getting rich from the performance of jazz and dedicated jazz clubs did not always exist in large numbers, there was, generally speaking, enough jazz-related musical activity to forestall the need for artist-run co-operative jazz spaces. In other words, there were enough venues in both Montreal and Toronto to provide playing opportunities for up-and-coming musicians as well as more lucrative work for established players in the larger clubs.

In 1952, pianists Paul Bley and Keith White, along with several other Montreal-based musicians, founded the Jazz Workshop,[41] which though initially a co-operative endeavour, differed from the organizations discussed so far in a few key ways. Membership in the Jazz Workshop was restricted solely to musicians, and its resources were offered in a more private capacity than was the case at the Cellar, Black Spot/Flat Five, Yardbird Suite, Foggy Manor, or 777 Barrington Street clubs. The Jazz Workshop was not a response to any lack of performance space for the musicians involved, most of whom were playing on the Montreal scene, but was instead conceived as a supplement to their performance activities. Indeed, in order to raise the funds necessary to rent a dedicated space for the Jazz Workshop, the musicians involved played concerts at Montreal club Chez Paree, and allocated the door fee to the Jazz Workshop rather than paying themselves.[42] Pianist Keith White recalled,

> The Chez Paree would open at one p.m. on any Saturday agreeable to both the Jazz Workshop and them and they would provide all of the necessary services such as the stage, lighting, drinks, etc. and would keep all proceeds from whatever they sold in the club. We would be allowed to charge whatever entrance fee we wished and we could keep all proceeds from this.[43]

In the other cities we have examined, the co-operative jazz spaces that emerged were required to provide the performance opportunities that already existed in Montreal at venues such as the Chez Paree, Café St. Michel, Rockhead's Paradise, Black Bottom, Algiers, Little Vienna, and others.[44] In contrast, the Jazz Workshop, which rented space above the Video Café in September 1952, was intended as a private space where musicians could practice, socialize, and learn from one another in addition to their professional activities. The Workshop also sought to import American jazz artists to Montreal to engage in private jam sessions with Workshop members, and to perform concerts with local musicians.[45] Montreal's Jazz Workshop was thus primarily an exercise in pedagogy rather than the type of do-it-yourself performance opportunity represented by co-operative jazz spaces in Canada's smaller cities.

Toward the end of the Workshop's existence, control had shifted almost entirely into Paul Bley's hands and it was no longer operating as a co-operative venture. Indeed, the actions of Bley at times served to exclude dues-paying members of the Workshop, or at least, offered them no advantage over the general public. Without consulting the membership, Bley contracted Sonny Rollins to perform at the Jazz Workshop in February 1953, an engagement that, although initially met with excitement by the membership, quickly turned sour. Keith White recalled, "The Jazz Workshop members that came to hear Rollins, however, were in for a big surprise. They were asked to pay admission. This was bad enough, but to add insult to injury, Paul was asking them to pay full price without a discount!"[46] Meanwhile, the co-operatively led Jazz Workshop big band, which had been conceived as a vehicle for members to practice composition and arranging, shifted into the hands of Workshop member Steve Garrick and became the more conventional Steve Garrick Big Band.[47] The last concert presented under the Jazz Workshop's auspices occurred in June 1953, and the entire experiment seems to have ended by late 1953 or early 1954.[48]

In Toronto, the Musicians Incorporated Club (MINC) came closer to mirroring the Cellar, Black Spot/Flat Five, Yardbird Suite, and 777 Barrington Street, but also differed from those clubs in several key ways. Formed in April 1959, the MINC occupied space at 282 Parliament Street in Toronto's east end and included as initial members such musicians as guitarist Sonny Greenwich, pianists Connie Maynard and Robert Johnson, trumpeters Art Williams and Rod McTaggart, drummers Larry McDonald, Billy McCant, and Terry Hawkeye, and saxophonists Bill Holmes and Moe Pryor (Prieyr), among others.[49] Terry Hawkeye and Bill Holmes were of course already familiar with the concept of musician-controlled performance spaces from their experiences in Edmonton and Vancouver, and one wonders how much influence they may have had in the formation of the MINC, in particular Hawkeye, who had been a key factor in the establishment of the Yardbird Suite only three years earlier. Based in *Coda*'s hometown of Toronto, the MINC did not have to wait long to find coverage in that publication.

> MINC stands for Musicians Incorporated, a group of thirteen young cats who formed a business venture because they had "no place to play and practice – and to play jazz, you have to blow it." The premises at 282 Parliament Street are open for sessions on Thursday, Friday, Saturday after midnight. Sunday from 10:00 pm–2:00 am.[50]

Much like other co-operative clubs, the MINC did not hold a liquor licence, and required the possession of a membership for entry. Andrew Scott reports that MINC memberships were five dollars, which in 1959 was not an insignificant amount and would surely have dissuaded casual jazz fans from attending the club's late-night sessions. Predominantly though not exclusively a club run by and for Toronto's black jazz community, the MINC occupied slightly different territory than the other co-operative clubs examined thus far. With limited exception, MINC members were reasonably experienced musicians with a list of professional engagements and, in some cases, even recordings to their credit.[51] As well, Toronto provided ample opportunity to hear and to play jazz at such venues as the Colonial Tavern, the Town Tavern, the House of Hambourg, and George's Spaghetti House. While the Town Tavern and the Colonial tended to feature American artists and the most experienced Canadian groups available, George's drew primarily from the local studio scene (e.g., the CBC), and the House of Hambourg and a variety of other coffee houses and informal spaces provided younger players the space and opportunity to hone their craft. John Dawe, who spent nearly a year in Toronto just before the opening of the Cellar in Vancouver, recalled:

> In the early 1950s, Toronto was just out of sight. It was just ... everything was cooking there. You know, there was a circuit there, that all the guys from New York played. Montreal, Toronto, Buffalo, Detroit – that kind of circle that went around. They had all of those big cities, in sort of the same area, you know, that they could drive to, within a day to each city and they had all these incredible bands come through ... one of the places that really knocked me out was a place called the House of Hambourg ... Bill Boyle and I noticed all these little side clubs that were off the beaten track, where all the young guys were playing. The guys that weren't in the studio scene and who all played jazz. And they were playing in these funny old converted houses where people were turning their basements into clubs.[52]

The MINC, then, was not a response to any lack of venues in Toronto that welcomed jazz and jazz expression, nor to a shortage of places where young musicians could learn their craft, but rather to the professional difficulties faced by newly arrived players in the city. Due to the insular nature of the Toronto studio scene and the strength of the Toronto chapter of the American Federation of Musicians, those newly arrived had particular difficulty finding steady, well-paying employment because the union limited access for those transferring into the Toronto local. American musicians at times faced further complications with the union, and those who failed to secure the documentation necessary to work in Canada also found themselves at odds with the immigration service.[53] The MINC provided a space for these players.

Additional barriers were experienced by black musicians, who were often excluded from lucrative studio work and employment at the main downtown nightclubs.[54] Most working black musicians in Toronto were unable to support themselves by playing jazz exclusively, and took work in rhythm-and-blues and dance bands to make ends meet. Guitarist Sonny Greenwich, for example, a regular at the MINC, was hindered both by his inability to read music and by his early adoption of avant-garde developments in jazz that were still several steps ahead of the musical offerings at Toronto's mainstream clubs. The MINC thus also served as a place for players who wished to work together on jazz performance and experimentation following their paying jobs.

It should be noted that Toronto was a notoriously difficult city for a musician to break into, regardless of race. In order to protect the interests of those musicians already active in the local chapter, the American Federation of Musicians required that all musicians transferring into a new local had to wait six months before they could accept regular employment. The Toronto chapter of the AFM was particularly strong during the 1950s and 1960s, and such rules were regularly enforced. While enduring this waiting period, a musician could accept "casual" engagements of a night's duration, but it was often quite difficult to piece together enough one-nighters to make ends meet. Halifax guitarist Bob Mercer recalled that upon being discharged from the Stadacona navy band and moving to Toronto in 1961, the strength of the union prevented him from finding any steady employment in town. He was forced instead to take employment in touring bands, working his way through Ontario and the United States.[55] A skilled sight-reader and session player, Mercer enjoyed a lucrative career in Las Vegas, Atlantic City, and for American television, yet he found the Toronto scene unforgiving as a young musician. In Toronto, there were too many skilled players vying for the necessarily limited number of well-paying engagements.

In any case, the MINC as a co-operative or communal endeavour was short-lived, opening in April 1959 and closing by the end of November 1959. In its wake, venues such as the First Floor Club appeared,[56] and the MINC itself was re-established on Yonge Street early in 1960, though this incarnation of the space operated on a more conventional business model along with an expanded music policy that ended the club's days as a purely after-hours venue.[57]

Conclusion

> *The Cellar, it was like going to school. Everybody knew everybody, everybody had something to offer, something to give, something to help. There will never, in my opinion, be another place like the Cellar. Never.*
>
> – *Chuck Logan*

The co-operative jazz spaces established in Vancouver, Edmonton, Calgary, and Halifax during the mid-1950s began with rather modest ambitions – simply to provide a place for aspiring young jazz musicians to play and learn. Nonetheless, the scenes that arose from that very basic musical desire evolved into complex, multilayered sites of artistic intersection, which in no small way laid the groundwork for the development of jazz in Canada as a domestic cultural interest. Profoundly effective on a local level in the cities in which they existed, these clubs and the communities that grew around them represent, in many ways, the origin story for current jazz practices in Canada. Though these scenes were the by-product of a particular historical moment and eventually succumbed to the ascendency of new modes of popular culture, these clubs and musicians helped to order and organize aspects of affinity for modern jazz in postwar Canada – to create the "grooves" to which Canadian jazz practices became fixed.[1]

The Cellar, Black Spot/Flat Five (Vancouver), Foggy Manor (Calgary), Yardbird Suite (Edmonton), and 777 Barrington Street (Halifax) were not born out of financial ambition, but out of necessity.

For those who wanted to play jazz, it was not a matter of seizing opportunities presented by the scene, but of creating the scene itself. Drummer Chuck Logan summed up the situation:

> The Cellar itself was ... I always call it the school of music ... It was the only place ... where young musicians trying to figure out who they are or what they are or what they wanted to play and where they wanted to go with it – it was an outlet for them ... And like I said, it was, in my estimation, one of the prettiest, most gorgeous, musical outlets I have ever come across.[2]

These co-operative jazz spaces often served as de facto clubhouses for those involved not only with jazz performance, but with literature, painting, dance, theatre, and film – all arts that reflected the widespread socio-cultural upheaval that marked North America's entrance to the 1960s. Filmmaker and drummer Don Cumming recalled a time of profound change:

> It was very important. We were all being quite creative ... this was all new to us in some ways. Like Ornette Coleman ... That was the big changeover, you know. From the 1950s into the 1960s, that changeover was quite ... I mean, that opened up a lot of consciousnesses. People [were] finding out their own potential.[3]

Though this intersection of art scenes is perhaps best exemplified by the activities at the Cellar in Vancouver, the Black Spot/Flat Five provided an alternate outlet for visual arts and theatre in Vancouver, the Yardbird Suite in Edmonton hosted theatrical presentations from time to time, the Foggy Manor in Calgary was home to a comprehensive lending library of beat literature, and the community surrounding the 777 Barrington Street club in Halifax provided a musical grounding for a variety of artists, including folk-rock icon Denny Doherty. In Vancouver, this multi-scenic activity was formalized as the Cellar Musicians and Artists Society and expressed through the Cellar's active support of poetry, painting, and theatre. Through these activities, the Cellar came to serve as a congregational space for those involved with the counterculture in Vancouver across a wide spectrum of expression.

The vastness of Canada and the relative isolation of its population centres have often posed challenges for the development and dissemination of jazz, but such conditions have also arguably fostered a certain self-reliance and vibrancy in its local music communities. The activities of the co-operative jazz clubs detailed here enabled musicians living outside the major population centres of Montreal and Toronto to pursue music as an integral component of their lives. John LeMarquand and Terry Clarke found that opportunity at the Black Spot:

> I was thinking back on our reunion, and how this club affected the lives of so many people, quite profoundly. Claire Lawrence, a fabulous saxophone player, flute player, musician, he was a backhoe operator [at the time]. It's like wow, you know? And I ended up getting to play music professionally for a few years, but I was never at the level of those guys. So [music is] something I've done off and on for fifty years, and had I not gone to the Black Spot, it probably never would have happened.[4]

> It was kind of a template for what I think the kids should be doing now. I always refer back to the Black Spot, and the concept of why don't you guys get together and form a club, make it a co-op, set it all up yourselves, get everybody to chip in, get a coffee machine and sell sandwiches and charge five dollars at the door, and it's all ... and the rent is covered, and it's just a place to play.[5]

Through these clubs (at times the only jazz clubs in their host cities) and the intimate, casual contact they enabled, jazz became a shared and immediate experience. Participation in the activity of the scene broke down the division between those on the bandstand and those seated at the nightclub tables – a broadening of the performative relationship to include members of the wider jazz community in a way that was participatory, personal, and quite new.

These scenes created a local network of memory, myth, and identity that tied jazz to their home communities. Taken collectively, they mark an evolution in awareness for both jazz in Canada, and Canadians in jazz (to borrow a phrase from Mark Miller).

However, these scenes were also the by-product of a particular historical moment – the 1950s – that prioritized and normalized jazz and jazz-like sounds in popular culture.[6] As the musical interests of the postwar baby boom generation subsumed those of the postwar counterculture and the beat aesthetic, jazz-based musical expression gave way to other modes of popular culture such as rock and roll. Despite a small but enthusiastic community of listeners, Canada offered few opportunities for career advancement as a jazz musician, as jazz lacked any real involvement with the Canadian entertainment industry beyond a tangential relationship with the CBC.[7]

In Vancouver, the Cellar was in some ways undermined by its own success and the depth of its resonance within the community. With the establishment of the Black Spot/Flat Five and Espresso Coffee House, along with high-profile jazz presentations at venues such as the Inquisition Coffee House, the Cave, and the Queen Elizabeth Theatre, jazz and the audience that supported it were dispersed across multiple competing sites, thereby diluting the energy of the scene that had previously centred on the Cellar. As a result, despite an overall increase in the amount of jazz offered in Vancouver, on a venue-by-venue and concert-by-concert basis, audiences for jazz appeared smaller and provided less reliable economic support.[8] Paradoxically, while this process of expansion ultimately led to a sort of scenic entropy and the eventual dissolution of both the Cellar and Flat Five, it may also have made Vancouver's jazz co-operatives the most widely remembered, as the multiplicity of jazz venues in the city ensured that both the music and the co-operative experience touched the widest cross-section of listeners. As the energy produced by the original scene based out of the Cellar dissipated, jazz practices took root in multiple other locations in the city.

Though none of these co-operative jazz clubs existed beyond 1964 in their original forms, they had a lasting and profound effect on the development of jazz in Canada as a domestic art form and on the construction of a domestic jazz industry composed of a network of jazz societies, commercially sponsored jazz festivals, record labels, and educational initiatives. Though most of the musicians involved with these early co-operative clubs did not achieve any sort of lasting national or international fame, the generation of musicians who emerged from these venues made significant contributions to the development of jazz in Canada across a variety of platforms.

In Vancouver, the Cellar and the Flat Five provided valuable early musical experiences for many local jazz musicians who would go on to nationally significant careers, perhaps most notably drummer Jerry Fuller, saxophonists P.J. Perry and Dale Hillary, pianist, author, and artist Al Neil, as well as drummer Terry Clarke and bassist Don Thompson, both of whom were launched upon the international stage following an engagement with John Handy at the Flat Five in 1964. In Edmonton, the Yardbird Suite provided a home for pianist Tommy Banks and drummer Terry Hawkeye; Banks would be involved with the operation of Calgary's Foggy Manor Jazz Society, and Hawkeye in the organization of Toronto's Musicians Incorporated Club (MINC). Hawkeye and Dale Hillary, through their attendance at the Lenox School of Jazz in 1957, became two of the first Canadian jazz musicians to undergo formal training in the United States. They then shared this experience through their participation in the activities of these co-operative jazz clubs – Hillary in Vancouver and Edmonton, and Hawkeye in Vancouver, Edmonton and at Toronto's MINC. Taken together, these efforts resulted in a newfound and infectious confidence; their experience was proof that Canadian players were able to participate in jazz performance at its highest levels.[9]

> Because here was [Dale Hillary], who had hit it big, sort of ... I don't know if hero's the right word ... I mean the corollary question is, Are people here inspired by P.J. Perry? Well, I guess they are. Sure. You know, [they showed that] you can play and live here comfortably [and] learn to play and [still] play on the world stage.[10]

> I remember when I first saw Terry Hawkeye, it was kind of another sort of legendary, serious guy, and he came in and went up onstage at the Cellar ... and he'd just been in New

> York, and he was the guy ... and this guy was a really good bebop player, and he took the tom-toms off, both the rack tom and floor, and moved them over to the side, so all he had was a snare drum and cymbal. And I said, "Wow, what is this guy going to do? Hey man, look!" It was thrilling, you know? Because bebop ... if you can't play on two drums, a cymbal and a hi-hat, you can't do anything else. So [seeing] that whole concept was pretty mind blowing.[11]

Likewise, the success of Halifax natives Dave Caldwell and Skip Beckwith during the early years of the jazz program at Berklee provided other Maritime musicians with the confidence to pursue similar goals.[12] Warren Chiasson's successful audition for George Shearing and subsequent New York career inspired saxophonist Don Palmer to relocate to New York, where he studied under Lee Konitz and Lennie Tristano. Following a successful fifteen-year career in New York, Palmer returned to the Maritimes, where he became the first artist-in-residence at the College of Cape Breton,[13] helped to found the jazz program at Dalhousie University, co-founded the Halifax-based jazz society JazzEast (parent organization to the Halifax International Jazz Festival), and served as an early teacher and mentor to several notable Canadian jazz figures including saxophonists Mike Murley and Kirk MacDonald. Arguably the most dominant Canadian saxophonists of their generation, Murley and MacDonald have in turn influenced the musical lives of countless Canadian musicians through their own teaching at York University, the University of Toronto, Humber College, and a host of regional and national music camps. Murley credits Palmer with helping him truly understand jazz and improvisation:

> By the time I met Don, I had all the Aebersold-type patterns and things down. I mean, I could play the instrument. What Don had to tell me though was quite a revelation. I could play the instrument quite well, but I didn't really understand the whole thing until he started to explain it to me.[14]

In 1972, when Toronto's York University began Canada's first jazz studies program, it was under the direction of John Gittins and

Robert Witmer, both active participants at the Black Spot and Flat Five clubs in Vancouver.[15]

The 1980s saw the establishment of jazz societies and jazz festivals in Canada from Vancouver to St. John's. Through a combination of corporate sponsorship, volunteerism, and government aid, these festivals created the first viable domestic touring circuit for Canadian jazz artists.[16] Though several Canadian cities had been host both to jazz societies and annual jazz festivals as early as the mid-1950s, most of these had experienced several periods of inactivity over the intervening decades. The 1980s, however, ushered in a resurgence of Canadian jazz societies and major Canadian jazz festivals in what would prove to be a much more stable and long-lasting form. Government funding enabled jazz societies to stage year-round presentations of concerts that featured local, regional, and nationally touring musicians (both established and emerging). Such regular touring activity, itself the product of increased government sponsorship, increased the recognition of Canadian jazz artists outside their home regions, often leading to subsequent performance opportunities, increased CD sales, and teaching appointments.[17]

Though the Toronto and Montreal festivals have long been the largest and most high-profile annual events, in terms of the year-round programming of jazz during the mid-1980s–early 2000s, the jazz societies in the smaller urban centres of Vancouver, Edmonton, and Halifax are perhaps most notable.[18] The year-round programming and volunteer activism of the Coastal Jazz and Blues Society (earlier the Pacific Jazz and Blues Society), the Edmonton Jazz Society (based out of the Yardbird Suite), and JazzEast meant that these cities were lynchpins for national touring activity during this period.[19]

With the advent of funding for recording projects through agencies such as FACTOR and the Canada Council for the Arts (1980s/1990s) and the formation of co-operative jazz labels such as Unity (1988) and Cornerstone (1993),[20] Canadian jazz recordings began to be more widely produced. These efforts, in conjunction with CBC programs such as *Jazz Beat* (1983–2007) and *After Hours* (1993–2007), created a well-connected, informed, and supportive listening audience for Canadian jazz artists both on tour and in their home regions. Indeed, the period from the mid-1980s through the early 2000s may very well have been a "golden era" for jazz in Canada, when a confluence of financial support (both private and public sector) and popular interest created a new and welcome status for jazz and jazz artists in this country.[21]

The case for direct causation between these earlier co-operative jazz clubs and these later developments is impossible to prove. What may be more persuasive is to imagine the current jazz landscape had these early co-operative ventures not existed. Though outstanding talents (such as Don Thompson, who worked professionally at the CBC while still a teenager) would probably still have found careers in music, without the supportive environment that the Cellar provided for the learning and performance of jazz, such careers may well have had a different character. For countless other musicians in Vancouver, Edmonton, Calgary, and Halifax musical career ambitions may have proved impossible, and the development of infrastructure and educational resources for jazz in Canada would have been badly delayed as a result.

We should be careful, however, not to insist that the significance of these co-operative clubs derives from the tangible gains or quantifiable end products with which they can be credited. Rather, these clubs and the musicians who sustained them hold objective value and are of interest in and of themselves. The history of these co-operative ventures provides evidence of organically conceived musical practices, pedagogical methods, and forms of socio-cultural organization that are increasingly rare, and are a seminal part of Canadian jazz discourse.

More than thirty-five years after the closing of the Cellar, drummer Chuck Logan wanted to ensure he closed his interview on the right note:

> I just wanted to say this about the Cellar, the important role of the Cellar and these ... rather rare birds, these co-ops which all emerged at about the same time. They gave an opportunity for the younger musicians, particularly the younger guys who were non-establishment musicians, to

> get out there and play. For themselves. They didn't have to play for a patron, or a sponsor ... they played for themselves. And this is where a lot of talent ... [was given] an opportunity to blossom. I think that's one of [the] – if not its most important – functions of these sort of off-off-Broadway jazz clubs.[22]

Appendix A
Gigography for the Cellar, 1956–63

What follows here is a partial list of the performances that took place at the Cellar between 1956 and 1963. It has been compiled through a combination of information gathered during interviews, in a few cases via performer booking diaries, via *Vancouver Sun* advertisements, and from surviving gig posters. I have done my best to present the information accurately, but I am sure that errors remain and that many performances have been left unrecorded. Information toward a more robust Cellar gigography can be directed to liveatthecellarbook@gmail.com.

1956

Late 1956 or early 1957: Don Cherry's Jazz Messiahs are perhaps the first American group invited to play at the Cellar.

1957

May 17–19: Art Pepper
August: Don Cherry
October: Paul Bley Quartet
November: Ornette Coleman Quartet
December 2: Jazz à la Carte jam session
Dates unknown: Lou Levy, Sonny Red, the Mastersounds, Harold Land

1958

November: Harold Land
Dates unknown: Howard Roberts, Herman Green, Dick Forrest

1959

February 20–22: Kenneth Patchen with the Al Neil Quartet

March 26–29: Jim Kilburn Trio
May 24–28: *Endgame* (theatrical production)
July 24–August 2: Art Pepper Quartet
July 27–30: *The Lesson* (theatrical production)
September 6: Chris Gage Trio
November 9–12: *The Apollo of Bellac* (theatrical production)
Dates unknown: Pete Jolly, Joe Gordon, Carl Fontana

1960

February 14–18: *I Rise in Flame, Cried the Phoenix* (theatrical production) (year is only probable)
April 14: Al Neil, Doreen Williams, Jim Kilburn
April 15–16: Al Neil Quartet with Doreen Williams
April 22–24: Howard Roberts Quartet
April 24–28: *The Wrecker* (theatrical production)
May 22–24: *Krapp's Last Tape* (theatrical production)
June 17–19: Harold Land Quartet with Shorty Rogers
July 16–17: Joe Gordon Quartet
July 8–9: Bill Perkins
August 7–11: *The Tender Edge* (theatrical production)
August 16–21: Barney Kessel
August 30–September 4: Montgomery Brothers (formerly the Mastersounds)
September 16: Bob Winn Quartet
September 30–October 1: Al Neil Quintet
October 28–30: Tony Clitheroe Quartet
November 22–27: Jean Hoffman Trio

1961

January 6–21: Charles Mingus Quartet
January 28–29: Conte Candoli
February 3–4: Ray Sikora
February 10–12: Dale Hillary Quartet
March 17–26: Barney Kessel
March 31–April 16: Montgomery Brothers
May 12: Dick Forrest Sextet
May 19–20: Dale Hillary Quartet
May 20: Chris Gage Trio

June 27–July 9: Ernestine Anderson
August 4: Jim Johnson Quartet
August 18: Paul Perry Jr. Quartet
Summer (dates unknown): poetry readings by bill bissett and Lance Farrell
October 6: Dale Hillary Quartet, featuring Don Thompson
October 13: Mike Taylor Trio

1962

May 5: John Dawe Quintet
May 6: P.J. Perry Quintet
May 19: John Dawe Quintet
June 15–28: Warren Chiasson
June 29: Glenn McDonald Quartet
August 3–30: Closed for remodelling
August 31–September 2: Warren Chiasson Quintet, featuring Ian McDougall
September 14–16: Warren Chiasson
September 22–30: Lee Konitz
October 5–6: Dale Hillary
October 13–14: Dale Hillary
October 19–20: James P. Johnson (unclear who this performer was; it clearly was not the famous stride pianist, who died in 1955)
October 26–27: Dale Hillary
November: Monty Waters Quartet
November 23–25: Jimmy Lovelace Trio

1963

February 9–10: Jim Kilburn Quartet with Barry Dale
March 1–2: Jim Kilburn Quartet with Doreen Williams
March 1–2: *The Red Sock* (theatrical production)
March 8–9: Claire Lawrence Quartet with Barry Dale
March 8–9: *Freddy* (theatrical production)
March 15–16: Barry Dale and the Jimmy Kilburn Quartet
March 15–16: *Freddy* (theatrical production)
March 23–24: Lynne McNeil with Jimmy Kilburn Trio and Barry Dale

April 5–6: *The Zoo Story* (theatrical production)
April 5–6: Jimmy Kilburn Trio with Lynne McNeil
April 13: *The Zoo Story* (theatrical production)
April 13: Glenn McDonald Quartet
April 20: Jim Kilburn and Ralph Dyck
April 21: Ray Sikora Orchestra
April 23–28: Freddie Gambrell Trio
May 4–5: Jim Kilburn Quartet
May 6: Bobby Hales Nonet
May 10–11: Chic Gibson and the Jim Kilburn Quartet
May 17–25: Barney Kessel Trio
June 7–8: Jimmy Lovelace Trio with Monty Waters
June 9: Ray Sikora's Twelve-Piece Orchestra and Jimmy Lovelace Trio
June 25–26: Joyce King with the Mike Taylor Trio
June 25–26: *The Red Sock* (theatrical production)
August 16–17: Freddie Schreiber plays jazz cello with his quartet, featuring Bill Ramsey
August 30–September 1: Glenn McDonald Quartet
September 20–21: Donna Wright with the Don Thompson Trio
November 1–2: Ray Sikora
November 15–16: Clinton Solomon Quartet (last Cellar ad)

Appendix B
Canadian Jazz Sources

Compared to other areas of musicological study, jazz history and research are still remarkably undefined and surprisingly under-represented. Though most colleges and universities now offer a jazz program, the emphasis is still predominately on performance rather than on scholarly research. Researchers concerned with the history, development, and socio-cultural meanings that underlie jazz are frequently left to pursue their work from within three major fields: (1) musicology, which until quite recently was struggling to bend techniques and approaches developed for Western Art Music into something of an awkward fit for jazz topics; (2) ethnomusicology, often mapping those methodologies onto performance practice and personal experience; or (3) non-musical disciplines such as English, History, and Cultural Studies, from which many important considerations concerning gender, race, community construction, and identity have originated. This situation is not new, and the question of where to locate jazz and engage with the study of jazz has long been the subject of some debate.[1]

Given that many major American jazz artists have received scant scholarly attention,[2] it is not surprising that the jazz practices and experiences of players active *outside* the United States have also not been well explored. Recent scholarship has sought to recontextualize jazz as a truly global and transnational music, but much work remains to be done in order to successfully reframe the dominant jazz narrative.[3] The common tendency is, of course, to locate that narrative exclusively within the borders of the United States, rather than situating American jazz practices as only one site of jazz expression, albeit a rightfully privileged one. Despite its origins as an African American cultural practice, jazz was being received, reconceived, and meaningfully expressed in a myriad of local, translocal, and transnational settings from nearly its earliest beginnings. Nonetheless, jazz practices in Canada have usually been considered, when they have been considered at all, to be either derivative of American influence and therefore inauthentic or inferior, or simply not exciting enough to warrant attention given the proximity and overwhelming influence of American jazz musicians. Though several Canadian researchers have done great work in documenting the lives and practices of Canadian jazz musicians, their efforts have also highlighted the problems facing Canadian jazz research.

In 1990, Mark Miller remarked that "in a list of theses and major papers prepared for the graduate program in music at York University, although a half-dozen since 1978 were jazz-related ... none of them had anything to do with Canada."[4] In the mid-2000s, despite a few notable exceptions, jazz in Canada remains largely devoid of scholarly attention, particularly when contrasted with work on jazz in other countries.[5] Exacerbating the issue is the vastness of Canada and the number of functional yet disparate local scenes that result from this geography. While some work has been done on the jazz scenes of Montreal, there has as yet been no comprehensive study of jazz in Toronto,[6] and no significant examination whatsoever of the jazz scenes in Vancouver, Edmonton, and Halifax, each of which supported co-operative performance spaces during the 1950s and 1960s and produced several players of note.

Ambivalence with regard to Canadian jazz practitioners is not a recent development, and the relative dearth of information in historical media sources further hampers historical research into Canadian jazz practices. There is often no way to substantiate or prove claims made by or about Canadian musicians. Discussing the lack of press coverage of the famous 1953 appearance of Charlie Parker, Dizzy Gillespie, Max Roach, Bud Powell, and Charles Mingus at Toronto's Massey Hall, Mark Miller made the point that "if Toronto newspapers showed little interest in the likes of Parker and Gillespie at Massey Hall, it seems unlikely that they would be interested at all in such Canadians as Herbie Spanier and Benny Winestone at the Horseshoe Tavern. In other words, there is little solid documentation of the music made by Canadian musicians."[7] What work that does exist on jazz in Canada, especially jazz by Canadians in Canada, has therefore been the result of a painstaking amount of ethnographic and archival research.

No work that attempts to discuss jazz in Canada can do so without referencing the efforts of Mark Miller. Jazz critic for the *Globe and Mail* from 1978 to 2005, Miller has contributed the most significant body of work on, as he has termed it, "jazz in Canada, and Canadians in jazz."[8] In numerous cases, Miller's work is the only documentation of the lives and careers of Canadian jazz musicians and forms an invaluable resource for anyone approaching a Canadian jazz topic. *Jazz in Canada: Fourteen Lives* (Toronto: University of Toronto Press, 1982), along with *Boogie, Pete, and the Senator: Canadian Musicians in Jazz: The Eighties* (Toronto: Nightwood Editions, 1987) and the encyclopedic *The Miller Companion to Jazz in Canada and Canadians in Jazz* (Toronto: Mercury Press, 2001) were the first, and indeed are still the only major attempts to profile the lives and careers of Canadian jazz musicians from across the country, and *Such Melodious Racket: The Lost History of Jazz in Canada 1914–1949* (Toronto: Nightwood Editions, 1997) is the only work thus far to attempt a comprehensive look at the development of jazz across Canada from its earliest beginnings. It is an astounding work in many ways, combining interviews, census data, and archival research from the Library of Congress, *Chicago Defender,* and newspapers from across the country, and it presents the fullest picture to date of the ways by which jazz entered the Canadian cultural discourse and the means by which it was promulgated. Regrettably, there is as yet no volume that continues this research in a similar vein past 1949.

Similarly, John Gilmore's *Swinging in Paradise: The Story of Jazz in Montreal* (Montreal: Véhicule Press, 1988) is the most comprehensive look at the development and evolution of jazz in a single Canadian city.[9] It is also the only such study to date. Funded in part by a grant from the Canada Council, Gilmore's landmark study of jazz in Montreal comprises two volumes, the narrative *Swinging in Paradise* and the encyclopedic *Who's Who of Jazz in Montréal: Ragtime to 1970* (Montreal: Véhicule Press, 1989). Gilmore, like Miller, notes the dearth of informed writing on jazz in Canada and the need to rely, and perhaps over-rely, upon the recollections of musicians and the news reported in *Coda,* the one reliable and regular source of information on Canadian jazz since 1958. Beyond interviews and archival work, *Swinging in Paradise* is heavily indebted to Jack Litchfield's *Canadian Jazz Discography 1916–1980* (Toronto: University of Toronto Press, 1982), the only comprehensive discography of its kind, and to Miller's *Fourteen Lives.* These works are essential reading, and also demonstrate in part how small and co-dependent the research community is in this area.[10]

Andrew Scott has provided some of the most valuable recent research into Canadian jazz history through his work on guitarist Sonny Greenwich. In the introduction to his as-yet-unpublished PhD dissertation, Scott writes,

> One of the outcomes of my research ... is that I have deduced a core group of musicians who were important on the Toronto jazz scene in terms of how they influenced and nurtured the talents of future generations of Canadian jazz players. By writing them into the history of Canadian jazz, I attempt to give many individuals a historical voice where no voice existed previously.[11]

Scott's work contains exceptional and long-overdue research into the life of one of Canada's most unique musical voices, and also fills in many gaps in the story of jazz in Toronto. His exploration of the Toronto club and studio scenes, the complex racial politics within the jazz community, the living places and playing spaces that supported the city's growing jazz scene, the existence of organizations such as the MINC (Musicians Incorporated Club), and Toronto's role as a hub for arriving and departing musicians from across the country is essential to understanding the nature and evolution of jazz in Canada.

Luckily, Canada had its own domestic jazz periodical for some five decades (1958–2009), and *Coda* magazine provides the longest-running source for news and reviews about Canadian jazz artists. Established by John Norris, *Coda* is the most comprehensive chronicle of the evolution of jazz in this country. However, its reliance upon its readership for contributions of jazz news outside Toronto and Montreal means that, for significant periods, details on jazz activity across much of the country remain obscure. Developments in Vancouver, for example, a city home to the Cellar co-operative, the Vancouver New Jazz Society, the UBC Jazz Society, and CBC's *Hot Air* radio broadcast, were not mentioned in *Coda* until 1959; the rest of the Canadian west (Edmonton, Calgary) not until 1960; and jazz developments on the east coast (Halifax) were not reported on before 1965. Given that the magazine was originally intended to cater to the "traditional jazz enthusiast,"[12] this is perhaps unsurprising and in keeping with the publication's mandate, but it is regrettable from a research perspective. Nonetheless *Coda* remains a vital resource for the study of jazz in Canada, and one hopes that a comprehensive examination of the clues it holds as to the changing place of jazz in this country will someday be forthcoming.

As with *Coda* in its early years, a great deal of research on Canadian jazz topics has come from the jazz community itself, through the work of fans and jazz societies. The most comprehensive community-based jazz resource was undoubtedly the JazzStreet Vancouver project, a website dedicated to the preservation and dissemination of Vancouver's jazz history through photographs, musician biographies, venue descriptions, and most importantly, oral history through interviews conducted for the project and hosted on the website in audio or video format. Sadly, at the time of writing the project is currently offline, with its future, and the future of its gathered resources, unknown.[13] John Dawe, one of the founding members of the Cellar, with the assistance of musician and visual artist Gregg Simpson, is behind an online blog that outlines a brief history of the space and has reconnected past members;[14] and VancouverJazz.com has an online forum that includes an active subforum on local jazz history.[15] The website for Edmonton's Yardbird Suite jazz club does not offer quite the depth or number of resources of the Vancouver pages, but does include a brief history of the club along with some historical photographs. Lastly, Toronto radio station JAZZ.FM91 has established what it calls the Canadian Jazz Archive,[16] consisting of thirty years' worth of the radio station's live concert programming, as well as numerous audio documentaries on significant Canadian jazz musicians. While a wonderful collection of concerts across the decades, the performance archive is only searchable by leader rather than by side personnel, which makes its usefulness limited for research purposes, and it only represents those who were resident in or able to tour to Toronto to perform.

Given recent moves within the field of jazz scholarship toward a reconsideration of the processes of canonization as well as an increasing interest in various local, regional, and national forms of jazz expression, one hopes that a more comprehensive consideration of Canada's rich jazz heritage will soon be available.

Notes

Introduction

1 The co-operative space first known as the Black Spot was renamed, following two changes in location, the Flat Five. Since the core group of musicians remained constant throughout the co-op's various iterations, at times I refer to the two clubs together in order to include both periods and locations.

2 The one major exception is saxophonist and long-time Cellar manager Dave Quarin, who, despite repeated requests, declined to participate in this project.

3 *In Search of Innocence,* directed by Léonard Forest (Montreal: National Film Board of Canada, 1964).

4 See Mark Miller, *Jazz in Canada: Fourteen Lives* (Toronto: University of Toronto Press, 1982), *Boogie, Pete and The Senator: Canadian Musicians in Jazz – The Eighties* (Toronto: Nightwood Editions, 1987); *Cool Blues: Charlie Parker in Canada, 1953* (Toronto: Nightwood Editions, 1989), *Such Melodious Racket: The Lost History of Jazz in Canada* (Toronto: Nightwood Editions, 1997), and *The Miller Companion to Jazz in Canada and Canadians in Jazz* (Toronto: Mercury Press, 2001). See also John Gilmore, *Swinging in Paradise: The Story of Jazz in Montréal* (Montreal: Véhicule Press, 1988), and *Who's Who of Jazz in Montréal: Ragtime to 1970* (Montreal: Véhicule Press, 1989); and Andrew Scott, "The Life, Music, and Improvisation Style of Herbert Lawrence 'Sonny' Greenwich" (PhD diss., York University, Toronto, 2006).

5 At least some of the American musicians also appear to have been in Canada illegally, and were therefore hard-pressed to find other paying work. Several were eventually deported (see Chapter 7).

6 For more on this see Scott, "Herbert Lawrence 'Sonny' Greenwich."

7 Though the MINC is an important and fascinating part of Toronto's musical history, it is unclear whether it operated as a musicians' co-operative in the same manner as the other clubs in this study, wherein the financial risk was assumed and shared by the same musicians who used and played at the club. The MINC, in its original form, was short lived, and its second incarnation in the early 1960s seems, from the

available evidence, to have operated on a much more conventional business model. The MINC has also already been well documented by Andrew Scott in his work on Sonny Greenwich (ibid.). The circumstances in Montreal and Toronto are briefly discussed in Chapter 7.

8 See Sara Cohen, *Rock Culture in Liverpool: Popular Music in the Making* (Oxford: Clarendon Press, 1991); Barry Shank, *Dissonant Identities: The Rock'n'Roll Scene in Austin, Texas* (Hanover, NH: Wesleyan University Press, 1994); and Travis Jackson, *Blowin' the Blues Away: Performance and Meaning on the New York Jazz Scene* (Berkeley: University of California Press, 2012).

9 Exceptions might be made here for some of the Canadian dance bands, such as that of Mart Kenney, who recorded a handful of tunes in Montreal for American label Bluebird in 1941 (Mart Kenney and His Orchestra, Bluebird B-4730, B-11540, B-4731).

10 The Phil Nimmons Group, *The Canadian Scene* (Verve MCV8025, 1957); Phil Nimmons, *Nimmons 'N' Nine* (Verve MGV8376, 1960); The Phil Nimmons Group, *Take Ten* (RCA LCP1066, 1964); The Phil Nimmons Group, *Mary Poppins Swings* (RCA PC1005, 1964); Lance Harrison's Dixieland Band, *The Vancouver Scene* (RCA PC1043, 1965); Fraser MacPherson, *The Shadow* (Pacific North Records, PNR700: records differ on whether the album was released in 1971 or 1973) and *Live at the Planetarium* (West End 101 1976, Concord CJ-92, 1979).

11 Jack Litchfield, *Canadian Jazz Discography, 1916–1980* (Toronto: University of Toronto Press, 1982).

12 Founded by Canadian broadcaster and radio executive Lymon Potts, the Canadian Talent Library (CTL) was created to increase the amount of Canadian programming available for broadcast and was funded initially by the Standard Broadcasting Corporation, which at the time owned CFRB Toronto and CJAD Montreal, with access to several hundred affiliated stations. From around 1966 some CTL recordings were licenced for commercial release by RCA, Sony, Capitol, and others. For more on CTL see Litchfield, *Canadian Jazz Discography;* Alan Guettel, "15 Years and 200 Albums Later," *RPM,* Vol. 25, September 18, 1976; and the Canadian Communications Foundation (http://www.broadcasting-history.ca/canadian-talent-library-canadian-content-struggle-bring-canadian-programming-canadian-radio).

13 These situations offered a finite number of performance opportunities, and during the late 1950s to 1960s were firmly occupied by experienced musicians a generation or so older than those engaged in the activities of the jazz co-ops.

14 Not to be confused with the television program produced by CBC Montreal that bore the same name, Vancouver's *Jazz Workshop* was a jazz radio series produced by George Robertson.

Chapter 1: Are You In or Out?

1 Christopher Small, *Musicking: The Meanings of Performing and Listening* (Hanover, NH: Wesleyan University Press, 1998). Coined by musicologist Christopher Small, "musicking" presents music as a verb – "to music" – rather than as a noun. Small was concerned with stressing that music making is a process rather than (or in addition to) an end product. To music, Small tells us, is "to take part, in any capacity, in a musical performance, whether by performing, by listening, by rehearsing or practicing, by providing material for performance (what is called composing), or by dancing. We might at times even extend its meaning to what the person is doing who takes the tickets at the door or the hefty men who shift the piano and the drums or the roadies who set up the instruments and carry out the sound checks or the cleaners who clean up after everyone else has gone. They, too, are all contributing to the nature of the event that is a musical performance" (9). In presenting music in this way, Small posits that the process of music is essentially dependent upon human relationships, and that it is in the negotiation and performance of these relationships that musical meaning resides, at least in large part.

2 Andy Bennett, ed., *Music Scenes: Local, Translocal and Virtual* (Nashville, TN: Vanderbilt University Press, 2004).

3 Sara Cohen, *Rock Culture in Liverpool: Popular Music in the Making* (Oxford: Clarendon Press, 1991); Barry Shank, *Dissonant Identities: The Rock'n'Roll Scene in Austin, Texas* (Hanover, NH: Wesleyan University Press, 1994).

4 Consider the use of the jazz standard as something of a lingua franca for performance, or generally accepted rules for jam session and performance etiquette, knowledge of which is spread translocally via recordings (repertoire), performance, storytelling, periodicals (e.g., *Downbeat*), and the mythologization of certain performers and events.

5 In recent years, Internet-specific scenes have developed around musical practices that are unique to the digital arena such as the early 2000s phenomenon of the musical mashup, of which Danger Mouse's 2004 *Grey Album* is perhaps the most notorious example. Vaporwave presents a more recent virtual scene and emerged in the 2010s.

6 This information was located in the "News and Notes" section of the magazine, which printed news from jazz scenes around the globe. *Coda* did not use staff writers for this feature, but rather encouraged its readers to write to the magazine about activities in their local areas.

7 Of course, the line dividing musical from non-musical members will differ from scene to scene, and from occasion to occasion within a particular scene.

8 Howard Becker, *Art Worlds* (1982; repr. Berkeley: University of California Press, 2008), especially Chapters 1, 2, and 10.

9 The scenes perspective seems to have found particular resonance with scholars from countries that may feel the need to privilege their perspectives against the weight of American cultural hegemony (e.g., in the UK, Ruth Finnegan and Sara Cohen; in Australia, Andy Bennett; in Canada, Will Straw and Alan Blum).

10 Shank, *Dissonant Identities,* 20–21.

11 Interview with Jamie Reid, August 16, 2013.

12 Interview with bill bissett, January 19, 2013.

13 Interview with Ricci (Quarin) Gotsch, August 29, 2013. She was married to saxophonist, charter member, and eventual club manager Dave Quarin, and frequently worked the door at the club, among other tasks.

14 Interview with John Dawe, November 28, 2012, and January 28, 2012.

15 Will Straw, "Systems of Articulation, Logics of Change: Communities and Scenes in Popular Music," *Cultural Studies* 5, 3 (1991): 368.

16 Ibid., 378.

17 Cohen, *Rock Culture in Liverpool,* Shank, *Dissonant Identities,* Bennett, *Music Scenes,* Aaron Fox, *Real Country: Music and Language in Working-Class Culture* (Durham, NC: Duke University Press, 2004); Ruth H. Finnegan, *The Hidden Musicians: Music-Making in an English Town* (Middletown, CT: Wesleyan University Press, 2007); Alan Blum, "Scenes," *Public* 22–23 (2001): 7–35. Blum is currently on faculty at York University.

18 Cohen, *Rock Culture in Liverpool;* Shank, *Dissonant Identities.*

19 Fox, *Real Country,* 31.

20 Ibid., 30.

21 Interview with Stan Perry, November 14, 2013.

22 Finnegan, *Hidden Musicians,* 1–30.

23 Ibid., 236.

24 Ibid., 298, 305.

25 Eric Hobsbawm, writing as Francis Newton, *The Jazz Scene* (New York: Monthly Review Press, 1960).

26 More so, for example, than the picture painted later by Howard Becker in *Outsiders: Studies in the Sociology of Deviance* (New York: Free Press, 1963).

27 See Nathan W. Pearson, *Goin' to Kansas City* (London: MacMillan, 1988); Anthony Briggs, "Memphis Jazz: African American Musicians, Jazz Community, and the Politics of Race" (PhD diss., University of California, Los Angeles, 2003); Mark Osteen and Frank J. Graziano, eds., *Music at the Crossroads: Lives and Legacies of Baltimore Jazz* (Baltimore, MD: Apprentice House, 2010).

28 Clora Bryant, *Central Avenue Sounds: Jazz in Los Angeles* (Berkeley: University of California Press, 1998).

29 W. Alex Stewart, *Making the Scene: Contemporary New York City Big Band Jazz* (Berkeley: University of California Press, 2007); Travis Jackson,

Blowin' the Blues Away: Performance and Meaning on the New York Jazz Scene (Berkeley: University of California Press, 2012).

30 Blum, "Scenes," 7.

31 Ibid., 8.

32 Yi-Fu Tuan, *Space and Place: The Perspective of Experience* (1977; repr. Minneapolis: University of Minnesota Press, 2001).

33 Doreen Massey, *Space, Place, and Gender* (Minneapolis: University of Minnesota Press, 1994), 120.

34 Howard Becker, "Jazz Places," in Bennett, *Music Scenes,* 18, 20.

35 Blum, "Scenes," 9.

36 Peter Hollerbach, "(Re)voicing Tradition: Improvising Aesthetics and Identity on Local Jazz Scenes," *Popular Music* 23, 2 (2004): 155, 162.

37 Blum, "Scenes," 26.

38 Will Straw, "Scenes and Sensibilities," *Public* 22–23 (2002): 255. As I write this, I am reminded of the recent state of affairs in the Toronto jazz scene, which, following the closures of the Top o' the Senator (2005) and Montreal Bistro (2006), fragmented into an unstable collection of coffee shops and other venues, none of which maintained a consistent jazz policy. With few regular performance venues beyond Queen Street's venerable Rex Hotel, remaining "on the scene" began to require a great deal more effort.

39 Ibid., 254.

Chapter 2: Laying the Groundwork

1 Mark Miller, *Such Melodious Racket: The Lost History of Jazz in Canada* (Toronto: Nightwood Editions, 1997).

2 Bill McNeil and Morris Wolfe, *Signing On: The Birth of Radio in Canada* (Toronto: Doubleday Canada, 1982), 11.

3 See Canadian Communications Foundation, "Canada's First Network: CNR Radio," October 1998, Canadian Communications Foundation, http://www.broadcasting-history.ca/listing_and_histories/canadas-first-network-cnr-radio.

4 Canada's first true national radio broadcast was by Prime Minister Mackenzie King, who addressed the nation from Parliament Hill on Canada Day in 1927. To reach listeners across the country, telegraph and telephone lines were used to link together the few dozen radio stations that were operating at the time.

5 Vancouver's *Jazz Workshop,* for example, aired from 1955 to 1957 on CBC radio but was not broadcast nationally. A CBC Montreal television program of the same name aired from 1953 to 1957, but was also not broadcast nationally. Likewise, radio programs featuring Edmonton jazz artists broadcast on local CBC stations (or CKUA from the University of Alberta) were not heard nationally, and so on. George Robertson, the producer of Vancouver's *Jazz Workshop* program, recalled that he "had no sensation of

an audience outside of BC" for the shows that they produced. Interview, March 18, 2014.

6 Canadian Communications Foundation, "CBC English Radio Networks," History of Canadian Broadcasting, http://www.broadcasting-history.ca/listing_and_histories/cbc-english-radio-networks.

7 Don McKim, "Canadian Bands Are Still in Diapers," *Downbeat,* November 15, 1939, 15.

8 One example is Vancouver's Panorama Roof at the Hotel Vancouver.

9 BC Radio History/Radio West, "Bob Smith," http://bcradiohistory.com/Biographies/BobSmith.htm; CBC Music, "CBC Hot Air Fetes 65 Years with Special Concert," June 2012, http://music.cbc.ca/#/blogs/2012/6/CBC-Hot-Air-fetes-65-years-with-special-concert, accessed November 12, 2013.

10 Interview with Neil Ritchie, February 13, 2013.

11 Bebop, as well as other jazz styles produced after the Second World War.

12 Interview with Jim Carney, December 2, 2012. "Wow" was recorded by Lennie Tristano for Capitol Records in 1949, featuring Tristano (piano), Warne Marsh (tenor), Lee Konitz (alto), Arnold Fishkin (bass), and Harold Granowsky (drums).

13 Interview with Walley Lightbody, December 13, 2012.

14 Interview with Neil Ritchie, February 13, 2013.

15 American Rails, "Northern Pacific Railway, Main Street of the Northwest," http://www.american-rails.com/northern-pacific-railway.html.

16 *Edmonton Bulletin,* November 26, 1915.

17 BC Ministry of Transportation, "Frontier to Freeway," 1992, https://www2.gov.bc.ca/assets/gov/driving-and-transportation/reports-and-reference/reports-and-studies/frontier_to_freeway.pdf.

18 CBC Archives, "One of Canada's Earliest Roads: The Cariboo," http://www.cbc.ca/archives/entry/one-of-canadas-earliest-roads-the-cariboo.

19 In the mid-1960s, trumpeter John Dawe and a handful of other Cellar members embarked on an impromptu road trip across Canada, attempting to gig their way to Toronto. They were unprepared for the lack of performance opportunities east of Calgary and Edmonton. John Dawe, personal communication.

20 Quoted in Becki Ross, *Burlesque West: Showgirls, Sex, and Sin in Postwar Vancouver* (Toronto: University of Toronto Press, 2009), 1.

21 Miller, *Such Melodious Racket,* 24–25.

22 *Vancouver Sun,* September 7, 1916, 3.

23 Alan Morley, *Vancouver: From Milltown to Metropolis* (Vancouver: Mitchell Press, 1969), 169.

24 *Vancouver Sun,* October 12, 1919, 26.

25 *Vancouver Sun,* March 21, 1920, 25.

26 Alan Lomax, *Mister Jelly Roll: The Fortunes of Jelly Roll Morton, New Orleans Creole and "Inventor of Jazz"* (New York: Duell, Sloan and Pearce, 1950), 170.

27 Vancouver Public Archives, Register 190–1947, #385. The leader of the Patricia group at this time is unclear, with credit alternately going to Jelly Roll Morton and to Oscar Holden, who would eventually settle in Seattle. Morton, as might be expected, said that he was the leader, though contemporary sources suggest that Holden was the leader (Miller, *Such Melodious Racket,* 67).

28 Lomax, *Mister Jelly Roll,* 170. Morton later returned to lead the house trio at the Regent Hotel, although problems arise with regard to the chronology of Morton's time in Vancouver. Both Alan Lomax's work *Mister Jelly Roll* and the Library of Congress interview tapes upon which it was based suggest a straight progression from the Patricia down the street to the Regent at 162 East Hastings. However, Lawrence Gushee writes that in June 1920 Morton was in Seattle, and worked his way as far south as Portland, Oregon, before returning to Vancouver in June 1921. Such a series of events is corroborated by "Ragtime" Billy Tucker who, in a letter to the black newspaper the *Chicago Defender* dated July 31, 1920, reported that "Kid Jelly Roll and Ralph Love, the Whirlwind Entertainers, are doing their stuff in Portland en route to the Entertainer's Café in Seattle." In any case, by January 1921, Morton was back in Vancouver and employed at the Regent Hotel. Lawrence Gushee, "A Preliminary Chronology of the Early Career of Jelly Roll Morton," *American Music* 3, 4 (1985): 405.

29 Bricktop [Ada Smith] with James Haskins, *Bricktop* (New York: Atheneum, 1984), 72.

30 *Vancouver Sun,* September 28, 1919, 38.

31 Wayde Compton, "Seven Routes to Hogan's Alley and Vancouver's Black Community," in *After Canaan: Essays on Race, Writing, and Region* (Vancouver: Arsenal Pulp Press, 2010), 140n2.

32 Morley, *Vancouver,* 165.

33 Ibid., 152; Daphne Marlatt and Carole Itter, *Opening Doors in Vancouver's East End: Strathcona* (1979; repr. Vancouver: Harbour Publishing, 2011), 74–77.

34 Morley, *Vancouver,* 152.

35 Compton, "Seven Routes," 88–90; Marlatt and Itter, *Opening Doors*, 84–88. Nora Hendrix, maternal grandmother to guitarist Jimi Hendrix, was among those who helped to establish the church.

36 Robin W. Winks, *The Blacks in Canada: A History* (Montreal: McGill-Queen's University Press, 1971), 286.

37 See the 1951 and 1961 censuses of Canada. These figures might under-represent the black population as many black residents may not have self-identified as black (or "negro" as the Census was worded at the time), but rather as British or French. Some 25,379 individuals in British Columbia were listed as undeclared or "other" with regard to racial classification in 1951, and some 5,590 residents of Vancouver were so described in 1961.

9th Census of Canada (Ottawa, 1953), 1951: Population, vol. 1, section 32–2; *1961 Census of Canada* (Ottawa, 1963), Population, vol. 1, part 2, section 5 (1.2–5), Ethnic Groups, section 38–17.

38 Compton, "Seven Routes," 98.

39 John Gilmore, *Swinging in Paradise: The Story of Jazz in Montreal* (Montreal: Ellipse, 2011), 29.

40 Miller, *Such Melodious Racket,* 78, 149. Miller's work in general makes numerous prescient points about the various rules that governed the working lives of professional (jazz) musicians, as does Andrew Scott, "The Life, Music, and Improvisation Style of Herbert Lawrence 'Sonny' Greenwich" (PhD diss., York University, Toronto, 2006).

41 Kathy J. Ogren, *The Jazz Revolution: Twenties America and the Meaning of Jazz* (New York: Oxford University Press, 1989), 26.

42 Ross Lambertson, "The Black, Brown, White and Red Blues: The Beating of Clarence Clemons," *Canadian Historical Review* 85, 4 (2004): 755–76. Although the degree of racial tolerance toward blacks in Canada has been overstated at times, the overt and officially sanctioned racism in British Columbia largely targeted people of Asian descent rather than black Canadians. For example, the Chinese Immigration Act of 1885 imposed a head tax on all immigrants from China, and the Chinese Immigration Act, 1923 prohibited most Asian immigration to Canada. It was rescinded only in 1947 as recognition of Chinese Canadian contributions in World War Two. Before the Canadian Citizenship Act of 1946, only British subjects were entitled to Canadian citizenship, a rule that barred most Asian Canadians from citizenship while accommodating many blacks, as well as those from India.

43 Robert A. Campbell, *Sit Down and Drink Your Beer: Regulating Vancouver's Beer Parlours, 1925–1954* (Toronto: University of Toronto Press, 2001), 84–86. "Mixed race" in this context did not explicitly mean black and white, and given the population demographics at the time this sort of discrimination was more often levelled against Indigenous people and those of Asian descent.

44 Ross, *Burlesque West,* 34, 66–67.

45 The evidence also paints a confusing and contradictory picture built largely on local myth. There is, for example, a somewhat famous photograph by *Vancouver Province* photographer John McGinnis, which purports to show Louis Armstrong sitting on his luggage in the lobby of the Devonshire Hotel, having just been turned away from the Hotel Vancouver, though this story is also linked at times to the Hotel Georgia and dates vary (ca. 1951 or ca. 1956). Becki Ross also reports that Lena Horne seems to have been turned away from the Hotel Vancouver, Hotel Georgia, and Hotel Devonshire in the early 1950s. By contrast, the *Vancouver Daily Province* reported on April 16, 1940, that Duke Ellington was lodged at the Hotel Vancouver, and trumpeter Jim Carney recalled meeting both Ellington and

Billy Strayhorn at the Hotel Georgia in the early 1950s. Interview with Jim Carney, December 2, 2012; Ross, *Burlesque West,* 122.

46 This point was repeatedly brought up in interviews with musicians such as Lance Harrison, Dal Richards, and Bobby Hales (who was the American Federation of Musicians local president at the time of the interview). Lance Harrison and Robert "Bobby" Hales, personal communication, July 1999.

47 See *Vancouver Daily Province,* December 9, 1939, 9.

48 "Swing Music O.K., Vienna Conductor Says," *Vancouver Daily Province,* August 20, 1938, 1.

49 Interview with Al Reusch, conducted by guitarist Mike Beddoes, May 1999.

50 Austin Phillips, quoted in Daphne Marlatt and Carole Itter, *Opening Doors in Vancouver's East End: Strathcona* (1979; repr. Vancouver: Harbour Publishing, 2011), 140–41.

51 Ibid., 180–84.

52 It's possible that this woman was Mrs. Rosa Pryor, owner of Rosa Pryor's Chicken Inn, a well-known Hogan's Alley restaurant.

53 Ibid., 183.

54 Ibid.

55 Campbell, *Sit Down and Drink,* 16–18.

56 "Coast Dope," *Chicago Defender,* July 31, 1920, 4.

57 Bricktop and Haskins, *Bricktop,* 71.

58 Campbell, *Sit Down and Drink,* 19.

59 Ibid., 20.

60 Working-class beer parlours were legally granted permission to remove the entrances and the separate areas only in December 1963 (*Vancouver Sun,* December 3, 1963, 1). Several parlours surviving from the period in both downtown Vancouver and New Westminster still retain signs indicating the separate entrances for men and women.

61 Campbell, *Sit Down and Drink,* 12–15, 84–86.

62 Ibid., 112.

63 Interview with Terry Clarke, February 20, 2013.

64 Interview with Dal Richards, June 14, 1999.

65 Aaron Chapman, *Liquor, Lust, and the Law: The Story of Vancouver's Legendary Penthouse Night Club* (Vancouver: Arsenal Pulp Press, 2012), 54.

66 Robert Campbell, *A Demon Rum or Easy Money: Government Control of Liquor in British Columbia from Prohibition to Privatization* (Ottawa: Carleton University Press, 1991), 120.

67 Ibid., 120, 122. The "snug" of British pubs would not have been permitted (a pub snug is a small, private room with direct access to the bar through a private window, constructed so other pub patrons cannot see its occupants), nor would private VIP rooms.

68 Ibid., 118.

69 Ibid., 127, 129.

70 Vancouver-born clarinettist, composer, and Order of Canada recipient Phil Nimmons was one of those who benefited from the sudden shortage of experienced musicians, and began to work professionally at the age of seventeen. Phil Nimmons, personal communication, autumn 1999. That this was not a situation unique to Canadian musicians during the Second World War was confirmed by saxophonist Lee Konitz, who began his professional career in earnest under similar circumstances. Lee Konitz, personal communication, March 19, 2018.

71 Interview with Dal Richards, June 14, 1999.

72 Interview with Terry Clarke, February 20, 2013.

73 Interview with Tony Clitheroe, November 29, 2012.

74 Interview with Al Neil, August 14, 2013.

75 Interview with Jim Johnson, August 14, 2013.

76 Interview with Tony Clitheroe, August 27, 2013.

77 Interviews with Tony Clitheroe, August 27, 2013, and Don Thompson, February 26, 2013.

78 Interview with Ken Hole, August 19, 2013.

79 Chapman, *Liquor, Lust, and the Law,* 43, 54.

80 Interview with Jim Carney, December 2, 2012.

81 Ibid. Saxophonist Fraser MacPherson worked in the downtown nightclubs (he would lead the band at the Cave), at studios, and at the CBC. MacPherson won the Juno for Best Jazz Album in 1983 and was awarded the Order of Canada in 1987.

82 Interview with Tony Clitheroe, November 29, 2012. Rendered obsolete by the newly constructed Knight Street Bridge, the Fraser Street Bridge was demolished in February 1974.

83 Interview with Walley Lightbody, December 13, 2012.

84 Interviews with Ken Hole, August 19, 2013, and Jim Carney, December 2, 2012.

85 Interview with Tony Clitheroe, August 27, 2013.

86 Interview with Tony Clitheroe, November 29, 2012.

87 Miles Davis, *Bags Groove* (Prestige, 1957).

88 Interview with Tony Clitheroe, November 29, 2012.

89 For more on Thompson, see Mark Miller, *Boogie, Pete and The Senator: Canadian Musicians in Jazz: The Eighties* (Toronto: Nightwood Editions, 1987), 262–70; and Mark Miller, *The Miller Companion to Jazz in Canada and Canadians in Jazz* (Toronto: Mercury Press, 2001), 196–97.

90 Interview with Don Thompson, February 26, 2013.

91 Interview with Ken Hole, August 19, 2013.

Chapter 3: The Making of a Jazz Scene

1 For example, the Fall 1957 edition of University of British Columbia student magazine *Pique* ran a full-page ad with the Watson Street address

(see Figure 16), while the majority of *Vancouver Sun* ads directed patrons to the rear of 222 E. Broadway.

2 At one point (ca. 1963), the building housed a gymnasium owned by former Olympic weightlifter Doug Hepburn, who developed an interest in singing and was employed on an occasional basis as a bouncer of sorts on busy evenings at the Cellar. John Dawe, personal communication, January 3, 2014.

3 Interview with John Dawe, November 28, 2012.

4 See Figures 22–28, 32, 41, 41a, 47, 48, 50, and 51.

5 A very small section of this work can be seen in the background of Figure 10.

6 Interview with Ken Hole, December 7, 2012.

7 Interview with John Dawe, November 28, 2012.

8 Interview with Tony Clitheroe, November 29, 2012.

9 Interview with John Dawe, November 28, 2012.

10 Interview with Ken Hole, August 19, 2013.

11 Interview with Lyvia Brooks, December 6, 2012.

12 Interview with Paul Ruhland, November 17, 2012.

13 Interview with Jim Johnson, August 14, 2013.

14 Interview with Tony Clitheroe, November 29, 2012.

15 Interview with John Dawe, November 28, 2012.

16 Ibid.

17 The Montgomery Brothers were known as the Mastersounds before the inclusion of Wes Montgomery. The Mastersounds comprised Charles Frederick "Buddy" Montgomery on vibes, Richie Crabtree on piano, William Howard "Monk" Montgomery on bass, and Benny Barth on drums. Both groups were regular visitors to Vancouver, where they sometimes stayed at the bebop house, and often parked their car and gear there. Wes Montgomery became friendly with Cellar guitarist Jim Kilburn, and spent a considerable amount of time at the Kilburn residence.

18 Interview with Ken Hole, December 7, 2012.

19 Interview with Ken Hole, August 19, 2013.

20 Ibid.

21 Interview with John Dawe, December 20, 2001.

22 I asked many interview subjects about the Cellar's capacity, including John Dawe, Tony Clitheroe, Al Neil, Jim Kilburn, Don Thompson, and Terry Clarke. They were consistent in their recollections of the club's size.

23 Interview with Lyvia Brooks, December 6, 2012.

24 Interview with John Dawe, November 28, 2012.

25 Ibid.

26 Interview with Terry Clarke, February 20, 2013.

27 Interview with Ken Hole, August 19, 2013.

28 Interview with Tony Clitheroe, November 29, 2012.

29 Interview with John Dawe, November 28, 2012.

30 Interview with Paul Ruhland, November 27, 2012.
31 Interview with Ken Hole, August 19, 2013.
32 Interview with Al Neil, August 14, 2013. Neil made this assessment in the course of a discussion about a CBC *Jazz Workshop* program from 1956 that featured Al Neil, John Dawe, and some of the other Cellar regulars. I had commented on how mature and accomplished the recording sounded given the age and experience level of most of the players. While Neil is correct that this particular recording is perhaps not on par with many of the commercial jazz releases of the period, it is nonetheless very good.
33 Interview with John Dawe, August 14, 2013.
34 Interview with Chuck Logan, December 17, 2001.
35 Paul Bley was at the Cellar for several nights, Ornette Coleman and Harold Land were each in town for more than a week, Art Pepper returned for ten days in the summer of 1959, Charles Mingus was in town for several weeks in 1961, Lee Konitz for a week in 1962, and so on.
36 Interview with Ken Hole, December 7, 2012.
37 John Dawe, "The Original Cellar Jazz Club" blog, December 7, 2010, http://theoriginalcellarjazzclub.blogspot.ca/2010/11/story-by-john-dawe.html. The first major jazz recording of this tune was on Miles Davis's now obscure 1958 LP *Jazz Track,* which did not reach Canada for several months following the Red engagement.
38 Interview with Doreen (Williams) Young, December 2, 2012.
39 *Art Pepper Meets the Rhythm Section* (Contemporary) was released in June 1957 (*Downbeat,* June 12, 1957, 28).
40 Interview with Walley Lightbody, December 13, 2012.
41 Interview with Al Neil, August 14, 2013.
42 It's also possible that Pepper simply did not have a horn at the time. His autobiography suggests that he often pawned his instruments to fund his drug habit. Art Pepper and Laurie Pepper, *Straight Life: The Story of Art Pepper* (1979; repr. New York: DaCapo, 1994).
43 Interview with Jim Johnson, August 14, 2013.
44 "Members of trumpeter Don Cherry's neo-bop quartet returned from their two weeks in Vancouver's Cellar flipping over the Musicians and Artists club there." *Downbeat,* September 5, 1957, 38.
45 The liner notes indicate that *Solemn Meditation* was recorded in August 1957, though it was not released until 1958 (on GNP Crescendo). Charlie Haden's second appearance on record was on Paul Bley's *Live at the Hillcrest Club,* recorded in October 1958. This recording is notable in that it features Ornette Coleman, Don Cherry, and Billy Higgins under Bley's direction, and is the first live recording of Coleman. This group, minus Paul Bley, would shortly become the Ornette Coleman Quartet. The original album release was titled *The Fabulous Paul Bley Quintet* (America Records, 1958). "As a Sideman," 2012, Charlie Hayden's website, http://www.charliehadenmusic.com/music/as-a-sideman.

46 No advertisements exist to prove the Ornette Coleman gig was in November 1957. Several of the musicians interviewed recalled late fall or November, and email correspondence with Gavin Walker, who attended most evenings of the Coleman engagement, corroborates these recollections. Coleman's appearance at the Cellar predates the Hillcrest Club engagement in LA and the formation of his influential quartet by only a few months. Indeed, the 1957 Cellar appearances of all these musicians were bookended by important early releases by the players involved. This period was an important moment for the development of jazz on the west coast.
47 Dawe, "The Original Cellar Jazz Club."
48 Interview with Ken Hole, December 7, 2012.
49 Interview with Ken Hole, August 19, 2013.
50 *Downbeat,* July 21, 1960, 32.
51 Bootleg tapes from CBC's *Jazz Workshop* list Al Neil leading a group on-air in June 1956 and Dave Quarin doing so in 1957.
52 Dawe, "The Original Cellar Jazz Club." This was Paul Perry Sr., not his son P.J. Perry.
53 *Vancouver Sun,* May 17, 1957; Al Neil, August 14, 2013. The name of the television show referred to musician and arranger Dave Pepper, whose big band was featured on the musical series, and had not been altered to reflect the guest star, Art Pepper.
54 Interview with Tony Clitheroe, November 29, 2012.
55 Pianist Chris Gage was widely regarded as Vancouver's top accompanist, and one of the city's finest piano players. Along with his regular working trio of Stan "Cuddles" Johnson (bass) and Jimmy Wightman (drums), Gage was a fixture at the CBC on radio and television, as well as in the house band at the Arctic Club for many years. Gage headlined a myriad of Vancouver New Jazz Festival presentations, was a staple at the yearly jazz festival, and was frequently employed by the large nightclubs downtown to accompany visiting American artists. In the 1960s, he led the house band at the Cave.
56 Interview with Al Neil, August 14, 2013.
57 Interview with John Dawe, December 20, 2001.
58 In later years, the Cellar's jam sessions were augmented by sessions at the Black Spot/Flat Five that catered to a younger, less experienced group of players than the Cellar, and at the Espresso Coffee House, which became the main venue for informal playing by the city's studio musicians (the downtowners).
59 Interview with Chuck Logan, December 17, 2001.
60 Advertisements in the Vancouver press billed the concert as "Irving Granz' Jazz à La Carte." Although advertising for the concert began in early November, the performance itself did not take place until December 2, 1957. *Vancouver Sun,* November 9, 1957, 51; November 23, 1957, 52.
61 Interview with Ken Hole, August 19, 2013.

62 Interview with Don Francks, July 30, 2013. Fletcher Henderson, one of the most influential bandleaders and arrangers in jazz, whose orchestra had provided important early employment for the likes of Hawkins, Armstrong, Benny Carter, Roy Eldridge, Chuck Berry, and Lester Young, died in December 1952.
63 For example, Art Pepper's engagement went unheralded apart from a brief mention on the Variety page of the *Vancouver Sun* (May 17, 1957, 7) about his appearance on the half-hour television program *The Cool Pepper Show*.
64 Walley Lightbody, "The Jazz Scene," *Pique*, Fall 1957, 35. Although Lightbody used the 222 East Broadway address in his article, the back cover ad featured the 2514 Watson Street address.
65 Interview with John Dawe, November 28, 2012.
66 Interview with Al Neil, August 14, 2013.
67 Interview with Walley Lightbody, December 13, 2012.
68 Interview with Jim Johnson, August 14, 2013.
69 *Coda* magazine was at this point still largely concerned with traditional jazz practices rather than with modern jazz expression, and was therefore not generally of interest to the Cellar membership. It is unclear how aware Cellar members were of the magazine, which was available only by subscription at this time. No subjects that I questioned about *Coda* mentioned it as being important to the Cellar, even though the magazine eventually included infrequent news items about the club.

Chapter 4: No Room for Squares

1 Interview with Tony Clitheroe, November 29, 2012.
2 Interview with John Dawe, November 28, 2012.
3 Interview with Ricci (Quarin) Gotsch, August 29, 2013.
4 Interview with Don Cumming, August 22, 2013.
5 Interview with John Dawe, November 28, 2012.
6 Interview with Tony Clitheroe, November 29, 2012. The first *Vancouver Sun* ad appeared on July 18, 1958, 17.
7 Interview with Ken Hole, August 19, 2013.
8 The ability to play more than one woodwind, for example, was a fairly basic requirement for employment in a studio or big band orchestra. A saxophonist would be expected to be able to play (and often to own) alto, tenor, and baritone saxophones, as well as flute, clarinet, and sometimes piccolo.
9 Interview with John Dawe, January 28, 2012.
10 Interview with John Dawe, December 20, 2001.
11 Interview with Paul Ruhland, November 27, 2012. An incredibly well-educated musician who had immigrated from Austria via Winnipeg, Ruhland was a key part of the Vancouver music scene at the time. In addition to being the first-call bassist for clubs such as Isy's and the Cave, he was a regular on CBC radio and television, where he also provided arrangements

and original compositions for the likes of Dave Robbins. In 1963, Ruhland moved to Los Angeles, where he worked for a variety of groups and in the studios. While there, he wrote an arrangement for the Stan Kenton Orchestra, played frequently with Warne Marsh, and appeared on several recordings, including Warne Marsh and Clare Fischer's *Report of the 1st Annual Symposium on Relaxed Improvisation* (Revelation Records, 1973) and Forrest Westbrook's *This Is Their Time, Oh Yes* (Revelation Records, 1971).

12 For more on Ray Norris, see Mark Miller, *The Miller Companion to Jazz in Canada and Canadians in Jazz* (Toronto: Mercury Press, 2001), 148–49.

13 Fraser MacPherson was fond of bebop, and in addition to working steadily at the CBC in Vancouver, continued to play in modern small group styles with some regularity. Between 1964 and 1970, he led the house band at the Cave Supper Club, and in 1975 his *Live at the Planetarium* album was released by American jazz label Concord. For more on MacPherson, see ibid., 127–28; and Mark Miller, *Boogie, Pete and the Senator: Canadian Musicians in Jazz: The Eighties* (Toronto: Nightwood Editions, 1987), 158–64.

14 The *Vancouver Sun,* September 5, 1959, 33, included an advertisement for the Sunday, September 6 performance of the Chris Gage Trio. Trombonist Ray Sikora graduated high school in 1957, the second year of the Cellar's operation. Almost immediately, he found work at the Cave Supper Club and on CBC radio. He attended Westlake College of Music in Los Angeles in 1958, after which he worked with the bands of Les Elgart, Jerry Gray, and Stan Kenton, with whom he toured extensively. Sikora split his time between Los Angeles and Vancouver, and in 1963 underwent surgery that removed portions of both lungs, the legacy of a childhood disease. He recovered, and in 1964 briefly moved to Toronto where he worked with Phil Nimmons and the Boss Brass. Sikora worked as an arranger for BMI music, toured with J.J. Johnson and Doc Severinsen, arranged music for Woody Herman and Louie Bellson, scored portions of the *Jackie Gleason Show,* and recorded with both the Guess Who and Lou Rawls. He passed away in November 1998 at the age of sixty-one.

15 Interview with Gavin Walker, December 3, 2012.

16 Interview with Stan Perry, November 14, 2013.

17 Interview with Jamie Reid, August 16, 2013.

18 Interview with Stan Perry, November 14, 2013.

19 Interview with bill bissett, January 19, 2013.

20 Interview with Jamie Reid, August 16, 2013. Fred Douglas and Curt Lang were key members of the Vancouver counterculture in the 1950s and 1960s. Douglas mixed writing, drawing, photography, and tableaus and became recognized nationally (he also taught for a time at the University of Victoria); Lang was best known as a poet, though he also worked with painting and photography. Along with Roy Kiyooka, Al Neil, Jock Hearn, and Judith Copithorne (who would be later associated with the Sound

Gallery and Intermedia), they were members of a group of writers unofficially known as the "downtown poets" (as opposed to those based out of the literary scene associated with UBC). bill bissett frequently supported the work of these writers through his blewointmentpress. Claudia Cornwall's book, *At the Worlds Edge: Curt Lang's Vancouver 1937–1998* (Vancouver: Mother Tongue, 2011), paints a vivid picture of Vancouver's "beat" arts scene. Douglas died in 2005 and Lang in 1998.

21 Interview with Tony Clitheroe, November 29, 2012.

22 Interview with Gavin Walker, December 3, 2012.

23 Interview with Al Neil, August 14, 2013.

24 *Endgame* was first staged in April 1957, and is now generally associated with the Theatre of the Absurd, a term popularized around 1960 by critic Martin Esslin. Samuel Beckett is, along with Albert Camus, John-Paul Sartre, and fellow playwright Eugène Ionesco, associated with both the French avant-garde and Existentialism.

25 Interview with Gavin Walker, December 3, 2012.

26 The 711 Shop was a family-run clothing store, and should not be confused with the convenience store chain 7-Eleven.

27 Interviews with Ricci (Quarin) Gotsch, August 29, 2013, and Joe Geszler, August 25, 2013. For comparison, ticket prices for 1957's Jazz à la Carte performance at the Georgia Auditorium ranged from $2.50 to $4.50. Local resident Joe Geszler, a regular Cellar attendee, recalled that he could afford to go and hear the local groups, but generally could not afford the higher cover charges for American artists. It is safe to say that admission charges for the Cellar varied.

28 The plays were often drawn from popular sources such as the *Evergreen Review,* which often published one-act plays.

29 *I Rise in Flame, Cried the Phoenix* is the only play besides *The Apollo of Bellac* with a poster stating that the publisher had licensed the material for performance. Liner notes for *Kenneth Patchen Reads with Jazz in Canada* (Folkways, 1959, FL 9718) written by Al Neil in October 1959 mention that a play by William Saroyan was produced in 1960, but no promotional material seems to have survived.

30 Michael Magee (1929–2011) had a long career in broadcasting as an actor, writer, producer, and sports commentator, but may be best known as a voice actor in the CBC animated series *The Raccoons,* which aired from 1985 to 1991. Tom Hawthorn, "Popular Media Personality Loved Horse Racing, Alter Egos," obituary, *Globe and Mail,* November 29, 2011, http://www.theglobeandmail.com/news/national/popular-media-personality-loved-horse-racing-alter-egos/article2254374.

31 Brock Brower (1931–2014) was an American journalist perhaps best known for *The Late Great Creature* (1972), nominated for the National Book Award.

32 Also see *Coda,* September 1960, 9, for a mention of this production.

33 Interview with Don Cumming, August 22, 2013.
34 An anagram for "shit," *TISH* (1961–69) was founded by Jamie Reid, George Bowering, Frank Davey, David Dawson, and Fred Wah and was closely linked to the attitudes espoused by Black Mountain College and introduced to the *TISH* members by UBC professor Warren Tallman. Wah and Bowering both went on to be named Canadian Parliamentary Poets Laureate. The influential Vancouver weekly the *Georgia Straight* (1967–) was an offshoot of *TISH,* as were several other Canadian literary journals and periodicals. For more on *TISH,* see Frank Davey, *When Tish Happens: The Unlikely Story of Canada's "Most Influential Literary Magazine"* (Toronto: ECW Press, 2011).
35 Interview with Jamie Reid, August 16, 2013.
36 Interview with Al Neil, August 14, 2013.
37 Interview with Adrienne Brown, December 3, 2012.
38 Lord Buckley, the stage name for Richard Myrle Buckley, was in fact white. He was a stage performer and recording artist often referred to as a "hip comic," who referenced aspects of black culture. His style foreshadowed such comedians as Lenny Bruce. In *Chronicles,* Bob Dylan states that "Buckley was the hipster bebop preacher who defied all labels ... Buckley had a magical way of speaking. Everybody, including me, was influenced by him in one way or another." Bob Dylan, *Chronicles: Volume One* (New York: Simon and Schuster, 2005), 260. Nonetheless, Francks's performances were also informed by the work of black comics, knowledge of which he gained through recordings collected on trips down the American west coast from Vancouver to Seattle, and later while living in California.
39 Race records were those made exclusively by, and marketed primarily to, African American audiences. They included recordings of jazz, blues, gospel, and comedy artists, and the term was commonly used from the early 1920s through the 1940s. Billboard introduced the "Harlem Hit Parade" in 1942, and replaced this with a "Race Records" chart in 1945. "Race recordings" and "race music" were phased out as industry terms following the implementation of Billboard's "Rhythm & Blues" chart in 1949, though the term remained in the popular vernacular for some time. A separate African American Billboard chart continues to this day – "Hot R&B/Hip-Hop Songs."
40 Interview with Al Neil, August 14, 2013.
41 Interview with Don Francks, July 30, 2013.
42 *Jackie Gleason Says No One in This World Is Like Don Francks* (Kapp, 1963), *Lost ... and Alone* (Kapp, 1965), *Live at the Purple Onion* (Art of Life, 2004/1962). Francks also had a considerable film career, with roles in movies and television on both sides of the border, including appearing with Fred Astaire in Francis Ford Coppola's musical film *Finian's Rainbow* (Warner Brothers, 1968). He remained active as an actor and vocalist right up until his death from cancer in April 2016.

43 Cadence, 1957. It is possible that Neil may also have heard Patchen's earlier 1942 radio broadcast with composer John Cage, *The City Wears a Slouch Hat* (released on CD in 2000 by the Cortical Foundation, Corti 14) as well as Kenneth Rexroth and Lawrence Ferlinghetti's influential *Poetry Readings in the Cellar* (Fantasy Records, 1957). This Cellar was a club of the same name in San Francisco, also established in 1956, that similarly played host to jazz music and beat poetry during the 1950s and 1960s, including important experiments in combining the two by such artists as Lawrence Ferlinghetti, Kenneth Rexroth, ruth weiss, Stan Getz, and Brew Moore. In *Desolation Angels,* attending the Cellar is one of the things Jack Kerouac fantasizes about doing once he reaches San Francisco following his summer's employment as a fire lookout in the Cascade Mountains of Washington State. *Desolation Angels* was not published until 1965, but was written close to a decade earlier, at the time of these early jazz-poetry experiments at the San Francisco club. Jack Kerouac, *Desolation Angels* (1965; repr. New York: Riverhead Books, 1995), 132, 136–39.

44 Al Neil may have had help in contacting Patchen from Warren Tallman, an influential English professor who helped found the creative writing program at the University of British Columbia in the mid-1950s, and who had close ties to both Black Mountain College and to the San Francisco beat movement. Such a connection cannot be ruled out, because Neil associated with social groups that included Tallman, Tallman was known to frequent the Cellar, and Patchen's Canadian sojourn included dates at UBC. That said, poet Jamie Reid, who developed a close relationship with Tallman, believed such a connection to be unlikely.

45 Larry Smith, *Kenneth Patchen: Rebel Poet in America* (1999; repr. Huron, OH: Bottom Dog Press, 2013), 247. Briseno was a member of the Chamber Jazz Sextet, with whom Patchen had recorded in 1957.

46 Larry Smith, January 27, 2014, email correspondence.

47 Interview with Adrienne Brown, December 3, 2012.

48 Interview with Al Neil, August 14, 2013.

49 Smith, *Kenneth Patchen,* 247–48. The American dates took place after February 22, during Patchen's return trip to California by rail.

50 Anecdotal evidence suggests that a late-night performance occurred on February 13, 1959, but it cannot be corroborated.

51 Pat LaCroix, email correspondence, March 18, 2014. Though now part of the University of Victoria, at the time Victoria College was associated with the University of British Columbia. That the group travelled to the island for this engagement and did not perform at a mainland college with the same name was confirmed by Carole Itter, Al Neil's domestic partner, on January 28, 2014.

52 Smith, *Kenneth Patchen,* 247.

53 *Vancouver Sun,* February 20, 1959, 21.

54 Al Neil, liner notes for *Kenneth Patchen Reads with Jazz in Canada* (Folkways, 1959, FL 9718), 2. Neil went on to publish several novels, and these liner notes offer a glimpse into his early written voice.

55 Interview with Tony Clitheroe, November 29, 2012. Nonetheless, many Vancouver poets did read at the Cellar, including bill bissett, Lance Farrell, and Fred Douglas. Douglas can be seen reading with the Al Neil Trio in the 1964 film *In Search of Innocence* (dir. Léonard Forest, National Film Board).

56 Interview with Al Neil, August 14, 2013.

57 Neil, notes to *Kenneth Patchen Reads*, 3. Neil's liner notes seek to separate Patchen from the beat scene as a whole, an effort Patchen himself would make repeatedly throughout his career. Smith, *Kenneth Patchen*.

58 At least some of the resistance to the presentation of other artistic modes at the Cellar was rooted in an unconscious performance of hegemonic masculinity and the entrenched notions of gender that have been, and in many cases continue to be, associated with jazz. Bound up not only in historically developed considerations of masculinity and femininity but with the complex politics of race, jazz performance placed its value, for the most part, on somewhat hypermasculine displays of skill, aggression, autonomy, and risk taking generally seen to be at odds with domestic respectability and approaches or character traits coded as "feminine." As a result, and somewhat unsurprisingly, participation in the jazz scene by women and by those men who did not present as "typically" masculine was highly unusual, and often not well received. For more on gender and performativity in jazz, see Trine Annfelt, "Jazz as Masculine Space," July 17, 2003, Kilden Information Centre for Gender Research in Norway, http://kjonnsforskning.no/en/2003/07/jazz-masculine-space; Benjamin Piekut, "New Thing? Gender and Sexuality in the Jazz Composer's Guild," *American Quarterly* 62, 1 (2010): 25–48; Sherrie Tucker, "When Did Jazz Go Straight?" *Critical Studies in Improvisation* 4 (2008); Sherrie Tucker, "Big Ears: Listening for Gender in Jazz Studies," *Current Musicology* 70–71 (2001–2): 71–73; Ingrid Monson, "The Problem with White Hipness: Race, Gender, and Cultural Conceptions in Jazz Historical Discourse," *Journal of the American Musicological Society* 48, 3 (1995): 396–422; David Ake, "Re-Masculating Jazz: Ornette Coleman, 'Lonely Woman,' and the New York Jazz Scene in the Late 1950s," *American Music* 16, 1 (1998): 25–44.

59 The exact date is unknown, but correspondence with bill bissett and with poet Jamie Reid seems to put the reading in the late spring or summer of 1961.

60 Interview with Don Cumming, August 22, 2013.

61 Interview with bill bissett, January 19, 2013.

62 Interview with Jamie Reid, August 16, 2013.

63 bill bissett, *Sailor* (Vancouver: Talonbooks, 1978), 7.

64 Interview with Jamie Reid, August 16, 2013.
65 Interview with bill bissett, January 19, 2013.
66 Ibid.
67 Neil's activities included events at the Sound Gallery (1965), the Al Neil Trio, and the happenings organized by the Intermedia society from 1967. Noted artist and musician Gregg Simpson's blog (http://www.gregg simpson.com) has many useful links, as does the website *Ruins in Process: Vancouver Art in the Sixties* (http://www.vancouverartinthesixties.com).
68 Interview with John Dawe, August 14, 2013.
69 *Coda,* February 1977, 16.
70 Interview with Jamie Reid, August 16, 2013.
71 Interview with Al Neil, August 14, 2013.
72 From "Cosmic Klangfarben," an interview with Al Neil conducted by Rick McGrath in Vancouver, December 4, 1972 (full transcript possessed by author, obtained from a defunct website).
73 Ted Berrigan, "Jack Kerouac, The Art of Fiction No. 41," *Paris Review* 43 (1968): 60–105, https://www.theparisreview.org/interviews/4260/jack-kerouac-the-art-of-fiction-no-41-jack-kerouac; Canada, *House of Commons Debates,* 30th Parliament, 3rd Session (Ottawa: Queen's Printer, 1977–78); see also Ryan J. Cox, "HP Sauce and the Hate Literature of Pop Art: bill bissett in the House of Commons," *ESC: English Studies in Canada* 37, 3–4 (2011): 147–61.
74 Robert A. Campbell, *Sit Down and Drink Your Beer: Regulating Vancouver's Beer Parlours, 1925–1954* (Toronto: University of Toronto Press, 2001), 123.
75 Ibid., 123, 157.
76 Interview with Chuck Logan, December 17, 2001.
77 Interview with Lyvia Brooks, December 6, 2012.
78 Interview with Ricci (Quarin) Gotsch, August 29, 2013.
79 Interview with Gavin Walker, December 3, 2012.
80 Interview with Ricci (Quarin) Gotsch, August 29, 2013.
81 Ibid.
82 Ibid.
83 Interview with Adrienne Brown, December 3, 2012. Jessie Webb herself was an artist of some significance in Vancouver. See Adrienne Brown, *The Life and Art of Harry and Jessie Webb* (Vancouver: Heritage House, 2014).
84 Interview with Chris (Hole) Birdseye, August 15, 2013. This quotation does not refer to the Cellar, but rather to other ventures started by Ken Hole in the late 1950s and early 1960s such as Victoria's Scene Club and Vancouver's Espresso Coffee House.
85 Interview with Lyvia Brooks, December 6, 2012.
86 Interview with Al Neil, December 2, 2013.

87 See Lewis A. Erenberg, *Swingin' the Dream: Big Band Jazz and the Rebirth of American Culture* (Chicago: Chicago University Press, 1998); Sherrie Tucker, *Swing Shift: "All-Girl" Bands of the 1940s* (Durham: Duke University Press, 2002); Tucker, "Big Ears," 71–73; and Piekut, "New Thing?"

88 Interview with Al Neil, December 2, 2013.

89 Erenberg, *Swingin' the Dream,* 200.

90 Ibid. As examples of this conundrum even today, consider the visual imagery used in marketing campaigns behind pianist Diana Krall and saxophonists Grace Kelly and Candy Dulfer, in contrast to those of male artists such as pianists Brad Mehldau and Vijay Iyer, or saxophonists David Sanborn, Mark Turner, and Chris Potter. See also the work, variously, of Sherrie Tucker and Ingrid Monson; the contentious 2017 interview by Ethan Iverson of pianist Robert Glasper on Iverson's popular jazz blog, *Do the Math,* and the ensuing furor it prompted (https://ethaniverson.com/glasper-interview/); and the recent code of conduct for jazz employers put forward in April 2018 by a fourteen-member collective of female and non-binary musicians in New York City known as the We Have a Voice Collective (https://www.nytimes.com/2018/04/30/arts/music/we-have-voice-jazz-women-metoo.html).

91 Interview with Doreen (Williams) Young, December 2, 2012.

92 In addition to reluctance to include a woman in an otherwise exclusively male society, working with a vocalist requires a unique set of skills and sensibilities, and at times presents an uncomfortable task for younger or less experienced musicians.

93 Interview with Ricci (Quarin) Gotsch, August 29, 2013.

94 *Vancouver Sun,* April 14, 1960, 30.

95 Interview with Doreen (Williams) Young, December 2, 2012.

96 Vancouver-based Lance Harrison employed banjo player Ruth Dewhurst during the early 1960s (Mark Miller, email correspondence, August 1, 2014).

97 For the gender associations of instruments, see H.F. Abeles and S.Y. Porter, "The Sex Stereotyping of Musical Instruments," *Journal of Research in Musical Education* 26 (1978): 65–75; J.K. Delzell and D.A. Leppla, "Gender Association of Musical Instruments and Preferences of Fourth-Grade Students for Selected Instruments," *Journal of Research in Music Education* 40 (1992): 93–103; D. Barber, "A Study of Jazz Band Participation by Gender in Secondary High School Instrumental Music Programs," *Jazz Research Proceedings Yearbook* 19 (1999): 92–99; C. Conway, "Gender and Musical Instrument Choice: A Phenomenological Investigation," *Bulletin of the Council for Research in Music Education* 146 (2000): 1–15.

98 Interview with Paul Ruhland, November 27, 2012.

99 Interview with Al Neil, December 2, 2013. American singer Pat Suzuki, though never a full-time resident of Vancouver, was a frequent and popular nightclub guest at such venues as the Arctic Club, Isy's, and the Cave.

100 Influential singers included Lena Horne, Peggy Lee, and Keely Smith, for example. In conversations about Eleanor Collins, she was often compared to Lena Horne in a manner that led me to believe that the comparison was offered on a musical, rather than racial, basis.

The first female vocalist to achieve significant fame in Vancouver was probably Juliette Augustina Sysak Cavazzi, who performed under her first name, Juliette, and began singing with the Dal Richards Orchestra in 1939 at the age of thirteen. Quickly nicknamed "Our Pet Juliette," she sang with the Richards Orchestra until she moved to Toronto in 1942; she was replaced first by Beryl Boden, and then by Lorraine McAllister in 1950.

Eleanor Collins, however, was undoubtedly the most famous vocalist in Vancouver during the period. Born in Edmonton to parents who had immigrated from the United States at the turn of the twentieth century,. Collins moved to Vancouver in 1939 and quickly became a staple on regional television and radio broadcasts. Notably, she was the first black woman to star in her own television show – *The Eleanor Show* – which was broadcast on the CBC in 1955.

101 Barry Dale was billed as a "crooner" in several of the *Vancouver Sun* advertisements for his engagements at the Cellar. He should not be confused with the Canadian actor and musician of the same name who became famous for his role on the popular children's program *Harrigan* (1969–85), and who has numerous credits as a vocalist.

102 *Coda,* January 1961, 8. Though the review did not appear until January 1961, Hoffman performed at the Cellar in November 1960, as noted in the article.

103 *Jean Hoffman Sings and Swings* (Fantasy Records) was reviewed in *Billboard Magazine,* April 7, 1958, 24.

Chapter 5: In the Swing of Things

1 *Vancouver Sun,* July 18, 1958, 17; November 28, 1958, 47; February 20, 1959, 21; March 26, 1959, 16; and September 5, 1959, 33. The advertisement for Chris Gage was probably taken out because the performance was a rare Sunday evening show, and one of the few appearances at the Cellar by the popular Vancouver group. Gage was in such demand that Sunday may well have been the only evening he was available to play the Cellar.

2 *The Harold Land Quartet: Jazz at the Cellar, 1958* (Fresh Sound/Lone Hill Jazz, 2007, CD B000PFU7VW). Dave Quarin intended these recordings to be private and never had any intent to release or broadcast them. They were meant only as a record of the activities of the club, and as a pedagogical resource. He is reportedly quite bothered that the leaked Harold Land recording does not pay royalties to Land's estate. Though the

microphones were well hidden and the recording of performances was a closely guarded secret, at least some musicians suspected what was going on. Lee Konitz, who played the Cellar in 1962, searched the club for recording devices, going so far as to inspect the bathrooms, according to Tony Clitheroe (interview, November 29, 2012).

3 See *Harold in the Land of Jazz* (Contemporary, 1958) and *The Fox* (HiFi, 1959).

4 Leonard Feather and Ira Gitler, *The Biographical Encyclopedia of Jazz* (Oxford: Oxford University Press, 1999), 328–29.

5 Interview with Gavin Walker, December 3, 2012.

6 Interview with Tony Clitheroe, November 29, 2012.

7 Jim Kilburn, personal correspondence. Heroin is often known by the slang name "horse."

8 Interview with Doreen (Williams) Young, December 2, 2012.

9 Interview with Tony Clitheroe, November 29, 2012.

10 Ibid.

11 John Dawe, "The Original Cellar Jazz Club" blog, December 7, 2010, http://theoriginalcellarjazzclub.blogspot.ca/2010/11/story-by-john-dawe.html. This story hasn't been corroborated but is a fitting piece of Cellar jazz lore.

12 John Dawe, email correspondence, February 17, 2014.

13 Interview with Jim Kilburn, February 8, 2001.

14 *Vancouver Sun,* April 14, 1960, 30.

15 *Vancouver Sun,* June 11, 1960, 28; July 17, 1960, 10.

16 The advertisement for the Bill Perkins gig on Friday, July 8, 1960, marks the first time that the Cellar shared the *Vancouver Sun*'s entertainment page (p. 13) with an advertisement for the Black Spot, another co-operative jazz space that had developed out of the scene at the Cellar.

17 Vancouver had long been home to a thriving drug industry, and the Opium Act of 1908 – Canada's first anti-drug law – was in large part a direct response to the opium industry in Vancouver's East End. In the 1910s, 1920s, and 1950s, a series of enforcement attempts and legislative reforms enacted harsher penalties for drug-related offences and increased the prohibitions to include morphine, cocaine (1911), and cannabis (1923). See Robert R. Solomon and Melvyn Green, "The History of Non-Medical Opiate Use and Control Policies in Canada, 1870–1970," in *Illicit Drugs in Canada: A Risky Business*, ed. Judith C. Blackwell and Patricia G. Erickson (Scarborough: Nelson Canada, 1988). These laws did little to stem the influx of drugs into the port city, and in 1955, Vancouver had the highest rates of drug addiction in the western hemisphere, at least according to *Maclean's,* which published a story entitled "The Dope Craze That's Terrorizing Vancouver" (February 1, 1955, 12–13, 50–54). In 1958, the magazine described the East End intersection of Columbia and Hastings Streets as "Canada's most notorious underground rendevouz [sic]," *Maclean's,* March 1, 1958, 13–17, 38–41.

18 Interview with Jamie Reid, December 7, 2012. Reid's point about marijuana is corroborated by Ingeborg Paulus, whose 1967 study on the developing use of psychedelic drugs in Vancouver found that marijuana did not "catch on" in Vancouver until much later in the 1960s. Marijuana was considered, among other things, too bulky a drug to carry for dealing purposes, as well as too ineffectual for users accustomed to heroin and other hard drugs. At a time when a pound of marijuana was reportedly worth $40 in San Francisco and $70 in Seattle, its rarity north of the border saw that same pound fetch up to $1,000 in Vancouver. Ingeborg Paulus, *Psychedelic Drug Use in Vancouver: Notes on the New Drug Scene* (Vancouver: Narcotic Addiction Foundation of British Columbia, 1967), 17.

19 Interview with John Dawe, August 14, 2013.

20 Al Neil, *Changes* (Toronto: Coach House Press, 1975). Filmed interviews with Perry on the subject were once available at the now-defunct "JazzStreet Vancouver: A History of Jazz in Vancouver," http://www.jazzstreetvancouver.ca/artists/25 (last accessed April 23, 2014). Saxophonist Dale Hillary was also an addict at one point, as were drummers Jerry Fuller and Terry Hawkeye.

21 Interview with bill bissett, January 19, 2013.

22 Anonymous interview, August 2013.

23 The Harlem Nocturne was at 343 East Hastings, at Gore Avenue (see Figure 6 for location). Just as the Cellar served to locate the countercultural arts movement in Vancouver, the Harlem Nocturne functioned as the nexus for the black music scene in Vancouver, providing a place for community, connection, the cross-fertilization of ideas, and a social space. Unlike the Cellar, the Harlem Nocturne did not mark itself through musical exclusivity, instead presenting and representing a broad cross-section of black music (including blues, soul, funk, and jazz).

24 Becki Ross, *Burlesque West: Showgirls, Sex, and Sin in Postwar Vancouver* (Toronto: University of Toronto Press, 2009), 67.

25 Ernie King quoted in ibid., 70.

26 Mark Miller, *Such Melodious Racket: The Lost History of Jazz in Canada* (Toronto: Nightwood Editions, 1997), 177–80; Ross, *Burlesque West,* 67.

27 Ernie King quoted in Ross, *Burlesque West,* 66.

28 Interview with Mike Taylor, May 8, 2014. Taylor was married to Ernie King's niece, and had a busy and varied career in Vancouver, playing regularly at the Harlem Nocturne and other East End clubs, at the Cellar and the Espresso Coffee House, on CBC television, as well as at the Cave, Isy's, and a host of other downtown locations.

Interestingly, Charles Mingus offered a similar, brief statement on racial discrimination unprompted, in an interview taped at the Cellar. Although he was speaking in 1961, and as a visitor rather than a resident, such commentary from as politically engaged a musician as Mingus is perhaps noteworthy: "Canada. I've always known it to be liberal and freer thinking than most places in the United States ... anywhere I've been in any part of Canada the people have made me feel that they thought I was a man, and I've been many places in America where I'm called not even a man, but less than that." "The Mind of Mingus," *Quest,* CBC, 1961; private recording provided by Don Thompson.

29 Interview with Don Thompson, February 26, 2013.
30 Interview with Jim Carney, December 2, 2012.
31 Interview with John Dawe, November 28, 2012.
32 Interview with Gavin Walker, December 3, 2012.
33 Interview with Paul Ruhland, November 27, 2012.
34 Interview with Chuck Logan, December 17, 2001. In addition to his musical pursuits, Logan worked as a traffic manager for Ernie King's trucking company, and later on in law enforcement.
35 Ibid.
36 Interview with Tony Clitheroe, November 29, 2012.
37 Given the Cellar's relationship with touring groups along the west coast, this does seem the more likely scenario.
38 Interview with John Dawe, November 28, 2012.
39 Holmes seems to have been in Canada illegally. In 1959 he was briefly part of the MINC in Toronto, before being deported back to the United States in August 1960. Andrew Scott, "The Life, Music, and Improvisation Style of Herbert Lawrence 'Sonny' Greenwich" (PhD diss., York University, Toronto, 2006), 46.

   Freeman was most probably officially playing with Archie Shepp at Amougies on October 26, 1969, though this is unclear (Freeman would record several albums with Shepp). A photo widely circulated on the Internet shows him in a jam session at the festival with Frank Zappa, Philly Joe Jones, Grachan Moncur III, Archie Shepp, and others. Freeman also spent some time in Chicago with Sun Ra, probably between his time in Vancouver and his appearance in Europe in 1969.
40 No Business Records, "Henry P. Warner/Earl Freeman/Philip Spigner/Freestyle Band/No Business Records," M-etropolis, https://m-etropolis.com/blog/henry-p-warner-earl-freeman-philip-spigner-freestyle-band-no-business-records.
41 Interview with Chuck Logan, December 17, 2001.
42 Interview with Don Thompson, February 26, 2013.
43 Interview with Jim Johnson, August 14, 2013.
44 I have worked as a producer for both a large Canadian jazz festival and a jazz society, and one of the chief ways that high-profile concerts are funded is through co-presentations with the CBC.
45 Interview with John Dawe, November 28, 2012.
46 Interview with Jim Carney, December 2, 2012.

47 The program featured the Al Neil group with Dale Hillary, and was the only live broadcast to emanate from the club on radio or television (aired March 21, 1961).
48 "The Mind of Mingus" was originally broadcast on January 12, 1961, and received a national rebroadcast out of Toronto on March 29, 1961, on a program entitled *Quest,* hosted by Andrew Allen and produced by Daryl Duke.
49 Interview with Jim Carney, December 2, 2012.
50 Ibid. Nagra was a Swiss-made brand of portable audio recorder that became standard equipment for film and television production from the 1960s through the 1990s.
51 Interview with Ricci (Quarin) Gotsch, August 29, 2013.
52 *Coda* was Canada's premier (and most times only) jazz publication from 1958 to 2009.
53 See *Coda,* May 1958–March 1959.
54 John Norris, *Coda,* May 1958, 1.
55 *Coda,* March 1959, 4. For more on Lance Harrison, see Mark Miller, *Boogie, Pete and the Senator: Canadian Musicians in Jazz: The Eighties* (Toronto: Nightwood Editions, 1987), 146–51.
56 *Coda,* March 1959, 5.
57 *Coda,* July 1959, 6. This issue also briefly mentions that the Foggy Manor Club in Calgary, the MINC club in Toronto, and the Yardbird Suite in Edmonton were organized as co-operative ventures. These clubs are all discussed in Chapter 7.
58 *Coda,* November 1959, 10.
59 John Norris refers to him as the Vancouver New Jazz Society secretary in *Coda*, October 1960, 11.
60 John Moller, in *Coda,* January 1960, 8.
61 Moller mentioned the Patchen engagement only in March 1960, more than a year after the event, and then in reference to the Folkways LP, which had recently been reviewed in *Downbeat*, and not the actual live performance. The magazine had awarded the album a three-star review and noted the playing of eighteen-year-old Dale Hillary. *Downbeat,* January 21, 1960, 36.
62 Pete Wyborn, "Jazz Is Where You Find It," *Coda,* May 1960, 9.
63 Wyborn, "Jazz Is Where You Find It," *Coda,* June 1960, 10.
64 Wyborn, "Jazz Is Where You Find It," *Coda,* August 1960, 13; September 1960, 9.
65 Wyborn, "Jazz Is Where You Find It," *Coda,* October 1960, 10.
66 Dawe, "The Original Cellar Jazz Club."
67 *Vancouver Sun,* August 6, 1960, 27; August 12, 1960, 29; August 13, 1960, 18; August 15, 1960, 17; August 16, 1960, 18; August 18, 1960, 25; August 19, 1960, 29.

68 Kessel returned to play the Cellar in 1963, so if he did cancel his last two nights in 1960, it may not have been in response to any issues with the engagement itself.

69 *Vancouver Sun*, August 12, 1960, 29. *The Poll Winners* (Contemporary 1957), featured Kessel, bassist Ray Brown, and drummer Shelly Manne, who had all won their instrumental polls for 1956 in *Downbeat, Playboy,* and *Metronome,* respectively. The album was a musically and financially successful attempt to leverage the commercial appeal of the musicians following their wins, and led to a series of five albums for the group, including *The Poll Winners Ride Again!* (1958) and *Poll Winners: Three!* (1959).

70 The section also mentioned that Gavin Walker, then vice-president of the UBC Jazz Society, was presenting a jazz show on campus radio, an occupation he continues to this day. He has presented *The Jazz Show* on UBC's CITR station since 1984.

71 *Coda,* October 1960, 12.

72 Interview with Don Thompson, February 26, 2013.

73 Interview with Terry Clarke, February 20, 2013.

74 Jim Blackley moved from the UK to Vancouver in 1957 and established Jim Blackley's Drum Village shortly thereafter. His impact as a pedagogical figure cannot be overstated: during his time in Vancouver and his later years in Toronto (after 1973), Blackley had a profound influence on Canadian jazz musicians for more than fifty years. Little known outside the jazz world, Blackley passed away at the age of ninety on July 16, 2017.

75 Interview with John LeMarquand, February 22, 2013.

76 *Coda,* December 1960, 12–13. Wyborn was probably not speaking of the American artists performing at the Cellar, but the programming presented by the Queen Elizabeth Theatre, the Orpheum Theatre, Isy's, and the Cave, all of which were regularly bringing in well-known artists from a variety of genres. See *Vancouver Sun,* February 4, 1961.

77 *Vancouver Sun,* January 6, 1961, 12; January 21, 1961, 10. Harry Webb designed a poster during the planning stages of the engagement that lists the dates as December 15–24. For reasons unknown, though evidently somewhat last minute, the gig was pushed to January 1961. Mingus performed at the Cellar only once.

78 *Vancouver Sun,* January 6, 1961, 12. The Mingus engagement at the Cellar was brought up by nearly every person interviewed for this project, whether they had attended the event themselves or not.

79 Interview with Tony Clitheroe, November 29, 2012.

80 Interview with Terry Clarke, February 20, 2013.

81 No anecdote was shared by more interview subjects than this tale about Mingus and the BC Lions players, which has become inextricably linked to the history of the Cellar in Vancouver. The details included in each

retelling of the story revealed which interviewees had indeed witnessed the events themselves, and which had only heard about it.

82 Interview with Jamie Reid, December 7, 2012.
83 Interview with Jamie Reid, August 16, 2013. Though at this time Tallman was known to Reid as a UBC professor, they were not yet close acquaintances.
84 Interview with bill bissett, January 19, 2013.
85 I am including several versions of this event because the descriptions differ, at times significantly, from one version to the next. I wanted to present a comprehensive view without privileging one retelling over another or setting out my own "definitive" version of events.
86 Dawe, "The Original Cellar Jazz Club."
87 Interview with Terry Clarke, February 20, 2013.
88 Ibid.
89 Interview with Don Thompson, February 26, 2013.
90 Interview with Jim Carney, December 2, 2012.
91 Mingus, "The Mind of Mingus."
92 John Clayton, *Coda,* February 1961, 11–12.
93 *Coda,* February 1961, 12.
94 Interview with Terry Hill, August 26, 2013.
95 Pianist Mike Taylor recalled that he arrived at the Cellar one evening just in time to catch Mingus's last set. After the audience dispersed, Taylor took to the stage and began to play the house piano, which was a common way to commence the evening's informal jam sessions. Mingus, who had remained behind at the club, commented favourably on his playing, and invited him to sit in with the group the following evening. Taylor was employed in the house band at the Harlem Nocturne, but was able to arrive just in time to play the last set of the next evening with the Mingus group. Interview, May 8, 2014.

Chapter 6: Altered Chords

1 *Vancouver Sun,* February 1, 1961, 21. I presume advertising on Fridays was to avoid paying the higher fees for advertisements in the Saturday issue.
2 *Vancouver Sun,* February 25, 1961, 8.
3 Though local groups were rarely paid to union scale, whenever the Cellar was financially stable enough to permit it, local musicians were paid for advertised performances at the club.
4 Interview with Tony Clitheroe, March 17, 2013.
5 *Vancouver Sun,* March 10, 1961, 14; April 1, 1961, 8.
6 *Coda,* December 1961, 10.
7 Interview with Stan Perry, November 14, 2013.
8 Interview with Terry Clarke, February 20, 2013.
9 In the late 1940s, Jerry Fuller Sr. led the house band at the Cave.

10 Michael Fitzgerald, "The Lenox School of Jazz," November 1, 1993, jazzdiscography.com/Lenox/lenhome.htm. An anonymous photo of Hillary presumably taken during his stay at the Lenox School graced the cover of the September 26, 1963, issue of *Downbeat* – the magazine's 11th Annual School Music Issue. Mark Miller, *The Miller Companion to Jazz in Canada and Canadians in Jazz* (Toronto: Mercury Press, 2001), 94. Terry Hawkeye was one of the chief organizers of the Yardbird Suite jazz club in Edmonton (see Chapter 7).

11 See program from the 1957 Lenox School of Jazz year-end concert, archived at jazzdiscography.com/Lenox/1957prog.htm. In 1958, Hillary returned to Lenox, where he played in a small ensemble led by Jimmy Giuffre and a large ensemble led by Bill Russo. The program from the 1958 Lenox School of Jazz year-end concert is archived at jazzdiscography.com/Lenox/1958prog.htm.

Oscar Peterson would cofound the Advanced School of Contemporary Music in 1960 in Toronto. The school operated until 1965, and included as instructors Ray Brown and Ed Thigpen, Peterson's working group at the time. In 1960, the school taught a seventeen-week term and charged $350 tuition. *Coda,* September 1960, 22–23.

12 Miller, *Miller Companion to Jazz,* 94. Hillary's tenure with Philly Joe Jones remains obscure. He held dual Canada–US citizenship through his mother, which enabled him to work in the United States, but little is known of his activities during this period. Hillary claimed to have recorded sessions with both Philly Joe Jones and vibraphonist Dave Pike, though neither has ever surfaced or been documented (ibid.; Gavin Walker, personal communication, March 8, 2014). In the 1970s, he worked with notable Canadian jazz-rock band Lighthouse. Hillary died in 1992.

13 Interview with John Dawe, December 20, 2001.

14 Interview with Don Thompson, February 26, 2013.

15 Ibid.

16 Don Thompson often played either piano or vibes on these telecasts, in which case Robert Witmer usually played bass.

17 Interview with Terry Hill, August 26, 2013.

18 Interview with Gavin Walker, December 3, 2012.

19 Lani Russwurm, "Black Spot, 1961," 2014, *Past Tense,* pasttensevancouver.tumblr.com/post/45208351699/blackspot1961. These are only two of many possible origins of the Black Spot name; nobody is certain to what the name referred.

20 Interview with Jamie Reid, August 16, 2013.

21 *Vancouver Sun,* August 22, 1959, 17.

22 Interview with John LeMarquand, February 22, 2013.

23 Recollections of clubgoers suggest it was as low as twenty-five or fifty cents.

24 Interview with John LeMarquand, February 22, 2013.
25 *Vancouver Sun,* July 8, 1960, 13.
26 Interview with Jamie Reid, August 16, 2013.
27 Interview with Terry Clarke, February 20, 2013.
28 Interview with John LeMarquand, February 22, 2013.
29 *Coda,* June 1963, 8. Though *Coda* did not print bylines during this period, the correspondent responsible for the "Notes from UBC" column that provided the bulk of the Vancouver news through 1962 and 1963 was most often Adrian Tanner. At the time a UBC student, Tanner is now an anthropologist at Memorial University of Newfoundland. Interview with Adrian Tanner, June 24, 2013.
30 Interview with John LeMarquand, February 22, 2013.
31 Interview with Terry Clarke, February 20, 2013.
32 *Coda,* July 1962, 7.
33 *Coda,* December 1962, 8–9.
34 Interview with John LeMarquand, February 22, 2013.
35 Ibid. The Flat Five experimented with bringing in American artists much as the Cellar had done, though most of this activity occurred later in its existence, after it had ceased to be a co-operative venture. In addition to Charles Mingus, the Flat Five presented John Handy, who played with a local band consisting of Don Thompson, Terry Clarke, and Bob Witmer. In 1964, Handy returned to play the Blue Horn, after which Thompson and Clarke joined his group and relocated to the United States.
36 Ibid.
37 Ibid.
38 *Vancouver Sun,* January 4, 1963, 18.
39 *Ubyssey,* March 7, 1963, 6.
40 *Ubyssey,* various issues, courtesy of John Le Marquand. John Gittins would become perhaps best known for his work in jazz theory, and for his role in the establishment of the jazz program at York University in Toronto. Ralph Dyck became both a composer and music technologist whose work with Roland helped to design the Roland MC-8 keyboard synthesizer.
41 Interview with John LeMarquand, February 22, 2013. Eleanor Collins performed September 27–28, 1963, and one of these evenings was broadcast. *Vancouver Sun,* September 27, 1963, 37.
42 *Vancouver Sun,* March 23, 1963, 13.
43 Howie Bateman was a music enthusiast and a regular host on CBC radio and television. In 1966, he relocated to Toronto, where he helped to found *Toronto Life* magazine. *Vancouver Sun,* October 11, 2012, D2.
44 The Inquisition also booked high-profile folk acts such as the Travellers, Ian and Sylvia, and, in July 1962, comedian Lenny Bruce, whose show at Isy's had been shut down by the authorities. The Inquisition engagement was hastily arranged and unadvertised (though well attended), and

managed to escape the notice of the morality squad. Strangely for Vancouver, the Inquisition had no reputation as a bottle club.

45 *Vancouver Sun,* March 9, 1963, 10; *Vancouver Sun,* February 3, 1963, 18; *Ubyssey,* October 4, 1963, 4.

46 John Coltrane had been booked to play the Inquisition in late December 1963, but the gig was abruptly cancelled when the club closed on December 17. Lewis Porter, Chris Devito, Yasuhiro Fujioka, Wolf Schmaler, and David Wild, *The John Coltrane Reference* (New York: Routledge, 2007), 293.

47 *Coda,* February 6, 1964, 9.

48 Conversations with Terry Clarke, John LeMarquand, and Gavin Walker bear this out.

49 *Vancouver Sun,* December 20, 1963, 20; interview with Chris (Hole) Birdseye, January 28, 2013.

50 The exact address of the Espresso has been forgotten, but it appears to have occupied space between 670 and 680 Howe Street.

51 Longton bought out Ken Hole's share of the business in 1961, a welcome move that enabled the Holes to purchase their first house. Interview with Chris (Hole) Birdseye, August 15, 2013.

52 Interview with Ken Hole, August 19, 2013.

53 Interview with Chris (Hole) Birdseye, August 15, 2013.

54 Interview with Don Thompson, February 26, 2013.

55 *Vancouver Sun,* March 3, 1962, 43.

56 Avoiding the appropriate American Federation of Musicians and Canadian government paperwork seems to have been standard practice for the American artists who played at the Cellar, though one would assume that those with high-profile CBC engagements, such as Charles Mingus, would have had to officially involve the union. Managing such paperwork and the associated fees was perhaps one more way in which the CBC aided the Cellar Musicians and Artists Society.

57 *Vancouver Sun,* March 8, 1962, 18; March 9, 1962, 10.

58 Interview with Tony Clitheroe, November 29, 2012.

59 Interview with Tony Clitheroe, August 27, 2013.

60 Interview with Stan Perry, November 14, 2013. Tommy Hunter was a popular Canadian country music performer who hosted *The Tommy Hunter Show* on both CBC radio and television, where it ran from 1965 to 1992.

61 *Vancouver Sun,* November 17, 1962, 30.

62 *Vancouver Sun,* February 9, 1963, 18.

63 *Coda,* September 1963, 11.

64 The recollections of musicians such as John Dawe and Tony Clitheroe are vague on this point, and Dave Quarin, the club manager, refused all requests to participate in this project.

65 *Vancouver Sun,* March 1, 1963, 54; March 9, 1963, 10.

66 *Vancouver Sun,* April 5, 1963, 30; April 13, 1963, 16; June 25, 1963, 4.

67 *Vancouver Sun,* February 9, 1963, 18; March 9, 1963, 10; April 6, 1963, 29.
68 *Vancouver Sun,* April 6, 1963, 29.
69 *Vancouver Sun,* May 10, 1963, 50; June 7, 1963, 22; August 16, 1963, 22.
70 Interview with John Dawe, March 9, 2013.
71 *Vancouver Sun,* September 20, 1963, 52.
72 *Coda,* October 1963, 8.
73 *Vancouver Sun,* November 15, 1963, 28; Gavin Walker, email correspondence, March 18, 2013.
74 Interview with Tony Clitheroe, March 17, 2013.
75 *Coda,* December 1963, 13.
76 *Coda,* March 1964, 10.
77 Interview with John LeMarquand, February 22, 2013.
78 Interview with John Dawe, January 28, 2012.
79 Ibid.
80 Interview with John Dawe, November 28, 2012.
81 Ibid.
82 Interview with Tony Clitheroe, November 29, 2012. Elvis Presley had actually played Vancouver much earlier, on August 31, 1957, at Empire Stadium. Clitheroe may be thinking of the Beatles, who played Empire Stadium on August 22, 1964, though it is more likely that he is simply making a general point about the popularity of rock and roll at the time.
83 Interview with Jim Johnson, August 14, 2013.
84 Interview with Ricci (Quarin) Gotsch, August 29, 2013.
85 Interview with Al Neil, August 14, 2013.
86 Rock and roll, but also free jazz and similar musical experimentation as exemplified by Vancouver-based organizations such as the Sound Gallery and Intermedia later in the 1960s.

Chapter 7: Co-ops from Coast to Coast

1 Terry Hawkeye (b. 1937) had been interested in jazz for some years, and it is rumoured that he travelled to California to take some lessons with Shelly Manne. Though this cannot be definitively proven, it would explain his appearance at the Cellar – travelling up the west coast to Vancouver, and then over the Rockies back to Edmonton. In the summer of 1957, he and fellow Edmontonian Dale Hillary were both chosen to attend the Lenox School of Jazz, where he played in a small ensemble led by Ray Brown. See the program from the 1957 Lenox School of Jazz year-end concert, archived at jazzdiscography.com/Lenox/1957prog.htm. In 1959, he was part of the MINC club in Toronto.
2 Collette Slevinsky, dir., *The House That Bop Built* (documentary, not commercially released, 2011).
3 Interview with Tommy Banks, February 8, 2013. Tommy Banks was a pianist, conductor, arranger/composer, and Canadian senator. From 1968 to 1983, he hosted the *Tommy Banks Show* on network television and

acted as musical director and/or producer for numerous high-profile events such as the Olympics (XV Winter Games), the Commonwealth Games, and Expo '86. In 1979, he won the Juno Award for Best Jazz Album (Tommy Banks Big Band, *At the Montreux Festival*). He was appointed to the Senate in 2000 and died in January 2018.

4 Ibid.

5 Ibid.

6 Ibid.

7 Ibid.

8 *Coda,* July 1959, 7.

9 This location, replacing the Club Anton, is not to be confused with the club's next address, 9801 Jasper Avenue, which has 106 Street NW as its nearest intersection. The reference to 106 Street is unclear.

10 Mark Miller, *The Miller Companion to Jazz in Canada and Canadians in Jazz* (Toronto: Mercury Press, 2001), 216.

11 *Coda,* October 1961, 8.

12 "Our History," Yardbird Suite website, http://www.yardbirdsuite.com/archives/history.

13 Interview with Tommy Banks, February 8, 2013.

14 Heather C. Hudak, "Glenbow Museum Presents the Very Early Days of Jazz," *Calgary Straight* 195 (2002): 5.

15 *Coda,* July 1959, 7. Bill Somers, "Blues in the Night: The Foggy Manor Story," *Calgary Magazine,* June 1988, 14.

16 Hudak, "Glenbow Museum," 5.

17 Somers, "Blues in the Night," 15.

18 The Canadian regiment Lord Strathcona's Horse, stationed in Calgary during this period, had a band.

19 Ray Mah, quoted in Somers, "Blues in the Night," 16.

20 Ibid., 15.

21 E. "Red" Ockwell, *Coda,* November 1960, 7.

22 *Coda,* October 1961, 8. A private recording provided by Don Thompson and marked "Vancouver Jazz Quintet 1962" lists Peter Dyksman (bass), Dale Hillary (saxophone), Ray Sikora (trombone), Don Thompson (bass), and Jerry Fuller (drums). While no names appear in this *Coda* review, it does mention that the bass player was from Holland and the drummer from Halifax, so there is a good chance that this version of the group consisted of Dyksman, Stan Perry (drums), Don Thompson (piano), and possibly John Dawe (trumpet) with baritone saxophone (unknown) instead of trombone.

23 John Uren recalled that he rented the space complete with the club's stage, furniture, espresso machine, and library of beat literature still in place. The Depression was one of the first venues to hire a young Joan Anderson, soon to be known as Joni Mitchell. Les Irvin, "A Conversation with John Uren," August 29, 2005, Joni Mitchell website, jonimitchell.com/library/view.cfm?id=1336.

24 Interview with Don Palmer, April 13, 2011.
25 The most famous of these were the bands of trumpeters Don Warner and Peter Power.
26 At some later point, the Halifax Jazz Society was officially incorporated as a not-for-profit organization.
27 Miller, *Miller Companion to Jazz,* 180. As late as the 2000s, some members of this jazz co-op continued to refer to it as the "bucket of blood."
28 Interview with Stan Perry, November 14, 2013.
29 Interview with Don Palmer, April 13, 2011.
30 Interview with Warren Chiasson, July 19, 2013.
31 Warren Chiasson, "Remembering Lionel Hampton," n.d., warrenchiasson.com/tribute.htm.
32 Interview with Charles "Buddy" Burke, March 13, 2014.
33 Interview with Don Palmer, April 11, 2012.
34 Chiasson had a remarkable career in New York, recording with Eric Dolphy and Gunther Schuller in 1963 (*Vintage Dolphy,* MCA, GM3005), and performing as a member of the original cast of *Hair* on Broadway.
35 Interview with Charles "Buddy" Burke, March 13, 2014.
36 On July 1, 1974, Don Palmer appeared at the Newport Jazz Festival playing tenor and soprano saxophones in a band that included Lee Konitz, Phil Woods, Stan Getz, Gerry Mulligan, Joe Morello, and Michael Moore, led by Teo Macero. On May 29, 1974, the group had recorded for Columbia Records with Pepper Adams replacing Mulligan, and while Adam's annotated discography lists the album as having been released in 2002, this remains obscure and the only reference data remains Macero's private listing (Teo CD SAX-003). Gary Carner, *Pepper Adams' Joy Road: An Annotated Discography* (Lanham, MD: Scarecrow Press, 2013), 272.
37 In 1962, Skip Beckwith also moved to Toronto and attended Peterson's school, where he studied under Ray Brown.
38 Interview with Paul Ruhland, November 27, 2012.
39 Interview with Tony Clitheroe, January 28, 2013.
40 Interview with John Dawe, November 28, 2012.
41 The founders included Paul Bley, Keith White, Hal Gaylor, Billy Graham, Bob Roby, Yvan Landry, Valdo Williams, Neil Michaud, George Kennedy, and Floyd Williams. White, "Noting the Scene" (unpublished manuscript, ca. 1988), 78.
42 John Gilmore, *Swinging in Paradise: The Story of Jazz in Montréal* (Montreal: Véhicule Press, 1988), 291–92.
43 White, "Noting the Scene," 78–79.
44 Though not all these venues were contemporaneous with the Jazz Workshop, this list nonetheless shows that venues for the performance of jazz were plentiful in Montreal. Not all these venues had a full-time jazz policy or were jazz clubs, but they represented spaces in which young jazz musicians could perform, even if irregularly.

45 Most famously Charlie Parker in 1953.
46 White "Noting the Scene," 87.
47 Gilmore, *Swinging in Paradise,* 292.
48 Ibid.; White "Noting the Scene," 89.
49 Andrew Scott, "The Life, Music, and Improvisation Style of Herbert Lawrence 'Sonny' Greenwich" (PhD diss., York University, Toronto, 2006), 37.
50 *Coda,* May 1959, 2.
51 Scott, "Herbert Lawrence 'Sonny' Greenwich," 30–47.
52 Interview with John Dawe, November 28, 2012.
53 Scott, "Herbert Lawrence 'Sonny' Greenwich," 42, 46.
54 A notable exception was black American pianist Calvin Jackson, who immigrated to Toronto in 1950. Warmly welcomed to the city, he hosted his own weekly TV program on the CBC (*Jazz with Jackson*) and was a featured soloist in a variety of settings, including a guest engagement with the Toronto Symphony Orchestra. Mark Miller, *Way down That Lonesome Road: Lonnie Johnson in Toronto, 1965–1970* (Toronto: Mercury Press, 2012), 17.

While the difficulties for black musicians were in part a product of the insular studio and downtown club scenes, in which gigs were closely guarded, Andrew Scott has suggested that many black musicians in Toronto were less proficient than their white contemporaries in professional skills such as sight-reading and doubling, largely due to systemic inequality in the availability of and early access to formal music tuition. Scott, "Herbert Lawrence 'Sonny' Greenwich." In any case, the studios and larger jazz clubs in Toronto remained largely white enclaves, and the MINC filled an important niche for black musicians.
55 Interview with Bob Mercer, March 12, 2014.
56 The First Floor Club was an after-hours club run by Howard Matthews near the site of the current Toronto reference library, which also catered to a black clientele.
57 Scott, "Herbert Lawrence 'Sonny' Greenwich," 44.

Conclusion

1 Will Straw, "Scenes and Sensibilities," *Public* 22–23 (2002): 254.
2 Interview with Chuck Logan, December 17, 2001.
3 Interview with Don Cumming, August 22, 2013.
4 Interview with John LeMarquand, February 22, 2013. Claire Lawrence went on to be a founding member of the rock group the Collectors, which was later renamed Chilliwack. He also worked as a producer for CBC radio, contributed musical scoring for numerous television shows, and produced CBC radio's *Jazz Beat* from 2000 to 2006. He remains active on the Vancouver scene.
5 Interview with Terry Clarke, February 20, 2013.

6 Straw, "Scenes and Sensibilities." Here I am including not only jazz, but also the jazz-based musical expression of dance bands and vocalists such as Frank Sinatra, Dean Martin, Peggy Lee, Bobby Darin, and Keely Smith.
7 The commercial aspects of pursuing music as an economic activity, and aspirations surrounding making records and going on tour, were, tellingly, almost completely absent from my conversations with the participants in these co-operative jazz clubs. By way of contrast, Sara Cohen's *Rock Culture in Liverpool: Popular Music in the Making* (Oxford: Clarendon Press, 1991) and Barry Shank's *Dissonant Identities: The Rock'n'Roll Scene in Austin, Texas* (Hanover, NH: Wesleyan University Press, 1994) are filled with the commercial aspirations of local musicians.
8 Straw, "Scenes and Sensibilities," 255.
9 Dale Hillary's tenure with Philly Joe Jones was perhaps particularly aspirational for young Canadian players, especially because the group played a widely attended engagement at the Yardbird Suite in the early 1960s.
10 Interview with Tommy Banks, February 8, 2013.
11 Interview with Terry Clarke, February 20, 2013.
12 Others include bassist Athan Katsos in the 1960s, and percussionist Tom Roach in the mid-1970s.
13 Now Cape Breton University.
14 Interview with Mike Murley, April 5, 2011. Jamey Aebersold is perhaps the leading publisher of jazz instructional books and play-along recordings, which he began to produce in the late 1960s. In addition to Aebersold's home-use materials, he has regularly hosted in-person summer jazz workshops for learners of various ages.
15 The University of Toronto followed York with a jazz studies class in 1979, though a degree in jazz was not to appear until 1991.
16 Before this network, almost nobody toured across Canada. The population centres were simply too widely dispersed to make cross-country tours economically viable. Even Oscar Peterson attempted only one national tour, travelling as a solo act and performing with local rhythm sections in each city. Interview with Mark Miller, April 7, 2011.
17 While I was in Halifax during the late 1990s and early 2000s, the regular presentations of concerts by JazzEast outside of the summer jazz festival had a profound effect on my musical education, and greatly broadened my awareness of Canadian jazz artists from across the country. Anecdotal evidence from this period suggests that my experience was far from unique. When Halifax-based players relocated for post-secondary studies, for example, they were generally already familiar with their instructors, having heard them perform at a JazzEast concert. Several chose their programs with the direct aim of studying with musicians encountered through a combination of festival and regular in-year programming.
18 Indeed, neither Montreal nor Toronto have a jazz society that functions in quite the same way as Coastal Jazz and Blues, the Edmonton Jazz Society,

or JazzEast, which make use of paid employees, interns, and volunteers to present jazz concerts, workshops, and a variety of outreach activities on a regular basis.

19 As a producer for JazzEast Rising in 2002–3, my experience at national "block booking" meetings for the annual Canadian jazz festivals, as well as with assisting on numerous grant applications for in-year national touring by Canadian artists, bears this out. If an artist or group could secure firm commitments from Vancouver, Edmonton, and Halifax, a successful tour was much more likely than one without support from these cities. Engagements in Calgary, Winnipeg, and St. John's were generally scheduled after such support had been secured. These regional jazz societies had little or no involvement with presenting venues in Toronto and Montreal, which operated independently on a for-profit business model. That said, numerous tours did include dates in these major centres.

20 In addition, commercial label Justin Time, established in 1983, devoted a large part of its efforts toward recording and promoting Canadian jazz and blues artists.

21 Interview with Mark Miller, April 7, 2011. The changing rules surrounding tobacco advertising during this period certainly aided the expansion of jazz festival presentations in Canada; Du Maurier was the title sponsor of most of Canada's jazz festivals into the 2000s. The presence of well-informed and enthusiastic jazz critic Mark Miller at the nationally circulated *Globe and Mail* newspaper from 1978 to 2005 also raised the profile of jazz in Canada. However, we may now be in a period of decline, as suggested by a sharp decrease in funding for the arts, the end of Canada Council recording grants, the loss of both weekly national CBC radio shows with a jazz focus, and the steep decline in programming by jazz organizations outside of their yearly festivals.

22 Interview with Chuck Logan, December 17, 2001.

Appendix B: Canadian Jazz Sources

1 See, for example, Lewis Porter, "Some Problems in Jazz Research," *Black Music Research Journal* 8, 2 (1988): 195–206; Travis Jackson, *Blowin' the Blues Away: Performance and Meaning on the New York Jazz Scene* (Berkeley: University of California Press, 2012), 3–23.

2 Students in my jazz classes are continually confounded by the lack of material available on seemingly obvious topics and/or jazz figures.

3 Those interested might consult, among others: E. Taylor Atkins, *Blue Nippon: Authenticating Jazz in Japan* (Durham, NC: Duke University Press, 2001); William Shack, *Harlem in Montmartre: A Paris Jazz Story between the Great Wars* (Berkeley: University of California Press, 2001); David Ake, *Jazz Cultures* (Berkeley: University of California Press, 2002), *Jazz Matters: Sound, Place, and Time since Bebop* (Berkeley: University of California Press, 2010), and *Jazz/Not Jazz: The Music at Its Boundaries*

(Berkeley: University of California Press, 2012); William Minor, *Unzipped Souls: A Jazz Journey through the Soviet Union* (Philadelphia: Temple University Press, 1995), and *Jazz Journeys to Japan: The Heart Within* (Ann Arbor: University of Michigan Press, 2004); Luca Vitali, *The Sound of the North: Norway and the European Jazz Scene* (Mimesis International, 2015); Philip V. Bohlman and Goffredo Plastino, eds., *Jazz Worlds/World Jazz* (Chicago: University of Chicago Press, 2016); and Rashida Braggs, *Jazz Diasporas: Race, Music, and Migration in Post-World War II Paris* (Berkeley: University of California Press, 2016).

Despite a general paucity in the area of Canadian jazz studies, significant research is being done on localized jazz practices in other areas of the Commonwealth. I would mention David Boulton, *Jazz in Britain* (London: W.H. Allen, 1958), and Eric Hobsbawm, writing as Francis Newton, *The Jazz Scene* (1960; repr. New York: DaCapo, 1975), for their early efforts; Catherine Tackley (nee Parsonage) for her work on the history of jazz in Britain and, in particular, on the racial dimensions of British jazz: *The Evolution of Jazz in Britain 1880–1935* (Farnham, UK: Gower Publishing, 2005), *Black British Jazz: Routes, Ownership and Performance* (New York: Routledge, 2016), etc.; John Wickes, *Innovations in British Jazz,* vol. 1: *1960–1980* (Chelmsford, UK: Soundworld, 1999), and George McKay, *Circular Breathing: The Cultural Politics of Jazz in Britain* (Durham, NC: Duke University Press, 2005), for their work on innovations in British jazz practice following the 1960s and on the cultural politics of jazz in Britain, respectively; and Duncan Heining, *Trad Dads, Dirty Boppers and Free Fusioneers: British Jazz, 1960–1975* (Bristol: Equinox, 2012), and Dave Gelly, *An Unholy Row: Jazz in Britain and Its Audience, 1945–1960* (Bristol, UK: Equinox, 2014), for more recent efforts to detail stylistic variation in British jazz post-1960, and the often complicated socio-political makeup of the British jazz audience. In addition to these scholarly works, I must also mention the important contributions of journalist and music critic Jim Godbolt to the historical narrative of jazz in the United Kingdom: *A History of Jazz in Britain 1919–1950* (London: Quartet Books, 1984) and *A History of Jazz in Britain 1950–1970* (London: Quartet Books, 1989).

From Australia we receive the work of Andrew Bisset, *Black Roots, White Flowers: A History of Jazz in Australia* (Sydney: ABC Enterprises, 1987) and John Shand, *Jazz: The Australian Accent* (Sydney: University of New South Wales Press, 2008), along with the seminal efforts of Bruce Johnson: *The Oxford Companion to Australian Jazz* (Oxford: Oxford University Press, 1987), *The Inaudible Music: Jazz, Gender, and Australian Modernity* (Sydney: Currency Press, 2000); "Naturalising the Exotic: The Australian Jazz Convention," in *Jazz Planet: Transnational Studies of the "Sound of Surprise,"* ed. E. Taylor Atkins, 151–68 (Jackson: University of Mississippi Press, 2003); "Australian Jazz: A Cultural and Historical Overview," *Sonus: A Journal of Investigations into Global Music Possibilities* 26, 2 (2006):

1–22; "Jazz and Nation in Australian Cinema: From Silents to Sound," *NFSA Journal* 5, 1 (2009): 1–12; and "Deportation Blues: Black Jazz and White Australia in the 1920s," *IASPM Journal: Journal of the International Association for the Study of Popular Music* 1, 1 (2010), http://www.iaspmjournal.net/index.php/IASPM_Journal/article/viewFile/297/502. These contribute significantly not only to the understanding of domestic jazz and jazz practices within Australia, but to considerations of Australian jazz within the wider discourse of jazz as a transnational music.

Such scholarship, and the considerable conference and publishing activity in jazz research outside North America, show there is considerable interest in the perspectives and expressions of jazz outside the dominant American narrative. Canadian jazz expression thus seems strangely underrepresented in the discourse surrounding global jazz practices.

4 Mark Miller, "Oral History," in *Ethnomusicology in Canada: Proceedings of the First Conference on Ethnomusicology in Canada/Premier congress sur l'ethnomusicologie au Canada Held in Toronto 13–15 May, 1988,* ed. Robert Witmer (Toronto: Institute for Canadian Music, 1990), 197.

5 Recent efforts in the area of Canadian jazz research include: Stanley Pean, *Toute la Ville en Jazz* (Montreal: Trait d'Union, 1999); Michael Cado, "The Big Band: From Dance Band to Jazz Orchestra" (MA diss., York University, Toronto, 2004); and Andrew Scott, "The Life, Music, and Improvisation Style of Herbert Lawrence 'Sonny' Greenwich" (PhD diss., York University, Toronto, 2006). See as well: Valerie Breau St. Germain and Jeanne Twa, *Our Memories of Lenny Breau: The Love, the Music and the Man* (Winnipeg: Pemmican Publications, 2006); Ron Forbes-Roberts, *One Long Tune: The Life and Music of Lenny Breau* (Denton: University of North Texas Press, 2006); Margaret Sansregret, *Oliver Jones: The Musician, the Man: A Biography* (Montreal: XYZ Publishing, 2006); and Marie Desjardins, *Vic Vogel* (Montreal: Éditions du Cram, 2013).

6 For Montreal, see John Gilmore, *Swinging in Paradise: The Story of Jazz in Montréal* (Montreal: Véhicule Press, 1988), and *Who's Who of Jazz in Montreal: Ragtime to 1970* (Montreal: Véhicule Press, 1989). Andrew Scott's PhD dissertation, "Herbert Lawrence 'Sonny' Greenwich" may be perhaps the best examination to date of the Toronto scene. Also worth mentioning is Jack Litchfield's survey *Toronto Jazz 1948–1950: A Survey of Live Appearances and Radio Broadcasts of Dixieland Jazz Experienced in Toronto during the Period 1948–1950* (self-published, 1992).

7 Miller, "Oral History," 196.

8 Mark Miller, *Miller Companion to Jazz in Canada and Canadians in Jazz* (Toronto: Mercury Press, 2001).

9 It is unfortunate that Gilmore's work did not extend beyond 1980, and that no follow-up volume has been produced.

10 Thanks to Mark Miller, I was able to read portions of Keith White's currently unpublished manuscript "Noting the Scene" (written ca. 1988), in

particular Chapter 8, which deals with White's experiences as a young jazz pianist in Montreal during the 1950s, and his involvement with Paul Bley and the Jazz Workshop.

11 Scott, "Herbert Lawrence 'Sonny' Greenwich," 9.

12 *Coda,* May 1958, 1.

13 While I was researching this book between 2010 and 2013, ownership of the project was already unclear. Vancouver's Coastal Jazz and Blues Society was providing server space at the time, but no maintenance. The whereabouts of the original audio and video files were also unknown at that time.

14 John Dawe, "The Original Cellar Jazz Club" blog, December 7, 2010, http://theoriginalcellarjazzclub.blogspot.ca/2010/11/story-by-john-dawe.html.

15 There is also a Facebook group tied to this website; see https://www.facebook.com/vancouverjazz.

16 JAZZ.FM91, *The Canadian Jazz Archive Online,* www.canadianjazzarchive.org.

Selected Bibliography

Books and Articles

Becker, Howard. *Art Worlds*. Berkeley: University of California Press, 1982; repr. 2008.

–. "Jazz Places." In *Music Scenes: Local, Translocal and Virtual,* ed. Andy Bennett, 17–27. Nashville, TN: Vanderbilt University Press, 2004.

bissett, bill. *Sailor*. Vancouver: Talonbooks, 1978.

Blum, Alan. *The Imaginative Structure of the City.* Montreal: McGill-Queen's University Press, 2003.

–. "Scenes." *Public* 22–23 (2001): 7–35.

Bourdieu, Pierre. "The Field of Cultural Production, Or: The Economic World Reversed." *Poetics* 12 (1983): 311–56.

–. "Social Space and the Genesis of Groups." *Theory and Society* 14, 6 (1985): 723–44.

–. "Social Space and Symbolic Power." *Sociological Theory* 7, 1 (1989): 14–25.

Bricktop [Ada Smith] with James Haskins. *Bricktop*. New York: Atheneum, 1984.

Brown, Adrienne. *The Life and Art of Harry and Jessie Webb*. Vancouver: Heritage House, 2014.

Campbell, Robert. *A Demon Rum or Easy Money: Government Control of Liquor in British Columbia from Prohibition to Privatization*. Ottawa: Carleton University Press, 1991.

–. *Sit Down and Drink Your Beer: Regulating Vancouver's Beer Parlours, 1925–1954*. Toronto: University of Toronto Press, 2001.

Chapman, Aaron. *Liquor, Lust, and the Law: The Story of Vancouver's Legendary Penthouse Night Club*. Vancouver: Arsenal Pulp Press, 2012.

Coda (magazine). Toronto: Coda Publications, 1958–2009.

Cohen, Sara. *Rock Culture in Liverpool: Popular Music in the Making*. Oxford: Clarendon Press, 1991.

Compton, Wayde. "Seven Routes to Hogan's Alley and Vancouver's Black Community." In *After Canaan: Essays on Race, Writing, and Region,* 83–144. Vancouver: Arsenal Pulp Press, 2010.

Cornwall, Claudia. *At the World's Edge: Curt Lang's Vancouver 1937–1998*. Vancouver: Mother Tongue, 2011.

Davey, Frank. *When Tish Happens: The Unlikely Story of Canada's "Most Influential Literary Magazine."* Toronto: ECW Press, 2011.

DeVeaux, Scott. "Constructing the Jazz Tradition: Jazz Historiography." *Black American Literature Forum* 25, 3 (1991): 525–60.

Finnegan, Ruth H. *The Hidden Musicians: Music-Making in an English Town*. Middletown, CT: Wesleyan University Press, 2007.

Fox, Aaron. *Real Country: Music and Language in Working-Class Culture*. Durham, NC: Duke University Press, 2004.

Gilmore, John. "Issues and Directions." In *Ethnomusicology in Canada: Proceedings of the First Conference on Ethnomusicology in Canada/ Premier congress sur l'ethnomusicologie au Canada Held in Toronto 13–15 May, 1988,* ed. Robert Witmer, 184–91. Toronto: Institute for Canadian Music, 1990.

–. *Swinging in Paradise: The Story of Jazz in Montréal*. Montreal: Véhicule Press, 1988.

–. *Who's Who of Jazz in Montréal: Ragtime to 1970*. Montreal: Véhicule Press, 1989.

Grazian, David. "The Symbolic Economy of Authenticity in the Chicago Blues Scene." In *Music Scenes: Local, Translocal and Virtual,* ed. Andy Bennett, 31–47. Nashville, TN: Vanderbilt University Press, 2004.

Hudak, Heather C. "Glenbow Museum Presents the Very Early Days of Jazz." *Calgary Straight* 195 (2002): 5.

Jackson, Travis. *Blowin' the Blues Away: Performance and Meaning on the New York Jazz Scene*. Berkeley: University of California Press, 2012.

Lambertson, Ross. "The Black, Brown, White and Red Blues: The Beating of Clarence Clemons." *Canadian Historical Review* 85, 4 (2004): 755–76.

Lee, David. *Stopping Time: Paul Bley and the Transformation of Jazz*. Montreal: Véhicule Press, 1998.

Lees, Gene. "The Man from Powell River: Don Thompson." In *Friends along the Way: A Journey through Jazz,* 89–104. New Haven, CT: Yale University Press, 2003.

Lightbody, Walley. "The Jazz Scene," *Pique* (UBC student magazine), Fall 1957, 33–35.

Litchfield, Jack. *Canadian Jazz Discography 1916–1980*. Toronto: University of Toronto Press, 1982.

–. *Toronto Jazz 1948–1950: A Survey of Live Appearances and Radio Broadcasts of Dixieland Jazz Experienced in Toronto during the Period 1948–1950*. Self-published, 1992.

Lomax, Alan. *Mister Jelly Roll: The Fortunes of Jelly Roll Morton, New Orleans Creole and "Inventor of Jazz."* New York: Duell, Sloan and Pearce, 1950.

Marlatt, Daphne, and Carole Itter. *Opening Doors in Vancouver's East End: Strathcona*. Vancouver: Harbour Publishing, 1979; repr. 2011.

Massey, Doreen. *Space, Place, and Gender*. Minneapolis: University of Minnesota Press, 1994.

McKim, Don. "Canadian Bands Are Still in Diapers." *Downbeat,* November 15, 1939, 15.

McNeil, Bill, and Morris Wolfe. *Signing On: The Birth of Radio in Canada*. Toronto: Doubleday Canada, 1982.

Miller, Mark. *Boogie, Pete, and the Senator: Canadian Musicians in Jazz – The Eighties*. Toronto: Nightwood Editions, 1987.

–. *Cool Blues: Charlie Parker in Canada, 1953*. Toronto: Nightwood Editions, 1989.

–. *Jazz in Canada: Fourteen Lives*. Toronto: University of Toronto Press, 1982.

–. *The Miller Companion to Jazz in Canada and Canadians in Jazz*. Toronto: Mercury Press, 2001.

–. "Oral History." In *Ethnomusicology in Canada: Proceedings of the First Conference on Ethnomusicology in Canada/Premier congress sur l'ethnomusicologie au Canada Held in Toronto 13–15 May, 1988,* ed. Robert Witmer, 196–99. Toronto: Institute for Canadian Music, 1990.

–. *Such Melodious Racket: The Lost History of Jazz in Canada*. Toronto: Nightwood Editions, 1997.

–. *Way Down That Lonesome Road: Lonnie Johnson in Toronto, 1965–1970*. Toronto: Mercury Press, 2012.

Monson, Ingrid. "The Problem with White Hipness: Race, Gender, and Cultural Conceptions in Jazz Historical Discourse." *Journal of the American Musicological Society* 48, 3 (1995): 396–422.

Morley, Alan. *Vancouver: From Milltown to Metropolis*. Vancouver: Mitchell Press, 1969.

Neil, Al. *Changes*. Toronto: Coach House Press, 1975.

–. Liner notes for *Kenneth Patchen Reads with Jazz in Canada*. Folkways Records, 1959. FL 9718. https://folkways-media.si.edu/liner_notes/folkways/FW09718.pdf.

Newton, Francis. *The Jazz Scene*. New York: DaCapo, 1960; repr. 1975.

Piekut, Benjamin. "New Thing? Gender and Sexuality in the Jazz Composer's Guild." *American Quarterly* 62, 1 (2010): 25–48.

Porter, Lewis. "Some Problems in Jazz Research." *Black Music Research Journal* 8, 2 (1988): 195–206.

Ross, Becki. *Burlesque West: Showgirls, Sex, and Sin in Postwar Vancouver*. Toronto: University of Toronto Press, 2009.

Ross, Becki, and Kim Greenwell. "Spectacular Striptease: Performing the Sexual and Racial Other in Vancouver, BC, 1945–1975." *Journal of Women's History* 17, 1 (2005): 137–64.

Scott, Andrew. "The Life, Music, and Improvisation Style of Herbert Lawrence 'Sonny' Greenwich." PhD diss., York University, Toronto, 2006.

Shank, Barry. *Dissonant Identities: The Rock'n'Roll Scene in Austin, Texas*. Hanover, NH: Wesleyan University Press, 1994.

Small, Christopher. *Musicking: The Meanings of Performing and Listening*. Hanover, NH: Wesleyan University Press, 1998.

Smith, Larry. *Kenneth Patchen: Rebel Poet in America*. Huron, OH: Bottom Dog Press, 2013.

Somers, Bill. "Blues in the Night: The Foggy Manor Story." *Calgary Magazine,* June 1988, 12–16.

Straw, Will. "Communities and Scenes in Popular Music." In *The Subcultures Reader*, ed. Ken Gelder and Sarah Thornton, 494–505. New York: Routledge, 1997.

–. "Scenes and Sensibilities." *Public* 22–23 (2002): 245–57.

–. "Systems of Articulation, Logics of Change: Communities and Scenes in Popular Music." *Cultural Studies* 5, 3 (1991): 368–88.

Tuan, Yi-Fu. *Space and Place: The Perspective of Experience*. Minneapolis: University of Minnesota Press, 1977; repr. 2001.

Tucker, Sherrie. "Big Ears: Listening for Gender in Jazz Studies." *Current Musicology* 70–71 (2001–2): 71–73.

–. "When Did Jazz Go Straight?" *Critical Studies in Improvisation* 4 (2008), https://doi.org/10.21083/csieci.v4i2.850.

Weir, Austin E. *The Struggle for National Broadcasting in Canada*. Toronto: McClelland and Stewart, 1965.

Winks, Robin W. *The Blacks in Canada: A History*. Montreal: McGill-Queen's University Press, 1971.

Recordings

Al Neil Quartet/Quintet. 1956. CBC Radio Broadcast. Private recording. Courtesy Jim Kilburn.

Dave Quarin Sextet. 1957. CBC Radio Broadcast. Private recording. Courtesy Jim Kilburn.

Don Francks. 1963. *No One in This World Is like Don Francks*. Kapp Records. KRL-4501.

–. 1965. *Lost ... and Alone*. Kapp Records. KL 1417.

Harold Land Quartet. 2007. *Harold Land: Jazz at the Cellar 1958*. Fresh Sound/Lone Hill Jazz. CD B000PFU7VW. Recorded November, 1958.

Jim Carney and Nelson High School Kampus Kings. July 1, 1952. Private recording. Courtesy Jim Carney.

J.J. Johnson with the Chris Gage Trio. 1963. Side One: CBC RM 111.

Kenneth Patchen. 1959. *Kenneth Patchen Reads with Jazz in Canada*. Folkways Records, FL 9718.

Lenny Breau, Don Francks, and Eon Henstridge. 2004. *At the Purple Onion*. Art of Life Records. AL 1009–2 [CD]. Recorded August, 1962.

Montgomery Brothers. 1961. *The Montgomery Brothers in Canada.* Fantasy 3323. LP.

Monty Waters Quartet. February 1963. *Live at the Cellar*. Private recording. Courtesy Don Thompson.

Ray Sikora Big Band. February 1963. *Live at the Cellar*. Private recording. Courtesy Don Thompson.

UBC Jazz Society Campus Coolsters. January 27, 1954. Private recording. Courtesy Jim Carney.

Vancouver Jazz Quintet. 1962. Private recording. Courtesy Don Thompson.

Films and Television

Carney, James, prod. 1961. “The Mind of Mingus.” Vancouver: CBC Vancouver. Private recording. Courtesy Don Thompson.

CBC. 1966. *Fraser MacPherson: Diary of a Musician*. Television Documentary. Vancouver: CBC.

Forest, Léonard, dir. 1964. *In Search of Innocence*. National Film Board of Canada.

Rimmer, David. 1979. *Al Neil: A Portrait.*

Slevinsky, Collette, dir., *The House That Bop Built* (documentary, not commercially released, 2011).

Interviews

Banks, Tommy: telephone interview, February 8, 2013, Edmonton.

Birdseye, Chris (Hole): telephone interview, January 28, 2013; in-person interview, August 15, 2013, White Rock, BC; follow-up emails, August 12 and 26, 2013.

bissett, bill: in-person interview, January 19, 2013, Toronto.

Brooks, Lyvia: telephone interview, December 6, 2012, Vancouver.

Brown, Adrienne: in-person interview, December 3, 2012, Vancouver; follow-up emails, January 21, 2013, through March 18, 2014.

Burke, Charles "Buddy": telephone interview, March 13, 2014, Halifax.

Caldwell, David: in-person interviews, October 10 and 26, 2013, Toronto.

Capon, John: in-person interview, August 21, 2013, Salt Spring Island, BC; follow-up emails, February 20–March 1, 2014.

Carney, Jim: in-person interview, December 2, 2012,Vancouver; follow-up emails, through February 12, 2014.

Chiasson, Warren: in-person interview, July 19, 2013, New York City; text communication, March 13, 2014.

Chivers, Jim: telephone interview, March 3, 2013, BC.

Clarke, Terry: in-person interview, February 20, 2013, Toronto.

Clitheroe, Tony: in-person interviews, December 6, 2001, November 29, 2012, and January 28, March 17, and August 27, 2013, Richmond, BC; follow-up phone calls, through March 5, 2014.

Cumming, Don: in-person interview, August 22, 2013, Nanaimo, BC; follow-up telephone interview, February 22, 2014; email, February 24, 2014.

Dawe, John: in-person interviews, December 20, 2001, January 28 and November 28, 2012, March 9 and August 14, 2013, Richmond, BC; follow-up emails, through March 27, 2014.

Doran, Tom: telephone interview, December 17, 2012, Edmonton.

Fawcett, Bill: in-person interview, August 27, 2013, Vancouver.

Francks, Don: in-person interview, July 30, 2013, Toronto.

Geszler, Joe: telephone interview, August 25, 2013, Vancouver.

Gotsch, Ricci (Quarin): in-person interview, August 29, 2013, Maple Ridge, BC.

Hales, Bobby: in-person interview, Vancouver A.F.M office, summer 2001.
Harrison, Lance: in-person interview, June 1999.
Hill, Terry: in-person interview, August 26, 2013, Richmond, BC.
Hole, Ken: telephone interview, December 7, 2012; in-person interview, August 19, 2013, Parksville, BC.
Johnson, Jim: in-person interview, August 14, 2013, Richmond, BC.
Jones, Cliff: telephone interview, August 23, 2013, BC.
Kilburn, Jim: telephone interview, February 8, 2001; unquoted interviews, August 19, 2013.
Kilburn, Joyce: unquoted interviews, August 19, 2013.
LaCroix, Pat: email communication, March 18, 2014.
Lawrence, Claire: in-person interview, August 13, 2013, Vancouver.
LeMarquand, John: telephone interview, February 22, 2013; in-person interview, August 21, 2013, Salt Spring Island, BC; follow-up emails, February 22–25, 2013, and March 24, 2014.
Lewis, Frank: telephone interview, January 20, 2013, Vancouver Island, BC; follow-up emails, January 10 and 21, 2013.
Lightbody, Walley (QC): in-person interview, December 13, 2012, Kelowna, BC; supplemental assistance through donated documents, September 2, 2013.
Logan, Chuck: in-person interview, December 17, 2001, Vancouver.
McNeil, Lynne: telephone interview, March 17, 2014, Ladysmith, BC.
Mercer, Bob: telephone interview, March 12, 2014, Florida.
Miller, Mark: in-person interview, April 7, 2011.
Murley, Mike: in-person interview, April 5, 2011, Toronto.
Neil, Al: interview conducted by Rick McGrath, December 4, 1972, Vancouver (full transcript possessed by author, obtained from a defunct website); mail correspondence, January 18 and February 12, 2013; in-person interview, August 14, 2013 and December 2, 2013, Vancouver.
Nimmons, Phil: in-person interview, November 5, 2001, Toronto.
Palmer, Don: in-person interviews, April 13, 2011, and April 11, 2012, Toronto.
Perry, Stan: in-person interview, November 14, 2013, Keswick, ON.
Reid, Jamie: in-person interviews, December 7, 2012, and August 16, 2013, Vancouver.
Reusch, Al: interviews conducted by guitarist Mike Beddoes on May 1, 8, and 15, 1999. All quotations from May 1 unless otherwise noted.
Reynolds, Jack: telephone interview, August 5, 2013, BC.
Richards, Dal: in-person interviews, June 14 and August 8, 1999, Vancouver.
Ritchie, Neil: telephone interview, February 13, 2013.
Robertson, George: telephone interview, March 18, 2014, Vancouver.
Roop, Ed: telephone interview, January 4, 2014, Vancouver.
Ruhland, Paul: in-person interviews, December 17, 2001, and November 27, 2012, Vancouver.

Simpson, Gregg: telephone interview, December 6, 2012, Bowen Island, BC; follow-up emails and Facebook communication, through March 10, 2014.

Slater, Dennis: email correspondence, March 19, 2014.

Slevinsky, Collette: telephone interview, December 15, 2012, Edmonton.

Tanner, Adrian: Skype interview, June 24, 2013, St. John's, NL.

Taylor, Mike: telephone interview, May 8, 2014, Banning, CA.

Thistlewaite, Sheila: telephone interview, March 17, 2014, Calgary.

Thompson, Don: in-person interview, February 26, 2013, Toronto.

Vickery, Don: telephone interview, March 13, 2014, Toronto.

Walker, Gavin: in-person interviews, December 3, 2012, and August 14, 2013, Vancouver; follow-up emails, through March 30, 2014.

Wikjord, Blaine: in-person interview, November 27, 2012, North Vancouver, BC.

Young, Doreen (Williams): telephone interview, December 2, 2012, Vancouver.

Index

Note: Page numbers with (f) refer to illustrations.

Printed and bound in Canada by Friesens

Set in Georgia and Century Schoolbook by Artegraphica Design Co. Ltd.

Text design: Irma Rodriguez

Copy editor: Sarah Wight

Proofreader: Judith Earnshaw

Indexer: Judy Dunlop

Cartographer: Eric Leinberger